D1304839

The Macroeconomy
of the United States

Why the US Economy is Slowing
and the US Federal Government is Insolvent

Notes for Discussion

Bob Traa

ii

Sub Specie Aeternitatis

Baruch Spinoza (1632-1677)

Contents

Chapter Appendices		vii
Tables		viii
Figures		ix
Chapter 1	Introduction	1
Part 1	*Demographics*	7
Chapter 2	Population 1950-2100	9
Chapter 3	Working-Age Population and Dependency 1950-2100	19
Chapter 4	Demography and Labor Availability 1950-2100	29
Chapter 5	International Perspective	41
Part 2	*Labor Markets and Potential GDP*	51
Chapter 6	Labor Force, Unemployment and Employment	53
Chapter 7	Average Labor Productivity and Real GDP	69
Chapter 8	The Output Gap	87
Chapter 9	Inflation and Nominal GDP	97
Part 3	*The Objectives and Instruments of Government Policy*	107
Chapter 10	Structural Reforms to Support Aggregate Supply	109
Chapter 11	Cyclical Policy to Manage Aggregate Demand	131
Chapter 12	Money and Credit Policy	143
Chapter 13	Macroeconomic Balance: Internal and External Equilibrium	159

Part 4	*The Public Sector Finances*	
	and Fiscal Sustainability	169
Chapter 14	Federal Government Revenue,	
	Expenditure, and the Budget Balance	171
Chapter 15	A Long-Run Central Projection	
	for the Federal Public Finances	187
Chapte 16	Three Cheers for	
	the US Civil Service	209
Chapter 17	Simulations to Lower the Debt	223
Chapter 18	The US Federal Government	
	Balance Sheet	247
Chapter 19	Policy Considerations	257
Chapter 20	Preliminary Conclusions	267
References		275
Data Annex		283
Acknowledgements		303
About the Author		305

Chapter Appendices

1	Demographics and Generations	17
2	Populations in Nature	18
3	Male and Female Labor Force Participation Rates 15+	39
4	Average Labor Productivity per Person and Per Hour Worked	84
5	The Sources of Growth in the US Population	127
6	Labor Productivity Growth and Investment Spending	129
7	Debt Sensitivity Analysis	206
8	Intergenerational Accounting and the Fiscal Gap	242
9	How about the Inflation Tax?	244
10	Two Helpful Equations	270

Tables

1   Population and Growth Rates (2019)   42
2   Macroeconomic Internal Balance
    Indicators by Decade   161
3   Macroeconomic External Balance Indicators
    by Decade   165
4   Federal Government Revenue (1962-2019)   173
5   Federal Government Expenditure (1962-2019) 174
6   Coronavirus Assumptions for the Federal
    Budget   194
7   Overview of Central Scenario Primary
    Spending Assumptions (% GDP)   196
8   Implicit Interest Rate on Federal Debt
    held by the Public   200
9   Comparing Assumptions for
    the long-run Scenarios   213
10 Comparing the Baseline/Central Projections 218
11 Summary of the Central Scenario and
    four Adjustment Simulations   226
12 Operating Result of the US Federal
    Government   250
13 Balance Sheet of the US Federal Government 251
14 Intertemporal Balance Sheet of the
    US Federal Government   255

Figures

1	Population (1000s)	11
2	Percentage Change of the Population	12
3	Population and Sensitivity Scenarios	15
4	Percentage Change in the Population and Sensitivity Scenarios	15
5	Annual Number of Persons in the Working-Age Population 16-64	21
6	Percentage Change of the Number of Persons in the Working-Age Population	21
7	Annual Number of Persons <16 and >64	24
8	Annual Number of Dependents <16 and >64	26
9	Percentage Change of the Number of Dependents	26
10	Total Dependency Ratio (Dependents/ Working-Age Population)	27
11	Population, WAP 15+, and Employment	31
12	Participation Rates for WAP 16-64, and WAP 15+ (LF/WAP in percent)	34
13	Participation Rate Scenarios (LF/WAP 15+; percent)	38
14	UN Population Projections, Index 2020=100	45
15	Dependency Ratios ((<16, >64)/ WAP (16-64)), in percent	47
16	Labor Force Participation Ratios in OECD Countries (LF 15+/WAP 15+)	48
17	Working-Age Population and Labor Force	55
18	Unemployment Rate	58
19	Employment	62
20	Growth in Employment and its Trend (percent)	63
21	Employment Scenarios	67
22	Growth in Employment Trend (percent)	67

23	Employment and Real GDP (1950-2019)	69
24	Average Labor Productivity (Real GDP per unit of labor) (1950-2019)	70
25	Labor Productivity Growth and its Growth Trend (percent)	74
26	Employment and Real GDP (1950-2100)	77
27	Real GDP Growth and Growth Trend (percent)	78
28	Scenarios for Real GDP (1950-2100)	81
29	Scenarios for Real GDP Growth Trend (percent)	81
30	Real GDP and Potential Real GDP (1950-2030)	90
31	Real GDP Output Gap (Percent of Potential Real GDP)	92
32	Implicit GDP Deflator (2012=100)	98
33	Inflation in the Implicit GDP Deflator (percent)	99
34	Nominal GDP Scenarios (US$ billions)	104
35	Nominal GDP Growth Scenarios (percent)	104
36	The Business Cycle and the Output Gap— Stylized Version	133
37	OECD General Government Revenue	174
38	Federal Government Revenue and Primary Expenditure	177
39	Federal Government Budget Balance 1950-2020	182
40	Federal Government Debt held by the Public	184
41	OECD General Government Gross Debt	185
42	Federal Government Revenue and Primary Expenditures (1950-2100)	192
43	Implicit Interest Rate on Debt held by the Public	202
44	Primary and Overall Federal Budget Balance	204
45	Federal Government Debt held by the Public	204

46	Comparison of Real GDP Scenarios (Chained $ billions)	215
47	Comparison of Nominal GDP Scenarios ($ billions)	216
48	Comparing Scenarios for the Federal Budget Balance (%GDP)	220
49	Comparing Scenarios for the Debt held by the Public (%GDP)	220
50	Federal Government Debt held by the Public—Simulation 1	225
51	Federal Government Revenue and Primary Expenditure—Simulation 1	227
52	Federal Government Debt held by the Public—Simulation 2	233
53	Federal Government Revenue and Primary Expenditure—Simulation 2	234
54	Federal Government Debt held by the Public—Simulation 3	236
55	Federal Government Revenue and Primary Expenditure—Simulation 3	237
56	Federal Government Debt held by the Public—Simulation 4	238
57	Federal Government Revenue and Primary Expenditure—Simulation 4	239

Chapter 1—Introduction

Few score and many years ago president Lincoln said: "sometimes people get all their facts right, but they draw entirely the wrong conclusion." Even more years ago, in ancient Greece, the temple of the Oracle at Delphi had two mottos written up above its doorways. One was "know yourself" and the other was "nothing in excess." These pieces of wisdom stay good forever. That is why we remember them.

Herodotus tells us that when the fabulously wealthy king Croesus of the Lidyans asked the Oracle in Delphi whether he should go to war against the Persians, the Oracle answered that "if Croesus goes to war he will destroy a great empire." Croesus was delighted; these were the facts he was hoping for. In the battle that followed in Cappadocia, Croesus was defeated. His own great empire was no more and power in Greece shifted to the Spartans and the Athenians. One reckons that Mr. Lincoln must have been a classical scholar.

More recently, in the 1980s, president Reagan (R) introduced "the Reagan Revolution" and, in economic policy sphere "Reaganomics." The Revolution included a massive buildup of US defense spending, which, when they tried to keep up, destroyed the Soviet Union. The Pope was involved, and Mrs. Thatcher too. On the domestic economic front, Reaganomics was encapsulated by: tax cuts, deregulation, and starve the beast (the latter would morph into "deficits don't matter"). The Republican Party has followed these three characteristics of Reaganomics in one form or another since then.

In fact, Mr. Reagan's strategy left many so impressed that Mr. Fukuyama, an American political scientist, wrote a book called "The End of History and the Last Man (1992)." Wikipedia summarizes that "in this book, Mr. Fukuyama proposed that with the ascendancy of Western liberal democracy, which occurred after the Cold War (1945–1991) and the dissolution of the Soviet Union (1991), humanity has reached "not just ... the passing of a particular period of post-war history, but the end of history as such: That is, the end-point of mankind's ideological evolution and the universalization of Western liberal democracy as the final form of human government."" This conclusion surely was not for the weak of heart. Mr. Reagan's fans saw all this as the product of their hero. The facts spoke for themselves.

One wonders if Mr. Fukuyama's conclusion and interpretation of the facts was also Oracular. Yes, the Soviet Union could not keep up and fell apart, but what really came to an end was the long march to the top for the US as a world power and an unbeatable domestic economy. One can make the argument that from the 1980s onward, the US has gradually been losing its way and standing and influence in the world, as its economy became slowly but surely mortgaged to the point of insolvency. The instrument to wreak such havoc has been debt. Debt has become the cocaine of the modern capitalist economy that Reaganomics helped to create.

Tax cuts, starve the beast, and aggressive deregulation have become an ideology and have moved the US away from the flexibility and adaptability that marked its march to the top of the global pecking order in the previous 100 years or so. Gradually, Yankee Ingenuity became replaced with Identity Politics. The US has slowly but surely slipped downhill ever since—the end of history indeed. Mr. Trump seems to agree, which may explain why he wants to "Make America Great Again." So far, he is choosing to do this by isolating the US from global events and a rules-based order. It seems time to check our facts again and ask if we really drew the right conclusion. Mr. Fukuyama, for one, is said to have had regrets, perhaps sensing that he had sniffed the gas and became Oracular.

This book asks a connected question: why is economic growth in the US slowing on trend; why has that led to a debt addiction; and what does this mean for economic and fiscal sustainability? Economics is about the allocation of resources. Politics is about power to influence the allocation of resources. So, inevitably, economics and politics are joined at the hip in the management of the country and its economy. In the answers to the above question, we must try to find where the political economy shows markers of how this process is unfolding. If we can find clues, then, perhaps, this can inform us about a way forward, and we can see if we are making mistakes that would be good to reverse or avoid altogether.

A preliminary conclusion that this book suggests is that we may want to consider moving away from a blind faith in economic expansion and sacrifice everything on the altar of the holy growth rate. Instead, should we not move forward explicitly toward a system of resilience and sustainability, including giving up some short-term growth for better overall results in the long run? This would be a system of economic management that looks at the long run first and then works backward to policy implications for the present, not one that looks at the next election first and then takes whatever comes later for someone else to worry about.

Our children and grandchildren are going to pay the bills that we leave behind. The bills are piling up, and many new ones have already been incurred, but not yet received. For instance, the price for destroying our natural planet is not in our macroeconomic cost equation, because that remains largely an externality. The coronavirus curve is only the smaller hill we need to climb.

* * *

Writing this book has caused the author some distress and doubt, even to the point of reflecting whether mothballing this book would be in the better social interest. To some reviewers of the book, selected content appeared condescending, insulting, arrogant, too simple, and superficial, and for some otheres it was deemed, at times, "too political." None of this is intended. Instead, the author wanted to make the material available to as wide an audience as possible, including those who have no experience in macroeconomics.

Further, the US is going through a difficult phase as we write in 2020, and what happens in the macroeconomy cannot simply be divorced from the political management and policy instincts that have been built up. Politics is important, including for the economy--it is exactly this question that is so interesting: how may our experience today be rooted in political tendencies and political economy and preferences of the recent past?

So, I hope that the redrafting of earlier versions of this book have taken away, or at least lessened, the concerns of some early readers. Naturally, I am responsible for the views expressed in this book. The book is sub-titled "Notes for Discussion" for a reason. Readers are allowed to disagree with, and improve, what follows on these pages.

* * *

The book is organized in four parts.

Part 1 discusses demographics. It studies population growth and population aging, which fundamentally determines the size of the working-age population and dependency, and the number of people who can work to produce the nation's real GDP. The size of the economy is related to demographics, and the demographers tell us that population growth in the US is slowing. This is automatically slowing real GDP growth as well. Further, the emergence of identity politics is now slowing immigration, and this will further restrain population growth and real GDP growth from the demand and the supply side of the economy.

Part 2 makes some assumptions about the natural rate of unemployment to which the US economy is likely to return after the effects of the coronavirus settle down. We can then derive a possible central path for employment. This leads us to a discussion about how efficient, or productive, the average unit of labor input in the US production function is. Labor productivity is the second central variable in the equation, besides the number of labor units, that determines the nation's productive capacity and growth rate. Combining potential labor availability and labor productivity will yield a path for potential real GDP in the future. Combining this with a monetary policy objective to keep inflation under control, will lead to a notion of potential nominal GDP in the future.

Part 3 talks about the objectives of economic policy. How can economic policy be designed to support potential real GDP? How can economic policy be designed to keep the output gap as small as possible—to be a good counter-cyclical instrument to keep the economy on an even keel? The role of money and credit also needs to be discussed. Here the question is asked whether the ultra-accommodative monetary policy of late is contributing to a rise in inequality and to financial market instability? The role of internal and external macroeconomic balance is also discussed as further indications and diagnostic devices whether economic policy in the US may be contributing to imbalances that can come back to bite the country in the long run.

Part 4 investigates the role of fiscal policy. It discusses recent trends, and seeks to explain the reasons for concern that the US has become addicted to debt. The author will make an argument that the budget of revenue and expenditure is not the most important financial statement for the federal government, and therefor for the US people. Rather, it is the intertemporal balance sheet of the US Federal Government that tells us in a more fundamental way where the US economy stands. In the author's view, this balance sheet shows serious problems (the US Federal Government is insolvent) that need to be addressed to bolster the resilience and sustainability of the US economy. Readers who are interested in fiscal resilience and sustainability may skip the earlier parts and go to part 4 of the book directly. The earlier parts, in some way, are inputs developed to lead up to part 4.

Part 1. Demographics

Chapter 2—Population 1950-2100

How large was the US population in 1950? How large is it today (in 2020)? And, how large will it be in 2100? As this book is written in 2020, we are 70 years onward from the beginning of this interval, and 80 years away from the end of this interval. Thus, today we are around the middle of this 150-year period.

Population has an important impact on the size of an economy. When there are more people in a country, there will also invariably be a bigger labor force. With more people in the labor force, the ability to supply goods and services will grow (we measure this as gross domestic product, or GDP). Thus, the available input of the number of workers in a country is a critical variable on the supply side of the economy. Putting this intuitively, as more hands are available to do work, the economy can grow bigger. Bigger countries therefore tend to have larger economies than smaller countries. Demography matters.

Demographers are scientists who study the evolution of populations. They analyze why populations increase or decrease, or whether the growth rate in the population may go up or down over certain periods of time. They also make models to project how large the future population may become, using developments in fertility, birth rates, death rates, and immigration and emigration. Net migration may significantly influence the size of a country, especially in smaller countries. In bigger countries, the internal birth and death rates tend to dominate, but even a large country like the US has had significant immigration that has shaped the population and the country in many ways, culturally, politically, and economically.

There are many aspects of demographics that we can study, but for the purposes of this book, which is ultimately about macroeconomics, we are mostly interested in the size of the population—the number of people in a country, and its composition among age groups. The latter is relevant in the context of studying the macroeconomy for various reasons. For instance, not everyone in the country is of working age. Two big exceptions are the young who spend their time in school, and the elderly, who have reached retirement age. It is also important to know how these cohorts will develop in future.

After the second world war, the US went through a period of rapid birth rates, generating a pool of young people that would soon be called the baby boomers. This growth in the young population then duly enlarged the labor force as they became of working age—driving rapid growth of workers and GDP in the economy.

Right now, in 2020, the boomers are of an age between 55-75, and thus at a stage when they are entering their retirement age. As a result, we now have a rapid graying, or aging, of the population. These relative shifts in the population are important, because the cost of taking care of the young (schooling) and the elderly (pensions) can be high and depends on how many elderly and young people, respectively, are in the economy. So, not only the number of people is important, but also the structure (composition) of the population. Demographers study these phenomena systematically, and are therefore important colleagues of the economics profession.

The United Nations collects many data on demography from all countries in the world, including the US. This book uses these data from the UN, vintage 2019 (i.e. including the latest projections from 2020 onwards).

The US population between 1950 and 2019, and projections of the population for 2020 through 2100, are plotted in figure 1 below. The vertical line indicates the present (2020), more or less in the middle of our 150-year period of interest.

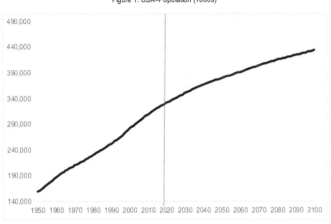

Figure 1. USA–Population (1000s)

Source: UN Population Division.

Several remarks may be made as we study this picture.

In a global context, the US is the third largest country with currently some 330 million people. The largest countries by population are China and India with over a billion people each (>3 times as many as in the US...).

The population line shows a tendency, or trend, that indicates continuous growth throughout the forecasting period. The US is projected to grow to 434 million people by 2100. This is interesting, because there are many countries in the world that show declining populations in the current century. As noted before, growing or declining populations have important economic and political implications.

Nevertheless, the rate of increase in the US population is slowing down, which is indicated by the gradual leveling off of the population. This is important too, because as population growth slows down, the rate of economic growth will also be restrained.

Figure 2 shows the annual percentage change growth rate of the population as derived from the data in Figure 1.

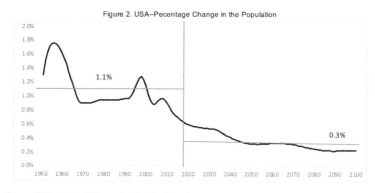

Figure 2. USA–Pecentage Change in the Population

Source: UN Population Division; calculations by the author.

The average population growth rate in the US in the period 1950-2019 was 1.1 percent a year. The average population growth rate projected for the US in the period 2020-2100 is 0.3 percent a year.

Population growth rates are not constant; they are variable and can be influenced in the short-term by many factors and temporary shocks. This is clearly visible in the recent past. The projections always tend to be smoother because scientists cannot predict what shocks will occur at what time. What matters for governing the well-being of countries is not the short-term variability, but the long-term underlying trends.

The higher growth rates in the 1950s and 1960s reflect the baby boom generation of people born in the 20-year period between 1945-1965. A smaller "baby boom echo generation" emerged some 20-30 years later during the period 1980-1995 as the large baby boom generation had its own children. The baby boom echo generation is often referred to as "the Millennials" or Generation Y (Appendix 1).

Political stability and prosperous economic times are often said to contribute to families being confident of having children. This hypothesis also coincides with the two peaks in population growth in Figure 2. The intervening 1970s and 1980s were more difficult times in politics (including the turbulent late 1960s and the Watergate years in the 1970s) and in economics (the oil embargoes of the 1970s and a period of stagflation into the 1980s, when low growth coincided with elevated inflation).

Nevertheless, if we abstract from the cyclical ups and downs and cast our eyes longer-term, then we see that the growth rate of the population *structurally* slows down as the population numbers get bigger. This is in part the Law of Large Numbers, but also reflects that larger populations put strain on the environment, resource availability, and, indeed the political process and governance. Thus, nature has a built-in mechanism to limit populations—they cannot keep growing forever. Vulnerabilities inherent in a biological mono-culture, including homo sapiens, eventually check the size of all populations (Appendix 2).

As the population experiences a *structural* slow down, the rate of growth of the economy will also *structurally* slow down. A country with zero population growth will have an economy that grows more slowly over time than a country where the population growth is 4 percent. When the public and political systems frame expectations of what an economy can deliver in future, it is important to keep this big-picture idea in mind. Misaligned expectations harm economies.

Sensitivity analysis. Figures 1 & 2 above give a single line of projections for the population in the US and its annual growth rates. But we don't know all the parameters and influences that will impact on the future. Therefore, it is helpful to do some sensitivity analysis around this "central forecast" or "baseline" as these projections are called. Helpfully, the UN also provides a "low" and a "high" growth scenario of the population for all countries in its database. These are based on differing birth rates, death rates, and assumptions on policies that will impact immigration and emigration. These sensitivity analyses use probability calculations, based on past observed events and behaviors, to calculate the low and high scenarios around the baseline. Figures 3 & 4 provide these low and high scenarios, forming an 80 percent probability band around the central scenario, and the respective growth rates.

These scenarios tell us that with 80 percent probability, the US population in 2100 will likely be between a low of 385 million and a high of 490 million, with a central projection of 434 million, as mentioned above. This is equivalent to an average annual growth rate from 2020-2100 of 0.2 percent in the low scenario (ending in zero growth by the end of the century), and 0.5 percent average growth in the high scenario (ending in 0.4 percent growth by the end of the century). This compares with 0.3 percent average in the central scenario.[1]

Figure 3. USA–Population and Sensitivy Scenarios(1000s)

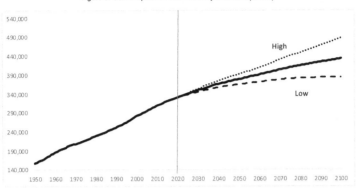

Figure 4. USA–Percentage Change in the Population and Sensitivity Scenarios

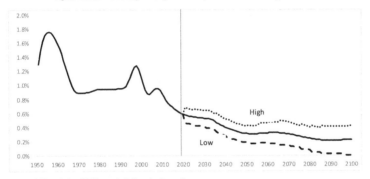

Source: UN Population Division; calculations by the author.

A difference between 0.5 − 0.2 = 0.3 percentage points on average over the long run may not sound much to the average reader, but for the size of the economy,

---

[1] In its 2020 Report on Social Security and Disability Insurance, the Trustees of Social Security project a central scenario for the US population of 475 million in 2095. This is at the high end of the UN population reports, and thus is a relatively favorable assumption for the outcome of the Trustees reports. The Trustees high growth scenario lifts the population to 570 million people, and the low growth scenario to 399 million people.

such a gap, compounded over many years, accumulates to an appreciable difference in the amount of GDP that the US can produce. We will return to this sensitivity analysis later as the book develops.

Appendix 1—Demographics and Generations

The oldest generation is the GI Generation born between 1900-1925. Then came the Silent Generation, born between 1925-1945. The baby boomers followed them (1945-1965). Then came Generation X (1965-1980), followed by Generation Y or the boomers echo (1980-1995). People born in the period 1995-2015 are called Generation Z. Thus, we have a veritable alphabet soup of 6 generations. The newest and youngest addition since 2015 is referred to as "Generation Alpha."

Different disciplines, such as economics and business, politics, public health care, psychology, and sociology are interested in different attributes of each generation. Each generation has its own concerns, opportunities, and outlook on life, and the business world has different ploys to tap into the needs of each generation. These big picture movements are sometimes referred to as "Mega Trends". It is only one example that makes studying demographics interesting.

Appendix 2—Populations in Nature

An evolutionary blip that we do not understand, has given human beings an unusually big brain. As a result, some believe that homo sapiens are somehow special and, indeed, not fully subject to the laws of nature. This is a mistake.

Robert Malthus (1766-1834) was an English economist who developed the idea of the "Malthusian Trap", which is to say that populations that do well economically will tend to grow instead of maintaining a high standard of living. If things go well, we multiply until nature calls in the constraints, such as having to use marginal lands to grow crops in Malthus' time. Indeed, we continue to multiply until people of less ability and less wealth suffer hardship such as famine and disease. Fertilizer and crop technique have allowed many countries to escape, to some extent, this Malthusian Trap—so far.

But then there are microbes and viruses that threaten mono cultures, as known from biology class. Black Death (1347-1351) killed 75-200 million people. Smallpox is estimated to have killed 500 million people in the last 100 years before it was eradicated, recently. SARS, HIV, Ebola, H1N1 (influenza and Spanish Flu (1918)), and now coronavirus, are also frightening diseases that can stop entire countries, bring down governments, and damage economies.

There is no evidence of unlimited growth in nature, so policies that advocate and promote resilience, sustainability, and wellbeing, instead of blindly gunning for growth, deserve all of our attention. Younger generations (ex. Greta Thunberg) are intuitively onto this; some older generations (ex. Mr. Trump) deny this. Perhaps the difference in age and moral sentiment focus the brain in a different way.

Chapter 3—Working-Age Population and Dependency 1950-2100

In chapter 2 we considered the outlook for the overall population of the US from 2020-2100. Now we need to drill down a level deeper to see what this means for the economy more precisely. While the entire population comprises consumers, who buy goods and services on the demand side of the economy, the gross domestic product is measured from the supply side—how many of these goods and services are produced (supplied) in the domestic economy.[2] Thus, to measure GDP, economists and statisticians ask all branches of business, households, governments, etc. in the economy how many units of goods and services they produce in a particular quarter, a year, etc. at constant prices. The answer to this question leads to the concept of "real GDP", disregarding for the moment that prices of output can change over time (we will return to "nominal GDP" later, including that prices can change over time).

For purposes of finding out how much real GDP a country can produce, we need to figure out how many people in the country are able to work. This leads us to split the overall population into three groups—the young (who need to go to school), the elderly (who retired), and the large middle group of so-called working-age population. From demographic data we can define the working-age population (WAP) in different ways. One intuitive and traditional way is to define it as all people between the ages of 16-64 years of age. Young people are

---

[2] When we measure GDP from the demand side, we make it equal to the supply side by subtracting that part of demand that is accommodated by imports and adding in that part of supply that is exported abroad.

then in the group from 0-15 and the elderly are defined as 65 years of age and over, which in many countries and for many years has functioned as a benchmark retirement age. As retirement ages are shifted up with longer life expectancies, in some countries the WAP could be defined e.g. as 16-67 years of age (or even older). It is now also becoming common in industrial countries to keep track of how many people are 15+ (i.e. including all the elderly), reflecting that elderly people nowadays tend to be healthier than before and can continue to be occupied in meaningful productive activity after reaching retirement age. We will switch to this definition in chapter 4 below.

For now, we can use the data from the UN to split the total population in the three groups of interest—the young (<16), the elderly (>64), and the WAP (16-64). Figures 5 & 6 show the total number of people in the WAP between 1950-2019 and a baseline, or central, projection for the WAP for the period 2020-2100, as well as the corresponding annual growth rates. As before, the vertical line indicates the current measuring point, 2020.

What we can see in these numbers is again interesting.

The level of the WAP is smaller than the level of the population as a whole. This is logical because we have subtracted the young and the elderly populations from the total.

The evolution of the WAP has a kink that is more pronounced than the gradual slowdown in growth of the overall population. For the period 1950-2007, the WAP grew on average by 1.2 percent a year. The effect of the baby boomers and the baby boom echo (Millennials or Gen Y) coming into the working-age population is clearly visible in the growth peaks in the 1970s and 1990s in Figure 6.

Figure 5. USA–Annual number of persons in the Working-Age Population 16-64 (1000s)

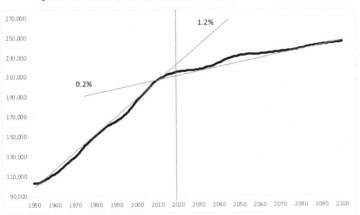

Figure 6. USA–Percentage Change of the number of persons in the Working-Age Population

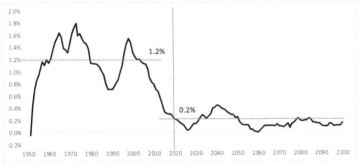

Source: UN Population Division; calculations by the author.

After the Millennials entered the working-age population, the number of new entrants in the critical WAP middle group for the economy slowed down *structurally* from 1.2 percent a year to some 0.2 percent a year on average. This structural slowdown is visible by the average lines in Figures 5 and 6.

If we make this rough split between the past and the future, then we can see that the growth in the number of people in the WAP shifts down over a period of only 20 years by as much as 1 percentage point. That is a lot. It has implications for how fast the economy can grow. If the number of potential new workers slows down by 1 percentage point from an average of 1.2 to 0.2 percent, then the potential rate of growth in output, or real GDP, that can be produced by the people in the working-age population will also slow down (unless there are important compensating changes elsewhere in the economy or in managing the production process—productivity per worker; more on this, later).

This rapid downshift in the growth of the WAP in only 20 years is due to two factors: one, the baby boomers started to retire. This retirement wave of boomers will end around 2025-2030 when all of them reach age 65. Since the boomers are a large cohort within the overall population, their advancing into elderly ages gets noticed. It is a Mega Trend. Second, for cultural reasons and with advances in medicine, such as the wide adoption of birth control methods and the anti-conception pill in the 1960s, pregnancies and birth rates started to slow down already at the end of the baby-boom generation. This is another Mega Trend.

With fewer young person's entering the working-age population (less inflow), and a wave of retirements as boomers started exiting the working-age population (more outflow), the WAP experienced the *structural* slowdown in growth. This important demographic phenomenon is visible in the numbers and has noticeable economic consequences. Society needs to be aware of these issues to make good policy decisions for a well-calibrated and sustainable economy—a central theme behind this book.

Dependency. The movements of people from youth to working-age population, and then to the elderly cohort, is important for demographers, economists, political scientists, and a host of other interested disciplines. We can look at the evolution of dependency (those <16 and >64 years of age) more closely.

Figure 7 shows the number of people in the US between 1950-2100 (projected) less than 16 years of age, and over 64 years of age—the two cohorts that make up the dependent population. The word "dependent" here is meant in a macroeconomic policy setting. It indicates that most of these sub-populations tend not to participate in the economic production function—generally, they do not produce GDP. But these individuals have economic needs like all people, and are part of the aggregate demand for goods and services that the economy offers. Thus, they *depend* on goods and services produced by the working population to meet their daily needs. It is only in this sense that these sub-groups are called dependents in this book.

Once again, it is immediately obvious that an interesting shift in composition is taking place even within the cohorts of dependents. The number of elderly people is about to overtake the number of youths (at around 60 million each in a few years from today). It is also clear that the growth rate of the elderly is consistently much higher than the growth rate of young people. Further, inspection of the line for the elderly demonstrates the acceleration in their numbers between 2010-2030—that is the effect of some 30 million (net) baby boomers entering retirement age.

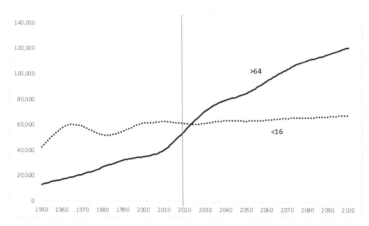

Figure 7. USA–Annual number of persons <16 and >64 (1000s)

Source: UN Population Division; calculations by the author.

Abstracting for a minute from the working-age population, this shift from mostly young people to elderly is again a Mega Trend—a change in the composition of dependency; and that is important for many economic and political reasons. Young people need schools and general education infrastructure. Elderly people need pensions, healthcare assistance, and a different infrastructure than the young. Since both are dependents and require money transfers, it is important to know whether an average young person needs more transfers than an average elderly person (more on this later).

For political reasons, it is important to know who tends to participate more in voting, and who participates less—young people or elderly people? For our purposes, the elderly are more politically aware, and vote in larger numbers, than young people, and this has implications for policy. For instance, when society wants to reform pension systems to save costs in the budget, but most active voters are elderly, such a structural reform is very difficult to get approved. When schools need more money, but there are fewer children, how do you get such a change approved? Different cohorts vying for scarce resources can generate stress, even where social relations are cohesive. Thus, knowing demographics is important for politics and political economy alike, and we are only scratching the surface when considering the impact on society of big demographics trends.

We can aggregate the young and the elderly in a single group of dependents and see how this group evolves as a whole. This is shown in Figures 8 and 9.

Figure 8 shows that the combined total number of dependents in the US has doubled between 1950-2020 from around 55 million to 110 million people. This number is projected to grow further to almost 190 million people by 2100.

This growth (shown in Figure 9) is mostly coming from more elderly people. This growth in (overall) dependency is also faster than the growth in the population as a whole—the "graying" of the population, or the "aging" of the population. Thus, dependents are expected to make up a larger proportion of the population as we go into the future. Population aging is a Mega Trend.

Since dependents need money to live, and since people in the working-age population produce the GDP of a country, or the income that is available to the country, it is furthermore interesting to see how the number of dependents evolves relative to the number of working-age people. This relationship, called the "total dependency ratio," is depicted in Figure 10.

Figure 8. USA–Annual number of dependents – persons <16 and >64 (1000s)

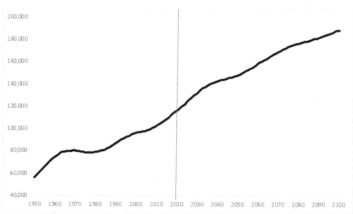

Figure 9. USA–Percentage Change of the number of Dependents

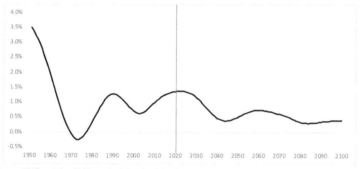

Source: UN Population Division; calculations by the author.

The total dependency ratio can be further divided into two groups: the youth dependency ratio and the elderly dependency ratio (not shown here). We will not dive deeper into these sub-ratios at this moment.

Figure 10 demonstrates that dependency is increasing from a low in 2010 of around 50 percent to nearly 80 percent by 2100. The number for 2010 means that for every person of dependency, there were two people of working age. By 2100, for every person of dependency there is projected to be only 1.3 person of working age.

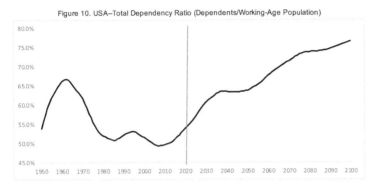

Figure 10. USA–Total Dependency Ratio (Dependents/Working-Age Population)

Source: UN Population Division; calculations by the author.

Thus, the dependency rate will go up and the carrying obligations of each average member of the working-age population will grow. In the 1960s, the previous peak in dependency came from young people; in future, the growing dependency comes from elderly people. Since elderly dependents cost more to care for than young dependents, aging will put economic pressure on society and on government budgets.[3]

---

[3] Empirical work suggests that the elderly cost 7 times more per capita than young people in the federal budget. But that is only part of the story, because state and local budgets carry the heaviest burden to provide schools and care for the young. When we combine the costs of dependency in general government (federal and state and local governments) then it remains true that elderly dependents cost more than young dependents. Thus, aging is important from a pure financial point of view, besides other effects that this generates in society.

Chapter 4—Demography and Labor Availability
1950-2100

In the previous two chapters we have looked at the total population and how it is projected to grow through the end of the century. Then we split this total population into three groups: the young, the elderly, and the working-age population. We have only scratched the surface as to what this information suggests to us, and what ideas are generated by deeper thinking about findings and tendencies in demographics. In this chapter, and to keep the focus on the economic implications of demographics, we will look deeper into the working-age population and ask the question: how many people in this working-age population are actually working (employed) to produce the nation's GDP?

GDP is produced by people who have work or who do work for some kind of sustenance in an independent capacity. Thus, we need to think of the factor labor (L) as everyone who contributes to generating output. This includes traditional payroll workers, self-employed, entrepreneurs, and all others who produce something, be it a good or a service, for which they get a wage, salary, or some other form of payment/compensation. The Bureau of Labor Statistics keeps track of the number of people who are over 15 years of age (15+) and are "employed" in the broad sense of the word. This involves the civilian population—the military is excluded. Within civilians, the incarcerated population does some work, but they are also excluded.[4]

---

[4] The US has among the highest incarceration rates in the world. The exclusion of over 2 million incarcerated people from labor force statistics raises some issues. One, this population is large. If we include parolees and people on probation, the number of adults under

The Bureau of Labor Statistics also collects numbers of people that are unemployed (U). Unemployed is defined as those people who would like to work, and are actively looking for work, but they do not have work at this moment. If you are not looking for work, you are not counted as unemployed, because unemployment, as defined for our economic purposes, is involuntary. Voluntarily taking time off is not the same as being unemployed.

The total number of people that are employed (L) and unemployed (U) is called the labor force (LF). Thus:

$$LF = L + U$$

As noted, the labor force is measured on the basis of all people that are over 15 years of age. This implies that the Bureau of Labor Statistics also considers all people over 15 years of age as potential labor resources available to the economy. Thus, we now need to make the shift mentioned earlier in our definition of the working-age population to align this with the statistics produced on the labor force by the Bureau of Labor Statistics. We will now use the broader definition of the working-age population (15+) in use in the US, rather than the narrower definition

---

supervision of the correctional system even jumps to almost 7 million (compared with unemployment in 2019 of below 6 million people)(BJS April 2018). Two, the summary statistics for the US and some other countries are not precisely comparable if other countries have much lower incarceration rates. For instance, the unemployment rate can seem quite low at times. But what happens if you have many people in jail of working-age population who could do some work, would be willing to do some work, but they are not counted as unemployed or otherwise included in different forms of participation rates? From a social and economic point of view, high incarceration rates involve a loss of potential labor resources and causes social distress.

of person between the ages of 16-64. We can easily adapt our earlier statistics above by adding back the elderly (>64) into our WAP. The new definition of the working-age population is thus the entire population minus the young (<16).

It is worth to have a brief look at this broader definition of the working-age population 15+ as summarized, together with the total population and employment, in Figure 11.

Figure 11. USA–Population, WAP 15+, and Employment (1000 persons)

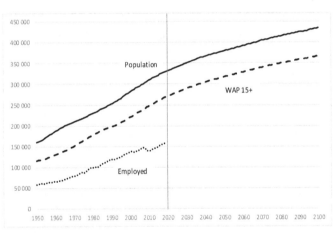

Source: UN, BLS.

We see in this Figure that the population data are unchanged from the earlier chapters, but the working-age population now tracks the overall population statistics more closely. This is logical because we are only subtracting the young population—the elderly remain in the WAP. The pronounced kink in the WAP (16-64), is gone. This is logical too, because that kink was largely a reflection of the baby boomers starting to enter retirement age. If we keep all people in the WAP, even if they pass 65, then this kink disappears.

The reason that high-income countries tend to shift to a WAP 15+ is because of the finding that more of the elderly continue to work in some capacity. This is a change from more traditional times in the past when 65 was the customary general retirement age. There is also a practical reason. As long as elderly can keep working, the costs for society and the economy to assist the elderly will be less. It reflects that elderly can continue to be a valuable resource for countries, given their work experience and as long as they enjoy good health. People involved in heavy or straining labor activity cannot continue working and sometimes have earlier effective retirement ages. The discussion of just what professions deserve earlier retirement ages is not a minor issue. Society holds vigorous debates on these issues in the political process.

The third line in Figure 11 is the new addition to our toolbox. It reflects the number of people who are working, or employed (L for labor). It is at once obvious that people actually working make up only a fraction of the WAP, let alone the entire population, and yet these people produce the entire GDP. It is also interesting to see that the employment line has dips in it, and that the gap between WAP and employment is slowly increasing. The dips take place during recessions, when employment declines even though the WAP and the overall population continue their steady increase. Indeed, upon inspection of this line, it takes some time for employment to revert back to the previous dynamics after recessions. This has implications for the political economy because we realize that recessions can do long-term damage, and we will look at this again a bit later.

The participation rate. We touched above on the *dependency ratio*, defined as the number of dependents (young and elderly) over the working-age population. Now we can look at a similar concept called the *participation ratio*, which asks the question: how many people out of the working-age population actually are active in the economy? The people who are active in the economy are those who have a job (employed or L) and those who are actively looking for one (unemployed or U). Thus, we would like to study the ratio between L + U = labor force, and WAP 15+. One key reason for studying this ratio is that as more people can participate in the economic process, the larger will be the potential to produce GDP; also called "potential GDP"—the more goods and services the society potentially has at its disposal. We are interested in policies that can encourage and promote sustainable participation.

Figure 12 shows two definitions of participation rates: the first based on the labor force over WAP (16-64) and a second based on the labor force over WAP (15+).

The top line in Figure 12 shows the labor force in percent of the working-age population 16-64 years of age. The lower line shows the same labor force as a percent of the working-age population 15+. Until recently, these two lines had a similar trend, with a notable increase in participation from the 1970s through the 1990s. Again, this reflects a shift in cohorts within the overall population as the baby boomers and boomer echo's entered their working age and looked for jobs.

An important second effect was the change in the role of women in society. Hitherto, participation by women was relatively low. In the 1960s everything began to change. Women gained better control over their own health and reproduction. With lower birth rates and steady increases in educational attainment, women used these added degrees of freedom to enter into the work place. Thus, the participation rate among females in the labor force has been rising, in turn contributing to lifting the overall labor force participation rates observed in many economies (Appendix 3).

Figure 12. USA–Participation Rates for WAP 16-64, and WAP 15+ (LF/WAP in percent)

Source: BLS, and author calculations.

When studying different national economies, we see that participation rates in the 60 percent range (with the WAP (16-64), top line) were common for many countries prior to the 1970s. Then, virtually all higher-income countries started to experience a shift up in participation rates toward the 75 percent range by the 1990s-2000s. The logical progression, if nothing else changes, is to expect that at some point, when the large baby boom and boom echo's start to retire, that the participation rates would start to level off again. This would be so, because, other things being equal, the working age population 16-64 and the labor force would both be shrinking by similar numbers, and that gives a mathematically smaller participation rate over time.

But we need to realize that the numbers for the labor force used here are those over 15+. Thus, if more elderly people continue to work, and they are included in the labor force statistics but not in the WAP (16-64), then we would expect that the participation rate can rise again. This is indeed what we see in the top line recently.

A second effect that plays a role is that during the Great Recession of 2008-2009, following the Lehman crisis and the collapse of financial markets beginning in the US, many people lost their jobs and a share of them became cyclically "discouraged" –these were workers who stopped looking for jobs and dropped out of the labor force altogether. Since they remained in the WAP, the ratio after 2007 or so would be expected to decline. This, too, is visible in the top line. But after a while, as the economy recovered through 2019, the discouraged workers may have become encouraged again, and re-entered the jobs market. That is a second factor why the participation rate, as defined in the top line, may have started to recover as well.

The lower line in Figure 12 allows further analysis of these thoughts. It differs from the top line in that the WAP is more broadly defined as including everyone 15+. What we see now, is that the decline in participation is still there after the Great Recession, but it has not yet been coming back up, in contrast to the top line indicator. Thus, here it seems that two opposing forces are in balance for now: baby boomers that leave the labor force stay in the

WAP 15+ (the denominator of the PR). This would, other things being equal, incrementally lower the participation rate. But if boomers continue to work in significant numbers after retirement age, then the labor force would be larger as well by these elderly workers and the participation rate would be cushioned. Further, if workers feel encouraged again and returned to the labor force, as in the narrative behind the first line, then the participation rate would also be supported for a while. Thus, the fact that the participation rate 15+ is stable recently, even though baby boomers are retiring, suggests that underlying participation in the labor force is again increasing (this view is also reflected in Eppsteiner et al, 2019).

The role of participation in the economic process is important for society. As population growth is leveling off, the natural growth in new workers in the economy will also level off, and thereby real GDP growth itself will be restrained. Out of a given population, the stretch that exists in economies, is thus gradually shifting to the question: how many people in society would be willing and able to participate and work? If participation can be increased, and if individuals and society believe that this is a good thing, then economic growth can be supported for a while by raising participation. Participation is not an unbounded variable in our economic equation, but it is an important one, and political systems need to discuss ideas to support participation in all the social, political, and economic complexities that surround this issue.

Projecting participation rates. If we want to explore how large the real GDP of the US economy can become in the future, we need to know something about the volume of labor (L) that will be available in the future.

As discussed above, this involves a chain of effects from total population growth, to growth in the population of working age (WAP 15+ as used in US statistics), and in the overall participation rate of the labor force within the WAP.

The general expectation is that participation will slowly decline in the next 10 years or so, reflecting the wave of baby boomers retiring (pushing participation down) offset to some extent by more elderly continuing to work, especially females (pushing participation up). The first effect is expected to dominate the second effect for a while.

Long-run projections are even harder to come by. As a result, we can make an *aspirational assumption* about the longer-run participation rates. Such an assumption presupposes that society cares about the participation rates and will try to keep it within certain bounds. It cannot go up forever, because there are legitimate reasons why some in the working age population cannot participate (e.g. families with very young children, handicapped, institutionalized people, people with health problems, people in extended education, growing share of elderly, etc.). There is also good reason to prevent a large decline, and policies can be designed to encourage labor force participation without becoming coercive.

For purposes of this book, we will assume that the participation rate will therefore ease off in the next decade before a gradual, slow, and small increase sets in for the longer run. Scenario analysis can be used to place a corridor around this central assumption with a low and high participation rate. What is important in such uncertainty is to monitor the data as time unfolds to see what nature is telling us. If we get surprised, then the model needs to be adapted.

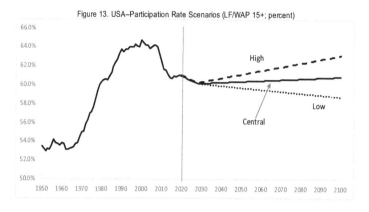

Figure 13. USA–Participation Rate Scenarios (LF/WAP 15+; percent)

Notes: BLS through 2028; then: High to 63 % in 2100; Low to 59%; central is gradual slow increase in between.

Figure 13 shows the results of our working assumptions for the participation rates 15+ through 2100. In the central scenario the participation rate first eases off to 60 percent and then slowly builds back up to 61 percent of the WAP 15+. In the low scenario, it gradually drops off further to 59 percent; and in the high scenario, it recovers to 63 percent of the WAP 15+ by 2100.

Appendix 3—Male & Female Labor Participation Rates 15+

Male labor participation rates have been gradually declining from high levels. Female labor participation rates have nearly doubled to 60 percent, before leveling off in the 2010s. One reason for downward pressure on participation in general is that younger adults stay in education longer than in the past—well beyond 15 years of age. As more time is used for education, participation rates drop.

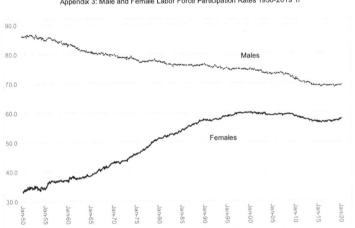

Appendix 3: Male and Female Labor Force Participation Rates 1950-2019 1/

Source: BLS and Federal Reserve Bank of St Louis.
1/ Seasonally adjusted monthly data.

The US BLS expects overall participation rates to decline in the future, as the advance for women has leveled off, whereas males continue to see a slow decline. The passing of baby boomers into retirement age (and especially as they reach 75 or 80 years or so—aging) is another key contributing factor why the participation rate could be expected to drop.

Chapter 5—International Perspective

In chapters 2-4, we have shown characteristics of the US population and US population dynamics. Now we can see more precisely how this looks in international perspective. Do other countries experience the same kind of developments in their population as the US? If there are differences, what does this imply? How should we interpret these differences and can it tell us anything about current and prospective affairs? Since international institutions collect comparable data, we can turn to them to get some preliminary answers or indications.

Population and population growth. Let us begin with population, the top line comparator. How big is the US compared to other countries? Table 1 gives an indication.

As of 2019, China was the most populous country on earth, closely followed by India. The US is the third largest country. If we were to consider the euro-zone as a single country for economic purposes, or as a single market, then this region would be the third largest entity, just a bit bigger than the US.

Table 1. Population and Growth Rate (2019)

		Persons Millions	Growth rate percent
1	China	1434	0.4
2	India	1366	1.0
3	USA	329	0.6
4	Indonesia	271	1.1
5	Pakistan	217	2.0
6	Brazil	211	0.8
7	Nigeria	196	2.6
8	Bangladesh	163	1.0
9	Russia	146	0.1
10	Mexico	128	1.1
11	Japan	127	-0.3
	Euro zone	342	0.2

Source: UN.

The population growth rates are also interesting. Emerging countries tend to grow more quickly than high-income countries. Russia is stagnating and Japan's population is declining. The euro-zone as a region has a lower population growth rate than China, India, and the US, so if population size means anything, then the euro-zone is destined to fall back gradually in this particular pecking order.

* * *

Political-economy interlude. Why would we care about population size and its growth? If economics is about the analysis of the allocation of resources (how can we be efficient in using the resources that we have?), then politics is about power (who puts more weight on the scale when the world has to make decisions?). It is especially the latter, political systems, that tend to care about the absolute size of the population.

From a politician's point of view, if you represent more people, then you put more weight on the scale of global affairs, and that helps in the competition for global resources. Larger populations proxy for market size which is important in things like global influence (especially in trade negotiations) and provides scope for growth of domestic firms. Population seems also to present a kind of (false) competition—the bigger you are, the more important you deem yourself to be.

The reason, however, that economists are interested in this phenomenon, is that bigger populations may benefit from scale economies, which can lift potential growth. Further, it influences the allocation of resources on a global scale—who gets what and for what purpose? That is the study of political economy. Enlightened politicians know that we should foremost care about *per-capita* well-being, not the absolute size of the economy, but this is not often an over-riding sentiment in political discussions.[5]

* * *

---

[5] On a per-capita basis Luxembourg is among the three richest countries in the world, together with Qatar and Macau. Luxembourg has a population of ½ million. The US ranks around 11th in the world. China ranks around 70, but is quickly rising. India is around 120th place. Thus, country population size is not the same as GDP per person.

If the growth rates in populations are not the same, what are the prospects for a possible realignment of relative rank order of future populations, as projected by the UN? We cannot compare all countries in this book, but let us look at some iconic examples. We will use the World population projections as a benchmark and construct index numbers for the future population, starting with a scalar of 100 in 2020. Thus, if, for any country, the population in the future is projected to go over 100, then that country has a growing population; if the index number travels below 100, then the population is projected to be smaller in future than today.

Figure 14 shows some results. The world population is projected to grow through the end of the century to some 9.9 billion people, from 7.8 billion in 2020.

Africa stands out for projections of population growth to reach a total population that is almost 3 times as large as today.[6] This makes Africa the center of attention in demography, politics, and economics. It is said that the future belongs to Africa if the African political leadership is able to manage this substantial population expansion for productive purposes. Europe is eyeing these numbers also, because if the politics of Africa misses this beat, then migratory flows to Europe, the neighboring high-income continent, will further grow. This would put great stress on the political management of Europe, in turn.

---

[6] By Africa is meant the geographic continent comprising the countries on the Mediterranean plus sub-Saharan Africa, from Egypt in the east to Morocco in the west and on down to South Africa. Middle East is not included.

Figure 14. UN Population Projections, Index 2020=100

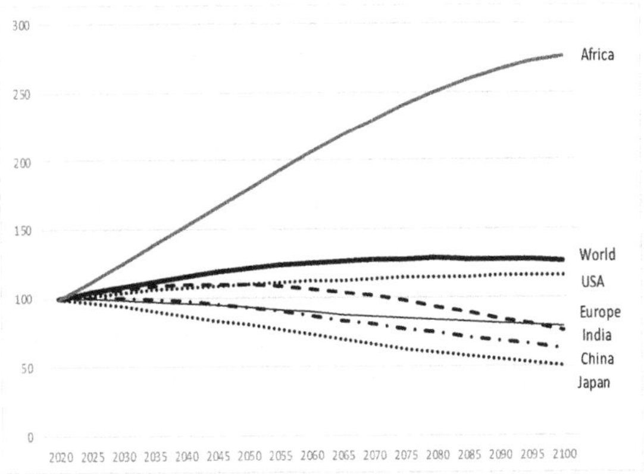

Source: UN, vintage 2019.

The US is also a growth country. This is interesting because the US is already very large as an economic power. Thus, the future is leaning in favor of the US, based on this metric. There is the impression that US financial markets present a more exiting value for investors, and that much capital flows to the US and out of other parts of the world, including those who should receive capital, in relative terms. This "flowing uphill of water" as this curious phenomenon is sometimes called, is partly caused by better growth prospects in the US, certainly as compared to Europe, where the population is projected to decline.

China, India, and Japan all are projected to lose population in the future as well, with Japan projected to almost halve in population by the end of the century. Japan today has one of the highest public debt ratios in the world. How is Japan going to evolve in its economy, and how is the country going to manage its debt with a progressively smaller population in future? This question has not been answered and remains a puzzle and question mark. Will potential solutions to Japan's debt burden spill over to the rest of the world, or will this be primarily an internal problem, given that most of the debt is held internally in Japan?

The projected population declines in China and India have raised their own questions to which we do not have a convincing answer. One is: can China and India become rich, i.e. have high-per-capita incomes, before they grow old? Population aging accelerates in declining populations, so this makes vigorous growth in per-capita incomes more difficult. On these various comparative metrics, the US still looks like a relatively promising economy, which is remarkable given the size of the US economy already.

Dependency ratios. As we have seen above, dependency ratios are important also because they give an indication of the number of people that are dependent on the number of working-age people in the economy—those who can produce GDP. If the dependency ratio goes up, then the burden on the working population increases; if it goes down, then the burden decreases. We can see in Figure 15 how the US compares internationally in projections for the dependency ratio. Data are from the UN. WAP is defined as between 15 and 65 years of age.

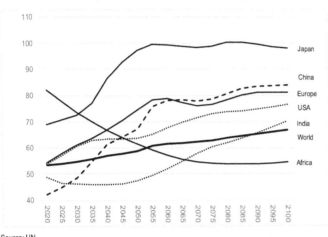

Figure 15. Dependency Ratios ((<16, >64)/WAP (16-64)), in percent

Source: UN.

The dependency ratio for the world population is the thick black line in the middle. It is projected to increases from 53 percent in 2020 to 67 percent in 2100.

This ratio for the US is shown to rise from 54 to 77 percent. A steady increase but not the fastest increase nor the highest level by 2100. It is indicative of growing dependency pressure, but relatively less than in partner countries in Europe, China, and Japan.

Japan is very advanced in aging, already at 70 percent, and projected to go to 100 percent by the 2050s. This increase is mainly old-age dependency.

Japan, China, and Europe are now in the rapid aging demographic cycle—their dependency ratios show a decided increase through the 2050s. It will put great pressure on the social security systems of these countries and slow growth of GDP, relative to the other countries that are later in aging, such as the US, India, and, especially Africa.

In Africa, dependency is high, but this is mainly youth dependency—Africa is a young continent in demographics. Its dependency ratio is significantly falling this century as all the young people are swept into the working-age population. If well managed, this could boost growth in Africa. Analysts say that in terms of dynamics, Africa is the continent to watch.

The bottom line for the US is that in comparison with other important economic powers in the world, aging is advancing, but the demographics still look relatively favorable. On this basis alone, and other issues being held constant, economic growth conditions in the US thus also look relatively favorable.

Labor force participation rates. A third interesting variable to compare across countries is the participation rate, measured as the labor force 15+ divided by the working-age population 15+.

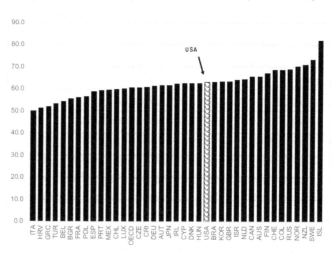

Figure 16. Labor Force Participation Rates in OECD Countries (LF 15+/ WAP 15+)

Source: OECD.

The reason that the participation rate is so important, is that we can maintain a sound growth rate even in a slowing population, if more people are willing and able to work. The OECD collects comparable numbers across the world and we can have a look at Figure 16 above.

Here, we see that:

The US is in the middle group with a participation rate of just over 60 percent of the WAP. France and Spain rank below the OECD average with lower participation rates, and Germany is barely above the OECD average.

Countries around the Mediterranean tend to have the lowest participation rates, such as Italy at around 50 percent, and Greece at 52 percent. Both are countries with declining populations and relatively advanced aging.

Japan and Germany also have participation rates below the US; both are more advanced in aging than the US.

Countries in Scandinavia tend to have the highest participation rates, such as Iceland at over 80 percent and Sweden and Norway at over 70 percent. These are countries that tend to rank high in gender equality across the world, so that it suggests that facilitating entry by females into the labor force, including by expanding part-time job opportunities and ample day-care facilities, is one way to increase participation.

The combined picture for the US from the above international comparisons is thus the following:

First, the demographics are reasonably favorable for economic growth in the rest of this century, based on the latest demographic projections by the UN. Compared to other countries, the US has somewhat more buoyant population growth.

Second, the US has a rising dependency ratio but it is not as acute a problem as in large trading partners such as Europe, China, and Japan.

Third, the US will feel downward pressure on participation rates as aging progresses, but it should also have some room to increase the participation rate from the working-age population, if policies can be designed to support participation, and provided that this is culturally accepted.

The combination of the noted factors suggest that, *from a demographic point of view*, the US has economic prospects that are somewhat more buoyant than many current important trading partners. The continent with the largest growth *potential*, based on demographic developments, would be Africa. If realized, this would be a catching up story, because Africa starts with low per-capita incomes and many basic needs still unmet.

Part 2. Labor Markets and Potential GDP

Chapter 6—Labor Force, Unemployment, and Employment

At the core of this book, we want to assess what a sustainable economy can deliver (how big can sustainable real and nominal GDP become?), and what this implies for policy. In the first part of this book, we looked at demographics as a fundamental issue for the size of any economy. More people in one market means a greater potential aggregate demand and also a greater availability of potential labor supply to produce these goods and services—this gets you a larger GDP (greater aggregate supply). Associated relevant cultural and policy questions include: do people enjoy work in its many broad dimensions (how do people choose between labor and leisure)? And what can public policy do to support and be efficient in producing as large a GDP as possible—what is the *potential GDP* of the country?

Real GDP is often represented by the symbol Q for quantity. We can thus write down the identity that:

$$Q = Q$$

Multiply and divide the right-hand-side by L (for labor) and we get:

$$Q = L * (Q/L)$$

This way of writing the definition of real GDP is economically meaningful. It is always and everywhere, and under any circumstance, correct, because it is still an accounting identity. It says that real GDP is the product of two things: the available units of labor (L) and the average amount of output (Q) that each unit of labor (L) can produce. This later concept is known as average labor productivity: how efficient is the average unit of labor at producing goods and services in the economy. In words:

Real GDP = Labor * Average Labor Productivity

Thus, if we want to know something about how large the economy can become in terms of real GDP, then we need to develop a view on how many units of labor are available, and how *efficient* these units of labor are on average in producing output. The potential availability of labor units is given by demographics and the interplay of policy to make work attractive—how many people have an interest in participating in the economic process. The efficiency of labor to produce output, on average, is a vast field of study and encompasses everything that private sectors and governments do, indeed, society does, to organize the economic process. We will have a look at this crucial aspect of producing real GDP shortly.

Labor force. So, to get a sense of how big the economy can become in the future, we need to focus on two things: L and (Q/L). Let us begin with L, labor. Labor availability is all about demographics. You cannot have more units of labor than people in the population, and we know that within the population, many people cannot work or are advised not to work for many different reasons. Thus, we split the population into the young and the working-age population in Part 1. Out of the working-age population, we determined a reasonable rate of participation in the economic process. Figure 13 provided three scenarios with a central outlook, a high and a low scenario for participation. Let us for the time being explore the central scenarios for the working-age population and for participation. Other combinations of these two variables, which are both uncertain in the future, will produce projections that lie, like a cone or a probability band, somewhere around the central scenario.

Figure 17 shows the multiplication of the working-age population 15+ (central scenario) with the participation rate (central scenario) to result in a central projection for the labor force (LF)—those people who wish to participate in the production of real GDP.

Figure 17. USA--Working-Age Population and Labor Force (thousands of persons)

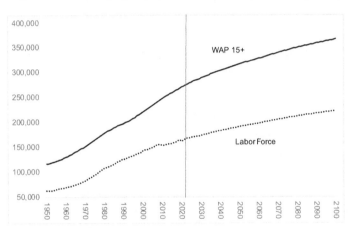

Source: UN and author's calculations.

The WAP is here defined according to the Bureau of Labor Statistics, thus all people above 15 years of age. This includes the elderly. As we look toward the future, the gap between the WAP 15+ and the labor force widens. This is so because in the future there are expected to be more elderly and slightly more young people, in absolute numbers, who do not participate in the labor process. We have also seen that this means that total dependency of young and old people is projected to increase in the future. These are demographic shifts that take a long time to play out and cannot be easily reversed or affected by policy (and there are (political) limits to immigration too). However, in the central scenario, we built in a slight increase in the participation rate of the labor force over the WAP as an aspirational assumption—society tries to get as many healthy and able-bodied people to participate as possible. As population ages, it is normal for participation rates to *decline* slowly over time. So, by assuming that policy can achieve a slight *increase*, we cannot be accused of using pessimistic assumptions in our model.

Unemployment. The labor force consists of two parts: unemployment (U) and employment (L). We have a time series projection for a possible central path for the labor force above. So, if we can find a sensible path for unemployment, then the number of employees, or workers or units of labor input (L) can be calculated as the difference.

We start with unemployment, because society presumably has a wish, an aspiration, to keep unemployment within bounds. If unemployment goes up too high, policies will presumably be reexamined to see if we can get unemployment down. If unemployment goes down very far to very small numbers, it turns out that economic effects can come into play, such as pressure for higher wages in the economy with scarcity of available labor that re-equilibrate the labor markets once again, and unemployment will then tend to increase back up. Somewhere in between the "too high" and the "too low" lies an equilibrium, or what some economists call, a "natural" rate of unemployment that is economically sustainable and socially acceptable.

Let us look at the past from 1950-2019 to see how unemployment has behaved as the economy went through business cycles and was affected by shocks and policy initiatives. We then make some assumptions for the future to see how unemployment might evolve in the period 2020-2100. Figure 18 gives the overview.

The US rate of unemployment in 1950-2019 averaged 5.8 percent of the labor force. Many things have happened during this period, and the volatility of the unemployment rate shows the negative shocks (peaks) and the years of a tight labor market when unemployment was low (troughs). For the future, we make an aspirational assumption that an average unemployment rate of 5 percent is economically, socially, and politically acceptable.[7] Of course, volatility will continue, but we cannot predict what shocks will come at what time and what policy mistakes or victories might emerge. Thus, for the future, we look through the ups and downs and reflect only the underlying aspirational average. This average in the future is 0.8 percentage point lower than the average for the past. That is a lot. We therefore also assume, implicitly, that we have learned from past mistakes and gotten better at keeping unemployment under control. Once again, our assumption cannot be said to be pessimistic. And, again, good monitoring over time is essential to see if and when we need to adjust our long-run assumptions.

---

[7] In the 2020 Report on Social Security and Disability Insurance, the Trustees of Social Security and Disability Insurance also assume as a central scenario an unemployment rate of 5.0 percent through 2095. The low unemployment scenario in the Trustees Reports assumes 4.0 percent; and the high unemployment scenario assumes 6.0 percent.

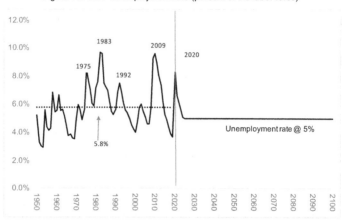

Figure 18. USA--Unemployment rate (percent of the labor force)

Source: BLS, Federal Reserve Bank of St Louis, and author's calculations.

The transition from the past to the future presents us with a puzzle, because as we are writing this book in 2020, the coronavirus has entered the global picture, shutting down economies, creating war-like situations in many countries, and upsetting conventional political regularities. Thus, we are now going through a huge bout of uncertainty where no-one can predict what will happen. What is a modeler to do in such circumstances?

We have opted for a scenario whereby unemployment will rise sharply in the short run, to be followed by a sharp contraction in unemployment when we get a better handle on how to treat the threat of coronavirus for human health and economic health of our countries. The orders of magnitude are anybody's guess at this time. We have modeled a monthly pattern for unemployment and real GDP growth for 2020 and 2021 with a V-shaped recession and inverse, and slightly delayed, unemployment picture. We will need to monitor the months as they go by to see if this pattern needs to be changed.

In short, unemployment is assumed to leap from 5.9 million people, or 3.6 percent of the labor force in February 2020, to a peak of 24 million people, or 14.1 percent of the labor force in May 2020, before starting to ease off. This path gives an average unemployment rate of 9.2 percent in 2020 for the year as a whole (the new peak in 2020 in Figure 17 above). Unemployment is then expected to fall as the shock wears off, and by 2029 the model is back to the underlying structural unemployment rate of 5 percent that we adopt, for these modelling purposes, as the long run average. This leaves open the possibility that the unemployment rate can come down much faster at first, or that it takes even longer, but what is indicated is that the rate will eventually return to some underlying "natural" rate. We can use different paths for this variable to conduct sensitivity analysis, but for now, we will use this clearly explained path as our "central" case, or baseline.

* * *

Political economy interlude: If we inspect the historical period of Figure 18, we see something that raises an interesting question. The peaks in unemployment are associated with presidencies of the Republican Party. Is this accidental or does this tell us something about preferences and risk management?

In 1973-74, the labor market weakened significantly with the first oil crisis while president Nixon (R) was in office; the unemployment rate then peaked in

1975 after Mr. Ford had taken over the presidency following the Watergate scandal.

The next peak came in 1983, during the first term of president Reagan (R). The difficult recession in the early 1980s was associated in the first place by the pursuit of very tight monetary conditions to lower inflation. Mr. Volcker, the new Chairman of the Board of the Federal Reserve, had been appointed by Mr. Carter (D), after inflation rebounded again following the second oil crisis. Mr. Reagan also played a role in combatting inflation by reducing significantly the influence of labor unions (to cut the wage-price spiral). His iconic policy step was the firing of traffic controllers (members of PATCO) who had gone on strike in August 1981, early in Mr. Reagan's first term, to ask for higher compensation and better and safer work conditions.

The third peak came during the term of president Bush Sr. (R), who found himself struggling with an exhausted cycle after the fiscal stimulus and recovery during the latter part of the Reagan administration and his own pledge of "no new taxes." He then increased taxes anyway and lost the election to president Clinton (D).

The next jump in unemployment started in the second term of Mr. Bush Jr. during the Great Recession. This bout of unemployment peaked in the first year of the Obama (D) administration in 2009. There is little doubt that this downturn in economic activity was caused by policy mistakes during the term of Mr. Bush Jr. (vice-president Cheney had famously said that "deficits do not matter.")

The latest peak in unemployment is now underway during the term of Mr. Trump (R) who is also of the view that deficits do not matter and what really matters, besides deregulation, is tax cuts to keep the economy going. The coronavirus has pointed out that economies are subject to large shocks and that it is good always to have buffers at hand to address them.

Economic troubles and high unemployment almost always occur following some trigger or shock to the economy (the oil shocks were adverse supply shocks; the Great Recession is associated with excessive deregulation and procyclical policies; the coronavirus shock has both demand and supply aspects, but also follows procyclical policies). Economic troubles are in this way opportunistic diseases that come when you are low on buffers, or after you make policy mistakes (Bush Jr. and Trump).

Any government of any political persuasion may be confronted with adverse shocks. What seems interesting for this unemployment picture is how administrations react to the problem—how does a government deal with risks? Are policies structured in such a way that they (wittingly or unwittingly) cause labor markets to absorb a lot of the shock, thereby tolerating in part high unemployment, or do they let financial markets absorb a lot of the shock by tolerating higher inflation and/or lower returns to capital? These questions are related to the Philips Curve, which posits that unemployment and inflation tend to move in opposite directions. If two people have different preferences and risk aversions, then one may choose for a bit more inflation and the other for a bit more unemployment in reacting to shocks. The shocks can be supply or demand shocks, and thus it is also important to understand where the bigger risks lie as policies aim for the subsequent economic recovery. This picture of unemployment peaks and their timing with republican administrations suggest that Republican policies lean toward risk weights that permit somewhat higher relative unemployment.

* * *

Employment. Now that we have a full time series for the labor force and unemployment, we can calculate how many units of labor (L) this provides to produce real GDP (L = LF − U). Figures 19 & 20 summarize the findings.

Figure 19. USA--Employment (thousands of persons)

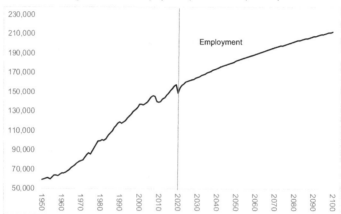

Source: BLS and author's calculations.

Employment in the central scenario is projected to increase from some 157 million persons in 2019, before the expected big dip during the Corona year 2020, to around 212 million by 2100. These data are determined largely by the demographic developments presented in Part 1, and our central assumptions on participation out of the working-age population 15+ and the evolution of unemployment. We will show some sensitivity analysis around these central forecasts, below.

It is clear that employment was not going up in a smooth straight line in the past, because shocks and recessions of various sorts presented bumps and dips in the employment line. In the future, these shocks will also occur, but we cannot predict when they will occur, so the projections always look like a smooth line representing an "average" or underlying trend forecast line. Reality will likely jump around this line as we move along in time.

Figure 20 shows the annual percentage change in employment as shown in Figure 19. This brings out more clearly how volatile employment growth can be, and it shows the dips with negative employment growth during the more difficult economic years, such as 1982, 1991, 2002 (after 9/11), 2009, and now 2020 (proj.).

Figure 20. USA--Growth in Employment and its Trend (percent)

Source: Figure 19, and author's calculations.
Trend line reflects HP-filter (λ=100).

The underlying trend line (the dotted line in Figure 20) is also interesting in that it clearly picks up the growth in employment as the baby boomers entered the job markets in the 1960-1970s. Since then, the demographic anchor of fewer entries into the working-age population has slowed down employment on trend, with a bad dip in the Great Recession of 2008-2009, and now another sharp dip in 2020.

While in individual years employment growth can still be between 1-2 percent, which is a good result for a high-income industrial country, the underlying trend clearly has slowed down and is projected to slow down even more in the future, to around 0.25 percent a year on average towards the end of the century. This is not a result that we designed to be so in any way; rather it is a result of an underlying data generating process. Thus, the intent is that without bias, we let the data tell us what the economy, in combination with demographics, is likely able to deliver in the future.

In the formula for real GDP, we noted that real GDP growth is the product of employment or labor (L) and average labor productivity (Q/L). Thus, we now have a projection for the first part of this equation, which is L. We see that the growth rate in L is projected to slow down over time, so real GDP growth, on trend, would also be expected to slow down, unless something is happening to average labor productivity that compensates the natural slowdown induced by the demographic anchor. We will examine this shortly.

What Figure 20 is also suggesting, is that the high growth rates in employment of recent years, before 2020, were above the trend line of employment growth. Since we can interpret the trend line of employment as a kind of "potential sustainable" employment growth line, it implies that the recent high growth rate in employment was not likely to be sustainable and had to slow down at some point, even ignoring the sudden stop from coronavirus in 2020.

Sensitivity analysis. We have now derived in a step-wise and careful fashion a crucial possible path for labor (L). The path we have derived we call the central scenario, because we consider it the most likely given what we know about how many units of labor might be available from the demographic process. But since we cannot predict with certainty what the future will bring and what loops nature may throw at us, it is therefore helpful to explore a low and a high variant of this central scenario to see how wide the cone might be of possible outcomes around this central scenario.

In Figure 3 of chapter 2 we presented a low, central, and high scenario for the *population* through 2100. Based on these three paths for population, we can thus get a low, central, and high scenario for the working-age population. In turn, we calculated a low, central, and high scenario for the *participation* rate, and hence the size of the labor force, out of this working-age population in Figure 13. Then, within the labor force, we calculated a path for *unemployment*. But this path is also subject to uncertainty—we picked a natural rate of unemployment of 5 percent in the future. But what if it is 4.2 percent instead, or 5.8 percent, as in the past?

So, here we have at least 3 steps that each have an uncertainty cone around it, and that leads to $3^2 = 9$ different possible scenarios. What we can do as an exploratory device is calculate the two extreme scenarios of a low version of employment and a high version of employment. The central version we already have in Figure 19. The extreme high version would assume the high population growth scenario of Part 1, combined with a high scenario for participation, and a low scenario for unemployment—that gives us a sense of upper bound for L. The low scenario does the opposite; we pick the low population growth scenario, the low participation scenario, and the high average unemployment scenario to get a lower bound for L. Figures 21 & 22 show the results.

The high employment scenario shows that there could be some 250 million employees by 2100, instead of 212 million in the central scenario. The low scenario would employ around 180 million units of labor (L) to produce the US real GDP.

In terms of the average, or trend, growth rates of employment, we see that the high scenario would be around 0.5 percent by 2100, the central scenario would be around 0.25 percent, and the low scenario would be at zero percent.

A difference of 0.5 percent in the growth rate of employment a year over 80 years by 2100 cumulates to the equivalent of a lot of real GDP. Indeed, looking at the number of employees working in the high scenario, the *level* of real GDP in 2100 would be much higher than in the low scenario. We will show shortly how big the difference in total real GDP could be. A much bigger real GDP would produce more goods and services for the public to enjoy, and also would make it easier to carry debt. Debt sustainability is a crucial issue in macroeconomics and in the public finances, as we will explore in Part 4 of this book.

Figure 21. USA--Employment Scenarios (thousands of persons)

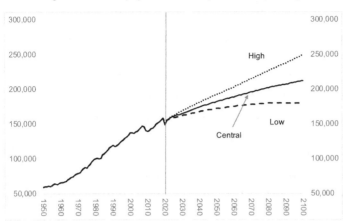

Source: BLS and author's calculations.

Figure 22. USA--Growth in Employment Trend (percent)

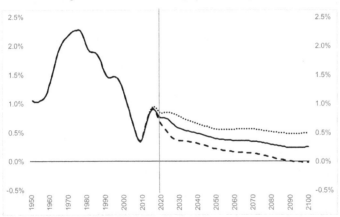

Source: Figure 21, and author's calculations.
Trend line reflects HP-filter (λ=100).

In contrast to the growth rates in Figure 20,
Figure 22 only displays the underlying trend line for
employment growth. The central scenario in both figures is
the same. Since we left out the annual ups and downs of
employment growth and only display underlying trend, it

is at once obvious how powerful the entry of the baby boomers into the labor markets was in the 1960s and into the 1970s. This powerful boost to employment is not in the offing for the future, given the aging of the population and other underlying demographics. We also see that the employment levels in all three scenarios are once again expected to recover once the US gets on the other side of the coronavirus recession.

Nevertheless, as time goes on, the demographic anchor is projected to slow employment growth in all three scenarios. Many high-income countries, such as Germany, Italy, and Japan, already have slowing employment growth or even negative employment growth, because they are more advanced in aging. Thus, by comparison, the US would be expected still to do relatively well.

At the outset of this chapter we derived that the *level of real GDP* is the product of the number of employees working in an economy and their average labor productivity—how many units of real GDP each worker can produce on average. This formula can be differentiated to find that the *growth rate of real GDP* can be proxied by the sum of the growth rate in labor (L) and the growth rate in average labor productivity (Q/L). If we look at Figure 22, we see that over time the (average or trend) growth rate of L will slow down, and hence that the growth rate of real GDP would be expected to slow down as well, unless productivity growth can accelerate.

Let us therefore look at productivity more closely, next.

Chapter 7—Average Labor Productivity and Real GDP

Average labor productivity (Q/L) is defined as the
level of output (Q) divided by the number of employees
that were used to produce this output (L). We can first
look at the historical record to see the level of average
labor productivity and how this has increased or decreased
over time. Figure 23 summarizes the level of real GDP and
the level of employment from 1950-2019; Figure 24 shows
the resulting level of average labor productivity (Q/L).

Figure 23. USA--Employment and Real GDP (1950-2019) 1/

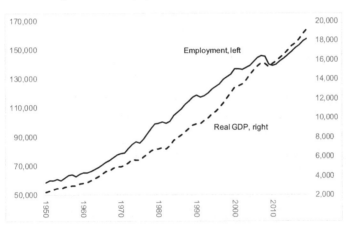

Source: BLS and Federal Reserve Bank of St Louis.
1/ Employment in thousands of persons; real GDP in billions of chained 2012 dollars.

Figure 24. USA--Average Labor Productivity (Real GDP per unit of labor) (1950-2019)

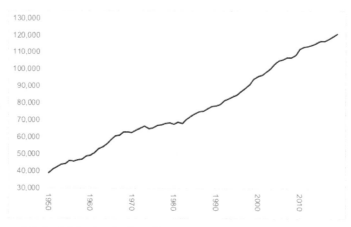

Source: Author's calculations based on Figure 23.

In Figure 23, we see that employment and real GDP have increased together. The dips in employment and real GDP also go together, indicating recessions. More precise analysis of these lines and this relationship shows that employment reacts to variation in real GDP with a slight lag—the labor market is always a bit late. This has an explanation.

When a downturn in activity comes, the business world needs to adjust employment and output plans, but doing so is expensive (severance payments, attempts to keep people on for social reasons, etc.). So, businesses study first to see if the recession will last and for how long. Based on that continuously adjusting assessment, they will keep personnel on, even if business is a bit slack, or they let them go. This process of finding out how serious the downturn is takes time. That is why labor markets are always a bit late to recessions, and they are a bit late to upturns also. Labor markets react with a lag; and this lag depends on how strong the signs of a variation in economic activity are.

Figure 24 shows that average productivity per employee in the US economy has steadily increased between 1950-2019. On the face of it, this is a good sign; not all economies in the world have steadily increasing productivity levels per employee. Those that do not, really do have problems of a structural nature. Productivity in the US has increased from about 40,000 constant dollars to some 120,000 constant dollars (dollars are chain weighted with reference year 2012 in this case. It means that we abstract from price variation and only focus on the real GDP measured in constant prices). Thus, Americans at work have become 3 times as efficient and productive over this time period.

To see just how important this issue is, we can do a thought experiment. Imagine an economy with 2 workers. Each worker can produce 10 units of output per day. The "real GDP" in this economy would be 20. Each worker can enjoy 10 units of output in their daily consumption. This would be the level of material wellbeing that they can enjoy.

Now imagine that these workers invent a machine that can help them to double their output to 20 units each per day (and they share the return on this machine in equal parts). This machine reflects investment in fixed capital. This investment in fixed capital makes each worker more efficient—it increases the productivity of each worker. Now the real GDP of this economy doubles from 20 units a day to 40 units a day. And, with the return on their machine and the return on their labor, each worker can now enjoy daily consumption of 20 units of output. Their material wellbeing has doubled. That is the power of labor productivity increases, helped, in this case, by fixed investment.

As workers become more productive, they may opt to enjoy more income (double in the above example), or work less and enjoy more leisure (Appendix 4). This choice is a cultural issue and different countries see different choices. Anecdotal evidence suggests that, for example, people in France enjoy more leisure when they get more productive, whereas the average person in the US tends to choose higher income, in relative terms. Such choices reflect preferences and are therefore sovereign and legitimate. Economic analysis is not about attaching value judgements to such choices or preferences.

Improvements in productivity can come from many different sources: better managerial abilities; better laws; better education (investment in human capital); better health; a better judicial system; better police; more honest citizens and politicians; better management of the natural environment; a discovery of a natural resource, etc. There are literally millions of factors that influence productivity, and that is why studying productivity and trying to increase it with sound policy is so important, but also difficult.

In relation to our equation for real GDP (Q) that is the product of labor (L) and productivity (Q/L), what would have happened to the above economy if not productivity increased, but only more people—a bigger population affording more workers? So, now we have the same 2 workers producing 10 units each for a total real GDP of 20. Each can consume 10 units a day.

Now two additional workers show up. These new people also produce 10 units a day. The real GDP doubles to 40 units a day. But each worker can now still only enjoy 10 units of consumption a day—just as before the doubling of the real GDP. The material wellbeing per worker in this country has not increased even though the size of the economy doubled, just as in the example before.

What we can conclude is that *productivity is the most important thing in any economy*, not just how many people live there. China and India are very large countries in population, but each worker in the US is much more productive than in China and India. This is the reason why the material wellbeing, or the standard of living, in the US is so much higher than in China and India. China and India are catching up with investments and improvements in organization and policies, but there is still some way to go.

What this thought experiment shows is that it is not important how big you are as a country, but rather how efficient you are and how well you can manage your resources and environment. As we have seen in footnote 5, Luxembourg, Qatar, and Macao are currently the most successful countries in the world economically, because they have the highest per-capita GDP in comparable dollars. These are tiny countries compared with China, India, and the US.

Figure 25 shows the growth in productivity per year (solid line), and the underlying trend growth line (dashed line). What we can see is that year-on-year productivity growth is very volatile. There are many disturbances each year that impact on productivity. But there is a gradual pattern that shows up—the trend. In the 1970s the economy went through serious supply shocks with the two oil crises. The economy needed to be retooled for much more expensive oil, and that took a while. As a result, during this period the economy was soft and productivity growth was low; it dropped to around 1 percent on average from around 2.5 percent a year before then in the

Figure 25. USA--Labor Productivity Growth and its Growth Trend (percent)

Source: Federal Reserve Bank of St. Louis, and author's calculations.
Labor productivity = Real GDP / Employment (persons).
Trend line reflects HP-filter (λ=100).

1960s. In the 1980s and 1990s productivity growth recovered to a peak of 2 percent toward 2000. This is thought to be the result of having overcome the damage from high inflation in the oil shocks (a big dividend from the anti-inflation policies of Messrs. Volcker and Reagan), but also because of the advent of personal computers and the acceleration of digital technology. Digital technology has now penetrated many aspects of life, and further productivity growth then becomes more difficult. A new wave of innovation would be necessary to boost productivity growth again.

In the last two decades of 2000-2019, productivity growth has slowed down again, to about 1 percent a year. There are good reasons to believe that productivity growth cannot stay very high for very long, and eventually may slow down even further. This occurs because efficiency levels in the US economy are already quite high, and to boost it further takes more and more innovation and inventiveness. This takes time. It is a kind of large numbers law. The bigger the number, the more difficult it is to make it even bigger in a world that is generally subject to diminishing marginal returns.

Nature is not unbounded, so getting ever bigger or more efficient is very difficult as this process runs into natural resistance and boundaries. For instance, how long will natural resources last before they are used up for economic purposes? By creating ever bigger economies and levels of consumption, can the planet carry the enormous effects this will have on the environment and our wellbeing?

Technology optimists believe that nanotechnology, artificial intelligence, and robots, to mention a few, can propel our economies ever further. Not all disciplines share this optimism, because there is so much more to a sustainable equilibrium, such as the environment and the climate, to make this possible. Robert Gordon, in his book "The Rise and Fall of American Growth" (2016) provides a well-documented historical view and analysis why productivity growth has slowed down.

Then, there is another line of thinking that does not see the decline in productivity growth as a bad thing per se. It says that as the country has gotten richer, people want other things besides the daily goods we can now fairly well supply. The cars we drive, the washing machines, the air-conditioners etc. all can be further perfected, but no-one is chomping at the bit that we are in a crisis in terms of the quality or quantity of manufactured goods. Wat societies want when they get richer is a higher quality of life and well-being, which depends more on services and time for ourselves then the boundless acquisition of goods. With higher incomes, we will purchase some more time for ourselves, and the production of services tends to have lower productivity growth, because these are often more personal and benefit less from automation and scale economies than the production of material goods. As we shift demand toward personal services and away from mass-produced goods, in relative terms, then average productivity gains per unit of labor will decline. Dietrich Vollrath in his book "Fully Grown" (2020) calls this phenomenon of slowdown a sign of success.

Further to the evolution of productivity growth. When we study macroeconomies in different countries, we have found that a marker that works reasonably well is to look for trend labor productivity growth of around 1.5 percent a year.[8] If countries can achieve this for extended periods of time, they make good progress in catching up with higher-income countries. China has had productivity growth above this level for several decades now, and that is truly a remarkable achievement—China is a strong catching up story. Some stagnant countries are not so lucky.

The inverse effects for countries that are already at very high productivity levels is also generally true—high-income countries have difficulties to keep growing at 1.5 percent productivity advancement a year. Therefore, in the view of this author, a more reasonable aspirational assumption to make for high-income countries like the US is that they aim to grow trend labor productivity at 1 percent a year in future. There are no guarantees that even this is possible, but neither can we rule out new

---

[8] This rule of thumb refers to growth in trend labor productivity. A related, and more technical concept called Total Factor Productivity (TFP), would then tend to show growth of around 1 percent a year.

inventions and technology. The assumptions we make in modeling are themselves an implicit or explicit exercise in balancing risk and return. As always, we can build scenarios around a central projection to explore alternatives. Then we monitor to see what new data tell us about the assumptions that we made. And we adapt the models as necessary.

Real GDP. Based on this path of reasoning, we can now attempt to project real GDP and its growth through 2100, first building a central scenario. The demographic anchor for the population gives labor availability (L). For productivity (Q/L), we assume that the US can sustain trend labor productivity growth of 1 percent a year. This allows us to complete the projections as summarized in Figures 26 and 27.

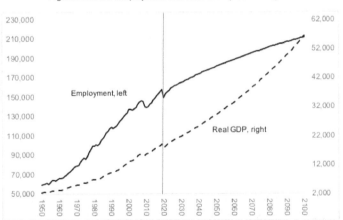

Figure 26. USA--Employment and Real GDP (1950-2100) 1/

Source: BLS and Federal Reserve Bank of St Louis; and author's calculations.
1/ Employment in thousands of persons; real GDP in billions of chained 2012 dollars.

Figure 26 highlights that labor will not grow at a constant rate in the future, but rather gradually decelerate. This is growth dampening. Labor productivity is assumed to continue at 1 percent growth rate a year, with a dip in the very difficult shock year 2020 and then a recovery in 2021, followed by a steady 1 percent growth rate thereafter. This is growth neutral. The deep recession and employment loss is clearly visible in 2020. Other than that, we can only project trends, not cycles, as we look further out. Slowing demographics will slow real GDP growth.

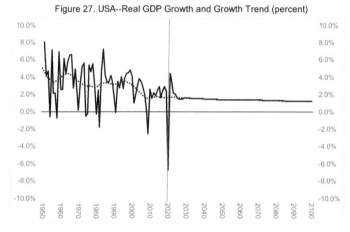

Figure 27. USA--Real GDP Growth and Growth Trend (percent)

Source: Federal Reserve Bank of St. Louis, and author's calculations.
Trend line reflects HP-filter (λ=100).

Figure 27 highlights that real GDP growth itself is also quite unstable. The business cycle causes ups and downs, with negative growth in recession years. 2020 is expected to stand out in its severity—a shock from coronavirus that we can do little about. The dotted line shows the underlying trend line in real GDP growth—we interpret this line as giving us an indication of underlying *potential real GDP growth.* In the 2010s, potential real GDP growth has been around 1.6 percent a year. The actual growth rates have been higher because the economy was recovering from the Great Recession and absorbing the many unemployed in its wake. Lastly, and importantly, fiscal and monetary policies have been pro-cyclical since Mr. Trump took office in January 2017, as we will see later, which also has pushed real GDP growth beyond the trend long-run path, and that is now being interrupted by the coronavirus crisis.

The projections in our central scenario result in a trend growth outlook of 1¼ percent a year by the end of the century (1 percent productivity growth and ¼ percent employment growth). Trend output growth in the next few years, after the shock of 2020, is projected to be around 1.7 percent a year. The actual rate of growth is projected to be higher than this trend underlying rate to catch up from the recession in 2020 and to bring unemployment down again to our long run assumption of 5 percent.

Sensitivity analysis. The central scenario above gave us a trend real GDP output growth of 1¼ percent a year by the end of the century (Real GDP to grow to $56 trillion by 2100). The average trend real GDP growth thus projected for the period 2020-2100 would be around 1½ percent a year (gradually declining from 1¾ percent currently to the 1¼ percent a year later on). In Figure 21 of chapter 5, we had calculated three scenarios for employment growth—a high, central, and low employment growth scenario. Now we can combine this with three scenarios for average labor productivity growth to see how sensitive the results are to more or less optimism.

For the low and high productivity scenarios, we will pick again a symmetric cone around our central scenario of 1 percent growth a year. The high productivity growth scenario will be 1.5 percent a year on average through the end of the century. The low productivity growth scenario will be 0.5 percent on average a year through the end of the century.

We will then calculate the extreme high real GDP growth scenario by combining the high employment growth scenario with a high productivity growth scenario; and the extreme low real GDP scenario by combining the low employment growth scenario with the low productivity growth scenario. Then we discuss results.

Figures 28 and 29 summarize the results. The high growth scenario combines the high employment scenario, which gave us employment growth of around ½ percent a year, with a high productivity growth scenario of around 1½ percent a year. This gives trend real GDP growth in the future of around 2 percent a year (Real GDP to grow to $97 trillion by 2100).

The low employment growth scenario was around zero percent a year, and if we combine this with a low productivity growth scenario of ½ percent a year, then trend real GDP growth will be around ½ percent as well (Real GDP to grow to $32 trillion by 2100).

The central scenario is in between, as we indicated above. It is interesting to consider that neither the high scenario nor the low scenario have a high probability attached to them, given the assumptions we have made. Why? This is so for two reasons.

One, each scenario is an extreme scenario whereby every step of the way of deriving the relevant result, we assumed that every turn would be favorable (high scenario) or unfavorable (low scenario). Thus, the high

Figure 28. USA--Scenarios for Real GDP (Chained 2012 $ billions; 1950-2100)

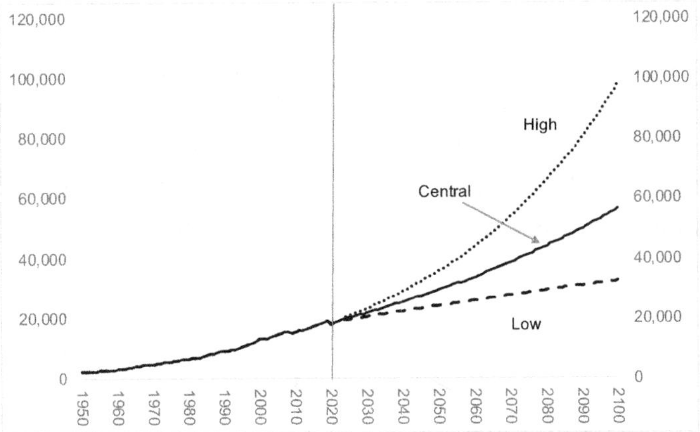

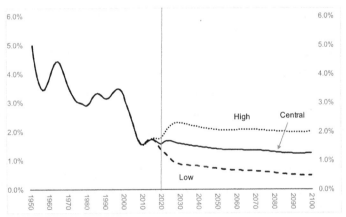

Source: BLS and Federal Reserve Bank of St Louis; and author's calculations.

Figure 29. USA--Scenarios for Real GDP Growth Trend (percent)

Source: Author's calculations.
Trend line reflects HP-filter (λ=100).

scenario calculates a high population growth rate, a high participation rate, and a low unemployment path, and vice-versa for the low growth scenario. But Mother Nature is an equilibrating machine whereby the probability that the odds either come out in favor or against in a continuous fashion are very low. It is more likely to be a mix between favorable and unfavorable developments that follow one-another. This line of thinking places more weight in the probability function around the central scenario, and less weight around the edges that we have calculated as our high and low growth sensitivity scenarios.

The second reason is that there tends to be a tradeoff between employment growth and productivity growth. When employment growth speeds up and unemployment is low causing labor markets to tighten up, business firms have to reach for less productive workers to pull them into employment. This will reduce average productivity growth. If employment growth is weak and unemployment is high causing labor markets to be slack, it becomes easier for business firms to find relatively high productivity workers in the economy. This supports average productivity growth. The high real GDP growth scenario in Figure 29 combines high employment growth with high productivity growth, and vice-versa. The probability that this will hold for any period of time is small. Again, the weight of probability lies around the central scenario and the more extreme our assumptions to get real GDP up or down, the smaller the probability that this is a realistic scenario.

* * *

Political economy interlude. Sustainability in many natural processes reflects some middle ground; it is never extremely favorable nor extremely unfavorable. This has important policy implications. Political systems have a tendency toward hyperbole and optimism. After all, who wants to elect a politician who is moderate and tells us that we can't have everything? Politicians tend to overpromise, and sometimes say that they are the only ones who understand how things work. But nature has no regard for this. It is best to calculate through the probabilities that nature offers, rather than take the electoral plans of politicians at face value—we always need to ask for documentation and we always need to check the numbers. The politicians that we elect to be in charge of the people's business must always be held fully accountable. If they don't like this, best to vote for someone else.

Appendix 4—Average Labor Productivity per Person and Per Hour Worked

In this book, we define average labor productivity as real GDP divided by the number of people employed in that year. We are interested whether this productivity number goes up, down, or stays the same. What causes productivity to go up, down, or stagnate is not at all easy to know. Sometimes, it is a statistical issue—it depends on how we measure things.

For example, for the workers in our small economy that each produced 10 units a day mentioned earlier, what do we mean by the word "day"? Is that 10 hours of work, 5 hours of work, or a standard 8-hour workday. Every concept matters.

Because working days have changed over time, and the number of working hours per day also has changed, many statistical offices are now switching to defining average labor productivity not in *per person* terms, but in *per hour worked* terms. Thus, our example workers above, working a 10-hour day to produce their 10 units each, would have a labor productivity of 1 unit per hour worked. Productivity per person is 10 units per day. If they were to invent a process by which they each could produce their 10 units in 5 hours instead of 10 hours, then they might wish to work only 5 hours and enjoy the rest of the day as leisure. If so, and if we measure productivity per person, we would see no productivity increase—they still produce 10 units each in one day. If we use the definition per hour, then their productivity would have doubled from 1 unit per hour to 2 units per hour. Their wellbeing (welfare) has gone up because now they can enjoy half a day of leisure, which they could not before. Thus, measuring productivity per hour is a more accurate indicator of efficiency to produce output.

But, we used number of people and productivity per person to get a view on real GDP in the future. Is this wrong? It is not wrong, but we have to be aware why productivity is changing to interpret whether this is welfare enhancing or subtracting. Let us say that the working week in the future, in hours worked, continues to decline slightly (we used to work 6 days a week, now most work 5 days a week; the workday used to be 8 hours, now many work fewer hours, etc.). If hourly productivity stays the same, then productivity per employee will go down if the number of hours worked slowly decreases. If productivity per hour increases, then some people will opt to enjoy more leisure, and their productivity per person may not increase—but their welfare will have been enhanced.

Thus, in the way we have set up our model of ascertaining how big the economy could get in the future, we have adopted a gradual increase in productivity per person employed. This may mean that productivity per hour worked is running somewhat faster, but people opt to "buy" a bit more leisure with the increased productivity that they achieve in the future.

In 2019, employees in the *nonfarm business sector* of the US worked almost 15 percent fewer hours per person than in 1950, according to Bureau of Labor Statistics data (roughly a reduction from 6 to 5 workdays a week). As a result, *productivity per hour worked* has increase 2.1 percent a year during this period (1950-2019), whereas *productivity per employee* increased by 1.8 percent a year. A bit of the increased hourly productivity was used for more free time.

Chapter 8—The Output Gap

We have seen above that real GDP has a trend line that steadily goes up. Over time, and with more employees in the country and underlying gradual improvements in productivity of these workers, the volume of goods and services that gets produced tends to increase. But we have also seen that shocks and policy experiments hit the economy all the time. The way up is not a steady smooth line, but one where recessions and booms occur with a certain frequency.

That real GDP goes up with considerable volatility was demonstrated in Figure 27. For the period 1950-2019, the annual growth rate of real GDP averaged 3.1 percent a year, with a peak of 8 percent in 1951 (recovery period from WW2) and a trough of -2.9 percent in 2009 (during the Great Recession). Regrettably, it looks as though the year 2020 will set a new post-war record for a downturn, because of the coronavirus recession that is unfolding combined with policy fumbling along the way.

In Figures 28 and 29, we calculated an underlying trend that smooths through the annual ups and downs. There are various statistical techniques to obtain such estimates of what the underlying trend growth line is, which all have some advantages and disadvantages. We have used a Hodrick-Prescott filter (HP-filter) that can have some bias at the end-points of the calculation. But since we are using very long time series with the end-points in 1950 and 2100 respectively, we keep finding that even in different scenarios, the underlying trend line for the long-time span in between these end-points, the results come out relatively robust. So, we worry less about the end-point problem of the HP-filter when we center our time period of analysis more or less in the middle of this long interval. Other researchers may use different and more sophisticated techniques, and if they find radically different results that are sustained over time, that would be a helpful comment on the findings we produce here.

The underlying trend growth line is not a constant. The growth rates that result from it also average 3.1 percent a year (this has to be, otherwise the filter would present a biased estimate even for the average and that would be a big problem), with a peak of around 4½ percent around 1965 (we ignore the first few observations in the early 1950s because of the end-period problem with HP-filters) and a trough of 1¼-1¾ percent in the low growth and high growth scenarios, respectively, of Figure 29 for more recent years. The central scenario that we prefer as a baseline to think about what is going on in the economy, estimates that underlying trend growth in the last few years runs at around 1½ percent. We can interpret the underlying trend growth rate as an indication of a potential growth rate over time even though we derived it with a statistical method. It is not an analytical explanation of potential growth, which would require a fully defined production function with separate capital and labor inputs. It is a growth rate that strips away the unusual ups and downs in growth (the outliers) that the economy is subject to because of various shocks, and reveals what is a sustainable growth rate for the economy over time.

If we interpret the trend line of Figure 29 as a *potential growth rate*, is it also possible to calculate what a *potential level of real GDP* is in balance—i.e. a level of real GDP that would indicate that demand and supply of resources in the economy are relatively aligned? The answer is yes, we can use the same technique to extract a potential *level* of real GDP along the time line as we did for the potential growth rate of real GDP.

Then we can do a second calculation that will prove helpful and interesting. This asks the question: if actual real GDP jumps around an underlying potential real GDP (or real GDP trend), can we calculate by how much the actual real GDP is removed from the potential real GDP? The answer is again: yes. This calculation gives us what is called the output gap. It is the difference between the levels of actual real GDP and potential real GDP, in percent of potential real GDP. Thus, for example, if actual real GDP overshoots its underlying potential level by 2 percent, then the positive output gap is +2 percent. If it drops below potential real GDP level by this amount, then we talk about a negative output gap of -2 percent.

This concept has an intuitive economic meaning. Namely, when demand in the economy is very strong and propels actual real GDP activity above its sustainable or potential supply level, then we may expect resources on the supply side of the economy to run low and inflation to raise its head. Inflation is something that we like to keep within limits otherwise it will damage the economy in due course, so having an indicator about how far removed the level of activity is from what we estimate as a sustainable level is quite important.

The same holds on the downside. If demand collapses and there emerges spare capacity, *supply* will shrink as businesses close down, and that damages the long-run productive capacity of the economy—the ability to bounce back when the sudden recession ends. Following this line of thought, now it makes sense why governments around the world are assisting companies to prevent too many closures and job losses in 2020 in the wake of the sudden coronavirus shock.

At the same time, this coronavirus recession also damages the *demand* side of the economy as people cannot interact normally in economic manner to exchange goods and services. Since this problem is considered to be temporary, governments want to assist both businesses to keep supply capacity up, and households to protect a certain level of demand.

Figures 30 and 31 show the levels of actual real GDP and potential real GDP (the underlying trend line), and the output gap, as calculated above. It is clear that Figure 30 is not easy to interpret because this is in levels and has large numbers, so the actual and potential real GDP are not so easy to distinguish. That is why Figure 31 is helpful, whereby we present the output gap only, as percent of potential real GDP.

Figure 30. USA--Real GDP and Potential Real GDP (1950-2030) 1/

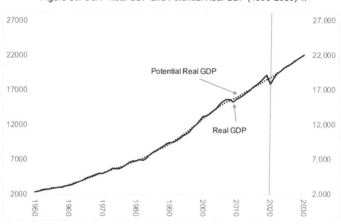

Source: Author's calculations.
Trend line reflects HP-filter (λ=100).

In Figure 30 we have presented data through 2030 only, because we need to cover the period after the coronavirus recession in 2020 to see how we envision the economy to come back to its potential level. Thus, the coronavirus recession causes a sizeable negative output gap to emerge (-4.6 percent)[9], which will take some time to recover. Beyond 2030, we can only project our sense of potential or trend real GDP, because we do not know what other shocks may come in the future. Thus, in the future beyond 2030, by logical design, the output gap becomes nil after a transition period. This nice smooth outlook is for calculation purposes only. As reality unfolds, a zero output gap will not remain every year, because we fully expect that more shocks or policy errors will come that throw actual real GDP off its path of underlying potential or sustainable real GDP. Careful monitoring of data as these come in will reveal what the future has in store.

---

[9] There is a catch, because if coronavirus damages the supply side of the economy on a lasting basis, then this way of gauging the output gap is overestimated. Supply potential would then be lower and the output gap would be lower as well. Thus, when a gap from trend opens up, we need to assess carefully whether it is demand or supply that has declined, and why.

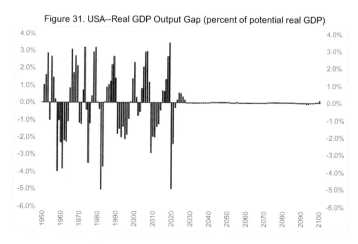

Figure 31. USA--Real GDP Output Gap (percent of potential real GDP)

Source: author's calculations.
Output gap = (Real GDP - Real GDP Trend)/real GDP Trend, percent.

For our purposes of seeing where the economy is relative to its trend, Figure 31 is thus more transparent and helpful. The idea of the business cycle is at once very clear: the economy takes turns cycling around the underlying trend real GDP, with periods of a positive output gap (demand running too hot or an adverse supply shock has reduced output) followed by periods of a negative output gap (demand running too cold or supply has sped up). It is worth repeating that it is important to know whether the gap has been caused by a demand or supply shock. Policies to deal with a gap, if necessary depending on duration and severity of the gap, are different in either case. Supply shocks tend to require structural reforms; demand shocks tend to require monetary and/or fiscal expansion or contraction.

* * *

Political economy interlude. It may surprise some readers to find that this analysis suggests that the recent years have seen a big overheating of the economy. The labor market has been very tight, new supply of workers (L) is being cut off with immigration restrictions and slower internal demographic developments, and productivity growth is declining on trend. This implies that the tax cuts have been procyclical in an economy that was already recovering. The tax cuts have thus not produced the higher growth rates that were envisaged. Instead, it seems that debt injections have been used to try and push the economy to a higher speed, against its natural tendencies.

One possibly good side effect that pushing against the grain of nature has achieved is that more people may have stepped into the labor market and joined the labor force than would otherwise have been the case. Underlying participation has increased.

A puzzle for many has been why inflation has not come back? Could this be the result of globalization and the fact that so many other countries still see the US as their largest potential market for their own growth? Furthermore, the US can pay for its deficits with dollars printed in the basement of the Federal Reserve, which also facilitates excess spending in the economy. Some economists say that labor has lost bargaining power relative to past periods of market tightness (say e.g. in the 1950s-1960s) so that dependent labor is less able to bargain for higher wages in the economy. The foreign pressures of competition through globalization may be contributing to keeping wage gains down in high-income countries (not just in the US). So, inflation seems to have occurred not in wages so far, but it seems to have migrated to profits and wealth, benefitting a smaller part of the population. This latter aspect is consistent with value increases showing not in the consumer price index, but rather in asset prices.

Now the economy has been set back by the coronavirus. Policy reserves had already been exhausted by the push into overdrive growth prior to corona, and that makes the task to deal with this crisis more difficult. As a result, what had gone up too high and overshot on the upside, will now need to go down and overshoot on the down side. Policy mistakes of this nature are common as political systems are often tempted to pursue procyclical policies and make promises they cannot keep. Often this results in tears. These tears are almost never those of the politicians.

* * *

Measuring the output gap is not easy and our indicator as presented above can be questioned, and alternative ones can be presented. Determining whether an output gap is caused by a demand or supply shift is not always so easy either, but important as a diagnosis and what to do in return. This is where the science part of economics meets the art part of economics—how do we interpret signals from reality? Many analysts look at a host of indicators to see if the economy is overheating (supply may have dropped or demand is too strong) or undercooling (supply has accelerated or demand has dropped), and that is certainly a good idea—we should never become a one-variable economist. But the idea of an output gap is still a powerful concept in economics and it can help us to put boundaries around the risks that policy makers should consider as they take difficult fiscal and monetary decisions. The emergence of the coronavirus was a surprise; but that surprises do happen is not a surprise and the economy should always have some policy cushions at hand to deal with them. The output gap suggests to us a consistent story that we should have built some cushions prior to this downturn—alas the cushions were all spent.

Chapter 9—Inflation and Nominal GDP

In the previous chapters we have calculated a long-run path for trend real GDP (in fact, three scenarios of it to deal with uncertainty), departing from demographics and considering that technology and policy learning contribute to lifting efficiency gradually and hence the average productivity per employee. We have also seen that just having more people does nothing per se for the wellbeing of the population; only productivity gains really lift wellbeing.

Government policy and managing the macroeconomy must always be oriented toward sustainability (which is the grain of nature). To assess whether government policy is sustainable in a fiscal sense (regarding the public sector budget and balance sheet), we will need to assess debt sustainability and how the public balance sheet is managed over time. To do this, in turn, we need to have a path for nominal GDP as well, not just the real GDP. To get to nominal GDP, we need to overlay the real GDP economy with prices. Real GDP combined with the price level prevailing over time will give us the nominal GDP that we are interested in.

So, let us first look at the price level and inflation that are the relevant variables in the context of the national accounts of real and nominal GDP. We have a record of nominal and real GDP from the past, so this is where we start. If we divide nominal GDP with the estimates of real GDP, then we get what is called the implicit GDP deflator. The implicit GDP deflator tells us how prices on average for the entire economy have evolved. Inflation can then be calculated as the rate of change in this deflator year by year. The consumer price index is another way to measure prices and inflation and, over time, these two measures should not provide radically different results.

Figures 32 and 33 present the level of the implicit GDP deflator and its annual rate of increase for the period 1950-2019.

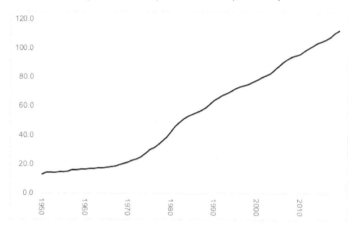

Figure 32. USA--Implicit GDP Deflator (2012 =100)

Source: Bureau of Economic Analysis and author's calculations.

Figure 33. USA--Inflation in the Implicit GDP Deflator (annual percent change)

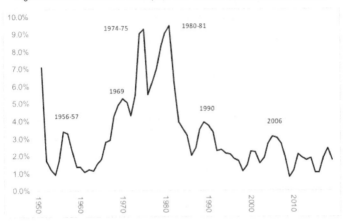

Source: Bureau of Economic Analysis and author's calculations.

The average inflation rate, as measured by the implicit GDP deflator, in the period 1950-2019 was 3.2 percent, with a peak of 9.5 percent in 1981 (the second oil crisis) and a trough of 0.8 percent in 2009 (the Great Recession). So far in this century since 2000, inflation has averaged 1.9 percent, which is just shy of the 2 percent inflation that has become an aspirational benchmark in most industrial countries. It is at once clear that the 1970s were difficult in terms of inflation, and indeed, that is when the two oil shocks took place and caused a lot of nominal pressure on all economies in the world. Energy is an essential input for all economies and oil prices increased from $3.60 in June 1973 to $39.50 per barrel in June 1980—more than a ten-fold increase.

Political economy interlude. We referred before to the Phillips Curve, which posits a trade-off between inflation and unemployment. In managing the risks inherent in such trade-offs, it is possible that some people could prefer to keep inflation under control, even if that is at the cost of somewhat higher unemployment. Others may prefer the opposite, wanting to keep unemployment down, even if that is at the cost of somewhat higher inflation. It would be interesting to know whether political parties, the Democratic Party and the Republican Party in the US, also make such inherent tradeoffs, and whether we can see in the record if they tilt the risk one way or the other.

We saw before that higher unemployment has been timed with the Republican Party in office, and we can now see if there are any indications that the Democratic Party was in power during higher inflation years. In the mid-1950s, president Eisenhower (R) was in office. These were turbulent years, with the baby boomers coming on stream, high demand and high economic growth, and significant growth in the labor union movement. The country was also entering the cold war after the Korean War ended in 1953. Then in 1969, president Nixon (R) assumed power following president Johnson (D), with even more turbulent years in the middle of the Vietnam War. President Nixon stepped down in 1974 and was followed by president Ford (R) until 1977, when he was succeeded by president Carter (D). President Carter then handed off the baton to president Reagan (R) in 1981. Federal Reserve Chairman Volker and president Reagan broke the back of high inflation in 1981-1989, as we noted before and as visible in Figure 33. The uptick in 1990 occurred during the term of president Bush Sr (R) following overheating of the US economy and a drop in the value of the dollar following the Plaza Accord in late 1985 against major other currencies that gradually worked itself through the economy with upward pressure on prices. The year 2006 shows the following overheating experience during president Bush Jr (R), which then resulted in the collapse of financial markets that triggered the Great Recession of 2008-2009.

If we examine this record, then we see that two democrats have presided over inflation upticks, president Johnson faced the inflationary costs of the Vietnam War and president Carter faced the second oil shock. The other 4 episodes all took place during republican administrations, with 2 episodes (Bush Sr and Jr) arguably related to government policy.

On balance, it seems that inflation has been somewhat less of a recurring problem for the economy than recurring bouts of unemployment, except during the oil shocks. It also suggests that the association of high inflation with any political party is less pronounced than the association of high unemployment bouts with republican presidents in office. Since monetary policy is the explicit task of the Federal Reserve Bank, as America's central bank, having an independent Federal Reserve Bank in charge of monetary policy, by and large, has worked well over time in learning how to manage inflation and keep it moderate.

Thus, if we set aside the special years of the oil shocks,[10] then US inflation has been running around 2.5 percent on average a year, which is relatively moderate. Even the upticks in between and around this longer-term average, again abstracting from the oil shocks, have not been that high. This evolution suggests that monetary policy has improved over time and has become more

---

[10] The two oil shocks were large adverse external supply shocks that acted like a tax on the economy. They gave rise to a learning process, because it was not immediately obvious how best to deal with them, and it took time to retool the production function in response to the jump in energy costs.

effective in keeping inflation under control. Globalization, which has brought online cheaper manufacturing from the rest of the world, and the effects of technology also have supported moderating inflation even with a good growth record. Monetary policy learning, globalization, and technology seem key factors behind this relatively good record in the US.

As already noted, what is really interesting in the context of the concept of inflation is that the phenomenon has migrated from everyday goods and services that all of us consume to asset prices. Inflation has now become more visible in asset prices than in consumer prices. Society has not placed this form of inflation on the radar screen in a similar way as with the conventional meaning of consumer price inflation. This may well have a political root and a political consequence. Wage inflation with moderate consumer price inflation (held down by globalization and technology) benefits working people; asset price inflation benefits high-income and wealthier strata of society. Low consumer price inflation and high asset price inflation is thus a boon for the wealthy. Since working people tend to lean democrat and wealthy people tend to lean republican, asset price inflation tends to be favorable for republican administrations. But this may bring a seed of instability, because asset price inflation then becomes the cause of growing inequality of income and wealth. This growing imbalance since the 1980s, can be a corrosive force on the wellbeing of society and lead to policy distortions in the political economy, particularly in monetary policy that is now seen as having to underwrite strong asset prices. It seems that republican presidents worry less about asset price inflation than democratic ones.

* * *

Inflation in the future. Even though the independence of the Federal Reserve Bank is under attack by Mr. Trump (R), we will assume that the FED will keep its good overall policy record and keep future goods and services prices inflation under control. For our modeling purposes, we will therefore maintain the aspirational assumption of 2 percent inflation per annum. Since populations are aging and economic growth is slowing down, there may be some risk of underperforming this assumption, so let us also explore a low inflation scenario of 1.5 percent in the future. But if asset price underwriting leads to a bias of too loose monetary policy, there is also a risk of a symmetric high scenario of 2.5 percent per annum, through 2100.[11]

Nominal GDP. We now have all the assumptions and steps in place to calculate a potential path for nominal GDP. We will use the three scenarios for real GDP and combine these with the three scenarios for the future implicit deflator. As before, we see most of the probability weight around the central scenario, with the low and high scenarios as less likely to occur but still informative with

---

[11] The Federal Reserve announced in August 2020 an evolution in its monetary policy framework. Instead of considering the inflation target as a type of ceiling of 2 percent, it now explicitly will target inflation of *average* 2 percent. This means that the FED will be patient in raising policy interest rates and allow inflation to overshoot the 2 percent limit with "moderate" amounts. The FED has not (yet) explained how it will calculate the "average" inflation performance, and what "moderate" means, so we will have to see what this evolution means in practice for the economy.

respect to allowing some uncertainty around this central scenario. Figures 34 and 35 summarize the results.

Figure 34. USA--Nominal GDP Scenarios (US$ billions)

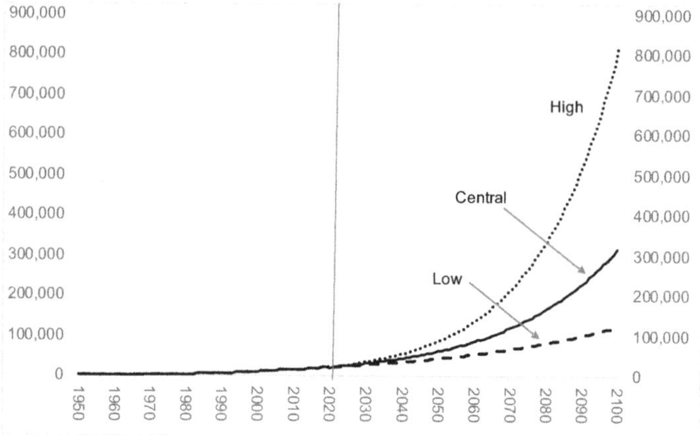

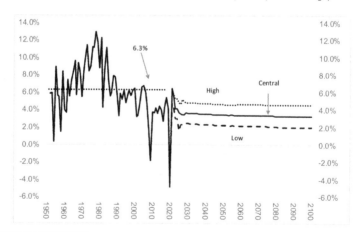

Source: Author's calculations.

Figure 35. USA--Nominal GDP Growth Scenarios (annual percent change)

Source: Author's calculations.
Note: does not include 1950,1951.

What we see in our findings is the following: inflation in the future is likely to be lower than average inflation in the past. This could change if new exogenous and important shocks occur, such as the oil shocks in the 1970s, or if too much debt and too loose monetary policy lead to an inflation boom. But we cannot predict such shocks, so we have smooth average scenarios for the future. Nominal GDP growth in the future central scenario would be around 4-5 percent in the near term (delivering a nominal GDP of $314 trillion in 2100), declining gradually to around 3¼ percent later. The high scenario would have a longer-run nominal GDP growth of nearly 4½ percent (nominal GDP of $806 trillion in 2100); and the low scenario would have a longer-run nominal GDP growth of 2 percent (nominal GDP of $121 trillion in 2100). These numbers contain important information about sustainable fiscal policy, as we shall see later in the book.

Part 3. The Objectives and Instruments of Government Policy

Chapter 10—Structural Reforms to Support
Aggregate Supply

In chapters 2-9, we analyzed how big the economy can get over time, both in real terms and in nominal terms. First, we started by considering how many employees there are in the country (L or labor input). This follows from the natural demographic profile and policies to encourage participation, as well as those that permit or reject net immigration. Second, we looked at how efficient the employees are at producing goods and services as measured in real GDP. We called this a sense of skill or efficiency: labor productivity (Q/L). Labor productivity is a function of education as a form of investment in human capital, investment in plant and equipment (fixed capital), the structure of aggregate demand between goods and services, and management and governance in all its diverse forms (how is society organized and what rules do people observe to live by?). Third, we considered that monetary policy by the US Federal Reserve aims to keep inflation within certain bounds around 2 percent a year (an aspirational target).

With the first two components we could project *potential real GDP*. Combined with the third component, we could project *potential nominal GDP*.

It is helpful to see the calculations we have made (including the scenarios to deal with uncertainty) as indicators of the macroeconomic *supply side* of the economy. We have calculated how many goods and services the US may be expected to be able to produce given its labor input and skill in any given year, in equilibrium. This is the output from the production function that the country is able to offer for domestic demand and net exports.

There is also a *demand side* of the economy, and that looks at how the goods and services produced are absorbed by the various aspects of demand, where we may classify different types of demand as: private sector consumption and investment, public sector consumption and investment, variation in inventory, and net exports, which is the difference between exports and imports—the well-known *aggregated demand components of GDP.*

In this chapter, we would like to say some words about the influence of policy and structural reforms on aggregate supply.

In the next chapter, we will say some words about the influence of cyclical policy on aggregate demand.

If in any year the GDP produced is equal to the GDP demanded, then supply and demand are in equilibrium and firms and stores will not see a noticeable change in their inventories. If supply exceeds demand, then the goods and services that have not been sold will end up in storage, and vice versa. Thus, at the end of the year, the variation in inventory, or "stock building" as it is sometimes called, is the residual product from the millions of decisions that consumers and business firms make regarding demand and supply in the economy every year.

If we believe that a plentiful supply of diversified goods and services is a good thing, how could government policy influence the supply side of the macroeconomy to maximize potential GDP? We have two variables of particular interest: the number of workers (L) and their productivity per worker (Q/L). Let us see what governments could do to influence each of these two variables.

Policy influence on Labor (L)

Population policies—natural birth rates. The government can explicitly encourage families to have more children or it can discourage families from having children. The US does not have explicit or intrusive population policies in this sense, but there are famous examples in the world, such as the one-child population restrictions implemented by China for a while. A regulation of this sort is called a "distortion" because it means that families are not free to determine by themselves, and thus voluntarily, how many children they wish to have.[12]

But there are also other, and less intrusive means of influencing birth rates. For example, France tends to have a relatively high natural birth rate. This is related in part to French social policy that provides relatively ample support for families and that allow women to bridge the time in childbirth and early childcare at lower cost. A country that extends generous maternity and paternity leave, has ample low-cost daycare facilities (at work and close to work), and good family healthcare plans supported by the state, will lower the economic and emotional cost of having children and the natural birth rate will tend to hold up.

But in general, and including in France, as the average income for families increases, the rate of

---

[12] Because of its one-child policy, there has been a sharp slowdown in births in China and the country is aging quickly. The gender distribution has also been affected, because Chinese couples preferred to have boys rather than girls. So there are now more boys than girls among the young generation. Distortions from policy can have intended and unintended consequences and good policy making should therefore always seek to go with the grain of nature to produce as few distortions as possible.

childbirth tends to decline. Higher-income countries have lower birthrates than lower-income countries. This is related to a higher marginal cost (more loss of income) for people in high-income countries taking time off from work. It is also related to better healthcare systems and social security systems in high-income countries, so that couples don't need as many children to take care of them when they get older and infirm. The nuances between countries around this declining trend are related to family, health, and social support policies noted above.

Population policies—Net Immigration. The US has always been an immigration country. More people have entered the US in its history then opted to leave for other countries. Some countries see their population decline because of net emigration. When looking at global statistics provided by the UN, we see that Canada, Australia, New Zealand, and the US are among the higher net immigration countries. Small island economies are losing population due to emigration, as is the continent of Africa (but the latter has a high natural birthrate so that its population is still taking off).

* * *

Political economy interlude. More recently in the US, the Republican Party has started linking immigration policy with identity politics. This would mean that immigration policy is becoming increasingly selective, with discrimination toward some groups. If that is a preference of the American people, then the politics can reflect such a preference as a sovereign choice. But this will have economic consequences. The natural birthrate of US citizens is declining and based on natural population increase alone, the US population would start to decline as a whole within a few decades. Nevertheless, the reason that the UN projects growth in the US population to continue through 2100 in its central projection is only because of net immigration (Appendix 5).

For the economy, immigration is thus not about identity, but rather about absorption and assimilation. Studies have shown that immigrants over a lifetime tend to contribute positively to society and economic growth, but they may impose costs in the short-term before they are fully assimilated to become "regular" citizens. Further diversification of the population is also seen by many to be net positive if society can find solutions to social stress in a harmonious way. This occurs because more diversification brings a potential wider array of ideas and possible solutions to problems that society may confront. As we have observed, mono cultures carry biological risks that, among humans, manifest both in physical and creative and innovative dimensions.

Immigration is a delicate issue for all countries. Preferences are sovereign but they do have consequences. Perhaps the concerns about immigration reflects innate fear of overpopulation and losing one's sense of community. The kernel of truth in Malthus' ideas also refuses to go away, including with new reminders recently in the environmental stresses that are becoming unmistakable. Populist movements in various countries seem to favor discrimination against people from other countries, but if one does not tolerate diversification, then tunnel vision may set in, and that is not optimal for humanity from any economic angle. A more humane policy that pays dividends to boot, compared with shutting the doors, would be to help reduce income inequality between countries through sustainable development and better healthcare, so that birthrates drop further in lower-income countries, population stress in these countries declines, and the need for economic migration diminishes.

* * *

Participation. Even if demographics are favorable, recall that not all people of working-age population actually participate in the economic process. Many governments analyze the participation rate, however, because if many participate out of the existing population and there are fewer dependents, then the (private and budgetary) costs of caring for the dependents is reduced. Participation can be influenced by several policies; we can only mention a few:

> $\Rightarrow$ Education. Better educated citizens tend to have higher participation.
> $\Rightarrow$ Health care. If health care is widely accessible, more people will work.
> $\Rightarrow$ Daycare. More daycare will allow more parents of young children to work.
> $\Rightarrow$ (Public) transportation. Better mobility boosts participation
> $\Rightarrow$ Housing. Good supply of affordable housing encourages mobility and participation (and productivity).
> $\Rightarrow$ Anti-discrimination. People in wheel chairs or with other physical limitations can work very well if they can get to work (or if work can get to them). Are streets and walkways smooth? Can they get on the bus or in the subway/metro, etc.? Combating any discrimination by age, gender, sexual orientation,

nationality, ethnicity, income, etc., can improve participation.

⇒ Tax system. Are income taxes so high that people feel discouraged to participate in work? Is the structure of taxes unfriendly for the supply side of the economy? Current thinking is that taxes on real property and consumption tend to be better for the supply side then taxes on income. But there are limits to this proposition, because the distribution of effective tax burden can be made worse, and that could create resistance and lower participation. Finding the right balance is a challenging task for government.

Unemployment. Going down the line of our analysis, once we have a certain population, and we have optimized participation, then, within the labor force, some still do not have or cannot find a job; but they wish to work. Thus, it is also important to keep unemployment as low as possible—high unemployment (and high incarceration) is a waste of productive people. Finding the right balance to help when they lose their job, and encouraging everyone to find a job quickly is difficult and different societies place this balance somewhat differently. Some aspects are:

⇒ Unemployment benefits. Are they too low (causing social stress) or too high (discouraging job search)?

⇒ Assistance to find a job. Can people find vacancies? Are they willing to move to a different city? How productive are employment agencies? These issues deal with the problem of "matching." There are unemployed people somewhere who are willing to work. There are jobs somewhere that could be filled with these people. Can we use technology and good management to help these two ends find each other? It is the dating game for the unemployed.

⇒ Retraining. Are there programs for those who want to learn new skills? Can they access vocational training or community college? Is society, i.e. government, willing to support funding for retraining? Germany is known for its large internship programs in the private sector, whereby businesses teach young people skills through on-the-job training. This may be worth emulating.

⇒ Hiring and firing costs. Are these costs so high that companies are reluctant to hire new workers? Do labor unions keep these costs high to protect their insider members?

⇒ Other regulations and flexible work hours. Sometimes government regulation can become so onerous that it causes unemployment to last longer or be higher overall. Governments need to be moderate and efficient in regulation. The Netherlands has reformed its labor market policies after the structural crisis in the early 1980s to liberate the labor market for part-time work and flexible work hours. This has materially increased female participation. Many in the

Netherlands work relatively few hours per person, but very many people participate in the economy.

We already have quite a long list, and this is only about the *number of employees* (L) in the production function. Proper governance and regulation is truly a difficult task and governments need to think long and hard about what is the right amount and the right kind of regulation in any economy. When there is a mistake or a big distortion somewhere, then all other aspects of the economy will feel this, because in the macroeconomy everything is connected to everything else—production may then be less than what it could be.

Policy influence on Labor productivity (Q/L).

If the discussion above opened up a long list, the second topic of labor productivity opens up an even bigger list. We cannot possibly begin to describe all the policies that are relevant for productivity growth. Let us therefore again give some examples, realizing that we are only scratching the surface.

Education. Education is investment in human capital. If people are better educated, they tend to be more productive. Do children get an excellent education in elementary and high school (the basis for higher learning)? Do universities strive for teaching and research excellence? Do all children in the country have access to a comparable high quality of education?

In the US, the system for funding schools is significantly based on the local real estate tax.

Neighborhoods with more expensive homes will raise more money for schools than those were housing is inferior. This can create poverty traps and economic segregation over time.

Does the state assist in paying tuition for universities, and if so, does most of this assistance go to students that come from relatively wealthier families where children come from better schools and have a better chance to make it into the university to begin with? On the one hand, it is sometimes said that university students are "heirs with rich expectations" (because they get the best jobs afterwards) and that, therefore, state-assisted funding is most important for day care, elementary, and high-school, where all children should get the basics. On the other hand, if university students have to borrow against their future income, this can lead to excessive levels of debt by the time the students get their degree. One would be tempted to think that a mix of solutions and assistance is best, so that one can learn from doing and adapt policies as society goes along.

Education also continues during work life. And this, too, contributes to becoming more productive and well-rounded in the job. Learning and education are life-long activities that show high rates of return for the productivity and wellbeing of people in the economy. Vocational training and community colleges can be important instruments for people to keep up their skills or to retrain for other types of employment.

* * *

Political economic interlude. An interesting question that has appeared in the US and Europe, is whether it is best for society and the economy's productivity that so many students with aptitude for mathematics are drawn into investment banking and other financial services, and away from engineering, medicine, and other high-value activities that have a direct impact on the real economy? As Kramer in the show Seinfeld says "I have always dreamed of becoming a banker!" China has no hesitation about pumping out many engineers in different fields as a matter of social quota. The US and Europe are very hesitant to apply such social engineering. Arguably, the US and Europe have a shortage of engineers and an excess of bankers. This could restrain the economy's productivity.

Thus, sorting out all the effects that determine if children have equal opportunities to get a good education is very complex and politically sensitive. Different countries with different sentiments and cultures will come up with different solutions and different degrees of success. There is not a one-size that fits all.

*   *   *

Healthcare. Ancient Greeks already established that healthy minds require healthy bodies; that is why they engaged in sports and physical activity—even developing an early version of the Olympic Games. Further, they believed in Asclepius as the god of medicine, and Hygeia as the goddess of hygiene and health. It made little sense to Greeks to educate children and then lead an unhealthy lifestyle. The coronavirus seals the point that healthcare is essential for a well-functioning economy. If we are sick, we can keep our jobs, but we won't produce anything, so productivity plummets and soon our incomes with it. The discussion in macroeconomic management is not about the need for good health, but rather how to pay for good healthcare.

The US system of healthcare and health insurance is substantially private sector based, with supplemental health care and health insurance from the public sector. Health outcomes in the US are not as good as in other well-functioning countries, but the cost of US healthcare outstrips all others in the world by a wide margin. More recently, as an ultimate indicator that something is wrong, the US experienced in several years a declining life expectancy—that is a true alarm bell. The US also is not doing well with the coronavirus—another alarm bell.

The discussion of what to do with healthcare, as with education, has become, regrettably, highly partisan and ideological. The political system struggles what to do, to keep the good outcomes of the US system, such as good R&D activity, speedy treatment, and high quality if you can pay for it, while improving the bad parts of the system, such as high cost, poor coverage of large groups of the population, and inequalities of access, even to primary care. Suffice it to say for this chapter that good health boosts productivity and poor health destroys it—this is why healthcare is not just a private issue, but also a public policy issue and a macroeconomic issue.

Investment climate. If labor has more access to capital (machines etc.), then it will be more productive (Appendix 6). Getting the right mix of labor and capital is a major intellectual challenge for any country. Are investors welcome? Are foreign investors welcome? Do we have concerns that they will steal our intellectual property, and therefore we restrict foreign investment? Governments tend to tax capital differently from labor. This is related in part to the higher flexibility of capital to move elsewhere (if taxes on capital go up, businesses move to another country more quickly than labor, which is more home-bound). Giving businesses income tax breaks to hope that they will invest more has met with uncertain outcomes, if not an absence of a strong link between lower income taxes and higher investment rates. What does seem to work is giving businesses the ability to accelerate depreciation for a while, when investment activity is cyclically down or needs to recover from a shock. The temporary nature of the benefit from accelerated depreciation gives businesses an incentive to boost investment now instead of waiting until depreciation rules are back to normal in the future.

Energy supply. Is the energy supply sufficient and stable? Electricity outages on a regular basis kill productivity and some US big cities, such as New York, have had noticeable energy failures. Energy is of course related to the overall investment picture. Is the grid safe? What mix of renewable and therefore environmentally friendly energy generation, nuclear and coal generation, or fossil fuel generation is optimal? We can use cheap coal, but if we poison our cities with coal emissions, are the gains only short-term followed by very large longer-term costs and productivity declines? Some have said that they favor to close the Department of Energy. But that seems odd, given how complex and important energy policy is and how critical the supply of energy is to productivity. The private sector or the market cannot easily produce an optimum outcome, because this industry is notorious for scale economies and for generating (negative) externalities such as pollution and geo-political stress. Energy is part of the productivity equation.

Infrastructure. When president Eisenhower (R) built the interstate highway system after the second WW, productivity in the US, and real GDP growth, increased. How are the roads and bridges today, not only for interstate traffic, but even inside cities? There is a noticeable difference driving on roads in Western Europe and driving on the US East coast—the roads in Western Europe are better. This leads to less vehicle damage, better logistics, and more money in society to dedicate to other important goals. Investments in (deep) seaports, efficient airports (and airport control systems), bridges, and water and sanitation systems, are all classical public good activities that would not be done by the private sector or in a pure market system—again because they create lots of (positive) externalities. Governments have a critical role to play in providing good infrastructure and efficient taxes are needed to pay for this.

The credit system. Is credit available to those who are most efficient in using it to create new output? Are banks safe, honest, and well regulated? Do the citizens have enough confidence to supply their savings to the banks, to be passed on at reasonable cost as credit to producers in the economy? The Federal Reserve, the Treasury Department, and a host of other important government agencies are in charge of regulating and monitoring the financial system. Again, one could easily spend one's life's career in just studying this material.

* * *

Political economy interlude. One key question that has arisen is whether an economy can become addicted to debt/credit, and that this addiction to debt can produce a collapse of its own in growth and productivity? It seems that way. Every time the US goes through an economic crisis lately, the outcome seems to be: more debt! (the equivalent of "This Time is Different", as the famous book by Carmen Reinhart and Kenneth Rogoff (2012) so aptly documents.) But surely, leverage ratios and debt ratios cannot rise forever, and the cycles of instability emanating from, not the real economy, but indeed the financial system itself, seem to have no end, and may well be afflicted by a "no-learning" syndrome. If debt is the cocaine of the modern capitalist economy, then we can safely assume that the mother of all global debt crisis is going to set us back to square one, one day. And given the shorter periods in which the crises in the US are now following one another (again always with the excuse that "this time is different"), this mother of all debt crisis may not even be that far away. We will illustrate in Part 4 of the book on fiscal policies and government debt, just how challenging the fiscal future looks for US policy in this regard.

*   *   *

The judicial system. How are the judges and the courts; are they honest and efficient? Is the judicial system transparent and does the judicial system, beginning with the minister of justice, explain to the public what it is doing and how it arrives at decisions? Is the justice department credible? Is access to the law open to all participants in the country, and are cases addressed relatively expeditiously? Is the process of appointing and confirming judges and other officials in the justice system open and transparent, and does the system of checks and balances between the three branches of government work satisfactorily? Does the political system strive to maintain a balance of different skills and political leanings in the judicial system, or does it make efforts to favor judges or officials with certain points of view (litmus tests or loading the courts) before they can get appointed? If you have doubts in your mind when you consider these questions, then there is a potential problem. If citizens lose trust in the law and the judicial system, and they wonder whether the scales of justice are still evenly balanced, then capital will not come, investments will be less than they could otherwise be, and productivity will suffer—potential real GDP will be lower than it could otherwise be.

* * *

Political economy interlude. There are countries where the most important minister of government is clearly the minister of justice, almost always because the administration of justice has been captured and the judicial system works very poorly. You cannot keep such things a secret. All citizens know that the country is governed with a lack of basic fairness. The citizens are unhappy, and they have a feeling that they cannot do much about it, because the same forces that pack the justice system will then be the judge and jury to consider complaints and requests for reform, sometimes even leading to outright reprisals for whoever brought the grievance.

Probity, or the willingness voluntarily to "do the right thing" and be honest, or at least to allow an open and transparent process to ascertain what is the best course of action, is a close cousin to having a strong, balanced, and independent judicial system. Probity is most important as a quality for office of politicians. Are politicians honest and do they set a good example? If politics is dishonest, why should the people have any confidence, and be honest themselves? Corrupt and dishonest politics is a cancer that infects whole societies from the top down, and this kills productivity. Output will suffer. Ethics affects the allocation of resources. And, whether economist like this or not, since we study the allocation of resources, we cannot ignore ethics.

*   *   *

Regulation. Is regulation lean and efficient or heavy and overburdening? Too heavy regulation can act like cholesterol in the body of the economy. The country is quickly out of breath and can even get an economic heart attack as too dense a web of rules can entangle and constrain the dynamic adjustments of economies. At the same time, some regulation is crucial, to deal with externalities, for instance (environmental damage comes to mind), for which market-based systems have no ready solution; or to avoid extreme concentration of market power, or trust forming, whereby the drawbacks from a lack of competition among a critical minimum number of players starts overwhelming the benefits that may be attached to economies of scale.

The reader will by now have an idea of just how massive this field of supply-side policy and supply-side political economy is to present the best possible actions in support of the economy. And, above, we have truly only scratched the surface and asked many more questions than provided practical answers. So many of these difficult choices have to be tested against the preferences of the population. This requires an arduous and continuous political process and discussion.

Genuine respect and admiration is due to politicians, public figures, and researchers who are able to navigate this vast field and come up with sensible options for the public, and who can compromise somewhere in the middle when in doubt. Those who cheat and are in it for a game of capture to represent a narrow interest should be summarily ejected, because the entire economy will suffer if there are bad decisions. Getting policy right is not a game of capture.

Appendix 5—The Sources of Growth in the US Population

It is interesting to see where the new (net) Americans come from: they can either be born, or pass away, in the US from the existing population, or they could come from abroad as (net) immigrants. The table below shows data to shed some light on this issue.

USA--Indicators of the Annual Change in the Population

	1990-99	2000-09	2010-19	2020-2100 UN Proj.
	(persons)			
Average annual change in population	3,268,595	2,773,136	2,146,799	1,293,691
Natural increase	1,706,091	1,703,071	1,289,167	224,282
Net immigration	822,835	914,776	842,071	1,061,358
Residual	739,669	155,289	15,561	0
	(percent)			
Average annual change in population	1.3%	1.0%	0.7%	0.3%
Natural increase (contribution)	0.7%	0.6%	0.4%	0.1%
Net immigration and residual (ccontribution)	0.6%	0.4%	0.3%	0.3%

Source: US Bureau of the Census; and UN Population Pojections.

From these data we see that the population grew by some 3.3 million people a year in the 1990s, 2.8 million a year in the 2000s, and 2.1 million a year in the 2010s. The UN projects that population increase will slow down to an average of 1.3 million people a year through the end of this century (central projection). A slowing share of this annual increase will come from natural increase (US births minus deaths); net migration has averaged around 860,000 people a year since WWII.

It is worth noting that during the term of Mr. Trump, net immigration is estimated to have slowed down significantly, so if this slowdown keeps up, then the projections from the UN for net immigration are far too optimistic and the US population will bend to the low estimates of total population that we have seen before. Indeed, as the years go by, the projected increase from the domestic source population continuously declines and even turns negative by 2070. It is only because of positive net immigration that the US population is projected to keep growing.

If net immigration were to fall permanently, then potential growth in the US economy will drop. So, immigration policy is not neutral for economic dynamism and growth. Europe and Japan have a combination of weak demographics and weak economic growth rates. The US outlook has been somewhat more favorable based on immigration. Perhaps, now this needs to be questioned.

Appendix 6—Labor Productivity Growth and Investment Spending

Some may find it counterintuitive to present the production function as:

$$Q = L * (Q/L)$$

because this does not seem to provide a role for investment/capital. Investment does not show in this equation, they say, and therefore there must be something wrong. This is incorrect. This formula is a tautology. What happens with this presentation is that all investment contributions to improving output are embodied in making labor more productive. I.e. the second part of this equation is a nested function of investment and many more things. One could say that:

$$(Q/L) = f \text{ (education, healthcare, investment, credit, energy supply, laws, regulations, diversity, probity, etc.).}$$

That is what makes productivity policy so complex but also interesting. A way of conceptualizing output is to say that output is a function of labor and capital together, or $Q = f(L, K)$ as in the Cobb-Douglass production function (where α is the fixed share of labor in output):

$$Q = A * L^{\alpha} * K^{(1-\alpha)}$$

This presentation seeks to show explicitly the contributions of labor (L) and capital (K) to output, and bundle productivity in "A" which is called Total Factor Productivity (TFP). We can now also see that:

$$(Q/L) = A * (K/L)^{(1-\alpha)}$$

Which shows that average labor productivity is a positive function of TFP and the amount of capital per unit of labor (K/L). The more investment that builds a higher level of capital per unit of labor (the more machines every worker has at his disposal), the higher will be average labor productivity.

Chapter 11—Cyclical Policy to Manage
Aggregate Demand

In the previous chapter we discussed structural policy. Economic structural policy, at the end, is about one thing only: how to optimize the efficiency at which the economy can produce goods and services. As such, structural policy addresses the supply side of the economy or, we could say, structural policy is about the slope (or trend) of the potential real GDP line. Efficient countries with excellent structural characteristics and policy will have a faster growing economy then less efficient countries. This means that the potential of the economy is higher and that growth is also higher. As growth is higher on a sustainable basis, the slope of the potential real GDP line over time, or trend line, will be steeper.

If structural policy is the instrument to guide or manage aggregate supply, then cyclical policy is the instrument to guide or manage aggregate demand. We can divide cyclical policy in many subcategories, but there are two that stand out from a macroeconomic perspective: fiscal policy through the government budget, and monetary policy through the actions of the Federal Reserve. Let us explore more closely how this works. In this chapter we give the general impression. In subsequent chapters, we delve deeper into how this works in the daily operations of the government, broadly defined.

Recall that demand intentions and plans in the economy are not always aligned with supply capacity and intentions. In fact, mostly these two are not aligned. Demand can be boosted by favorable events (a favorable shock) or depressed by unfavorable events (a negative shock) whereby the private sector (households and businesses) become more or less optimistic about the future. If they are more optimistic, they will be more willing to spend and demand accelerates. If they are less optimistic, demand will slow.

When demand accelerates, businesses need to adjust their offers of goods and services, and this make take some time (new investments, hiring more workers, etc.). So, typically, when demand accelerates above potential supply or trend real GDP, then businesses draw down their inventory of unsold goods, and when demand slows down below potential supply or trend real GDP, then firms see their inventories of unsold product increase. This cycling of actual real GDP around some underlying growing potential or trend real GDP gives rise to the term "business cycle".

In Figure 36 below, we provide a stylized version of the concept of the business cycle. The solid line in the top figure indicates the steady growth in potential or trend real GDP. At that line, demand and supply plans are relatively in balance and there will be no noticeable inventory accumulation or decumulation. But actual real GDP may at any time be more buoyant than underlying sustainable trend real GDP, or it may be below. This is shown by the dotted line that curves around the long-run steadily growing average or trend real GDP. The difference, or gap, between actual and trend real GDP, we have already called the output gap in Chapter 7, which is mapped onto the small diagram below the top one. The gap is calculated as the difference between actual and trend line, expressed as a percentage of the trend line.

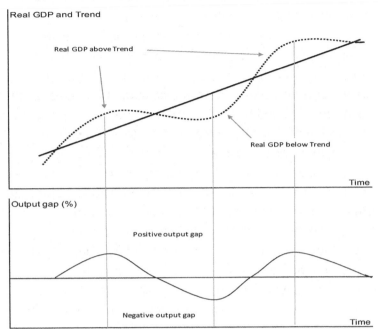

Figure 36. USA--The Business Cycle and the Output Gap--Stylized Version

When demand temporarily outstrips trend real GDP, inventories will decline and the economy could heat up or overheat as businesses scramble to find more employees and resources to expand output to meet the higher demand. As the economy tightens up, prices for goods and services could start to rise at an accelerated pace—that is inflation. Another possibility is that prices remain well behaved, but now we see the consequences of overheating in a bulging of the deficit in trade of goods and services with other countries—the so-called external current account of the balance of payments will then drop or become more negative. Thus, a positive output gap (actual demand outstripping underlying steady supply) may give rise to inflation and/or a current account deficit. Negative output gaps will do the opposite.

High inflation taxes different groups in society differently (yes, inflation is a kind of tax)—those that do most of their business on regular fixed contracts, with prices for their services determined some time in advance, might be surprised by this inflation as they see their real purchasing power of earnings decline (eaten away by general inflation). Those who have access to indexed assets or contracts would see the prices or returns on their holdings go up and down with inflation without major real effects, so they will not suffer or much less from unexpectedly high inflation. In any event, the economy and society react to higher inflation and as inflation gets higher and higher the disturbances within society get bigger. Moreover, if inflation in the US is higher than abroad, then the competitiveness of the US economy will suffer if the exchange rate does not adjust sufficiently to compensate, and foreigners will buy less and less from the US and the US will buy more and more from abroad—this is also not sustainable. Thus, the government will want to prevent inflation from running out of hand, and it has a stake in monitoring and managing inflation. In turn, since overheating is one cause of inflation and large external current account deficits, the government has a stake in monitoring and managing the business cycle.

In conclusion, we can say that cyclical policy, or aggregate demand policy, is all about aiming to keep the output gap as small as possible. The government will want to support supply capacity in the economy with structural policies, and manage demand in the economy with cyclical policies. Demand management needs to take place in the context of what underlying supply capacity is doing. Also, it needs to take place in the context of what the private sector is doing on its own initiative. Thus, if the private sector is very buoyant and spends a lot, the government should take its foot off the demand accelerator, so to speak; and if the private sector is temporarily holding spending back for one reason or another and the output gap turns negative, then the government could come in to support aggregate demand as a matter of policy.

This idea of watching what the private sector is doing and then compensating on the other side of private sector buoyancy or cautiousness is called counter-cyclical policy. Counter-cyclical policy is all about trying to keep the output gap as small as possible to prevent overheating or undercooling. Indeed, if the government were not to assist the economy when it is running very soft for a while, some business firms could go bankrupt that otherwise would be able to supply valuable goods and services to the economy. So, preventing undercooling is as valuable as preventing overheating.

In part, what makes counter-cyclical policies difficult, is that potential real GDP is a non-observable variable. We can calculate more or less where the economy is at one point in time, but telling what underlying potential real GDP really is with any degree of precision, is no minor issue. So, we also do not know exactly how big the output gap is. Furthermore, since it takes time to find out what the economy is doing, we may be initiating fiscal or monetary support policies just at the moment that the private sector is already repairing its course of action and is on the way to resolving the problem on its own. In the heat of reality, this uncertainty can lead to government policy mistakes and we find out only later that the government has provided stimulus when the output gap was in fact closing or already positive (a pro-cyclical policy), or it took money out of the market when the output gap was shrinking or already negative (this is also pro-cyclical). Pro-cyclical policies are those that move in the same direction as the private sector and magnify either a positive or negative output gap— precisely the opposite from what good policy is aiming to achieve.

* * *

Political economy interlude. We can point toward some examples of mistakes in government policy. One example occurred during the Bush Jr administration (deficits do not matter) in 2000-2008. President Clinton had achieved budget surpluses during a buoyant growth episode in his second term in office (even though assisted with a lot of new leverage in the economy). Then, president Bush Jr. took over and, in the words of the Economist Magazine, "found the keys to his mom's Ferrari [the economy moving on all cylinders], and he was now going to see if he could run this machine off the road and into the ditch." The US economy indeed did run off the road and into the ditch, as the financial collapse in 2007-2009 demonstrated. Note in Figure 31 the substantial positive output gaps during Mr. Bush's presidency in 2000-2008, but that did not prevent the administration from arguing that very large tax cuts were necessary to keep the economy growing (a pro-cyclical policy).

President Obama then assumed the presidency in January 2009 and put in place a counter-cyclical rescue plan (heavily criticized by republicans in Congress) to help combat the growing negative output gap (see again Figure 31) during the 2010s, and to stabilize the economy. This supportive policy during the Great Recession succeeded in resurrecting the economy, and by the end of his second term in 2016, the US was once again growing steadily; deficits were coming down; and the government debt was poised to peak.

Mr. Trump, however, in the election campaign of 2016, was of the view that the US was a disaster and that the economy needed a large tax cut to stimulate a "very weak" economy to growth rates of 4 percent a year or more. He pushed a large pro-cyclical tax cut into the recovering economy and thereby created once again a large positive output gap. Positive output gaps come to an end when the economy cannot keep up with even more stimulus and slows down on its own accord. The interpretation of this book is that Mr. Trump's policies were not aligned with the economy's growth potential, which has been lower than what Mr. Trump envisaged. Therefore, the tax cuts did not bring the higher growth rates that were promised, but they brought a windfall for wealthy Americans who received the biggest slice of the tax reductions.

When coronavirus came in 2020, US policy space had already been largely exhausted both on the fiscal side by the tax cuts and on the monetary policy side from putting pressure on the Federal reserve for lowering interest. The coronavirus was of course an unexpected event, but there are always unexpected events, and that is why all countries, including the US, need to maintain policy safety buffers.

* * *

If policies are pro-cyclical for an extended period of time, booms will be bigger and recessions will be deeper than they need be under counter-cyclical policies (a kind of manic-depressive economic reality). Cyclical policy cannot change growth potential, because for that you need structural (supply) policy. However, structural reforms are difficult to legislate and implement. Further, what pro-cyclical policies do is exhaust policy space, and when a recession comes under these circumstances, there is only one instrument left to pump up the economy: more debt.

Experience suggests that once the recession is over, taxes are not increased back up, so the new debt is not paid down. Consequently, pro-cyclical policies lead to debt buildup in difficult times, and do not lead to a debt paydown during booms. The bottom line is that this creates a debt ratchet whereby the debt rises on trend. This is unsustainable in the long run and will result, if not addressed, in ever-larger economic crises, followed with ever more desperate attempts to stop the recessions.

* * *

Political economy interlude. As we have noted already, debt has become the cocaine of the modern capitalist economy. Political systems have become addicted to it as the cure-all when the country feels down (and to push problems down the line to the next generation). But a debt addiction will not resolve the underlying sustainability problems in the economy (this requires reform), and as a result, many in society ask whether the capitalist system has lost its way? Politicians of a populist bent in the US and elsewhere are exploiting this stress to divide and conquer, and to capture power for narrow interests that have appropriated the moniker of being the only true "capitalists." Society needs to rescue capitalism from these "capitalists."

* * *

If business cycles are difficult to date with precision, what is a policy maker to do? One natural response is to use many indicators together to obtain information about the state of the output gap. This is what the government, the Federal Reserve, and the professional economic associations do—they use a dashboard of indicators to see whether the cyclical policy stance needs to be revised.

Another instrument that should be used more frequently is to place current events in a much longer context, as this book recommends. If we orient our policy to the long run, and use sensible assumptions to put boundaries around a future that we could accept, then the tendency to over-react to short-term business fluctuations will be reduced. Further, it is even unhealthy to over-react to short-term business fluctuations, because downturns are natural cleaning devices in which weaker businesses need to be removed from the economy. Propping up zombie banks or zombie corporations with new debt does not make for a healthy economy.

This re-orientation to long-run sustainability for a healthy economy brings out the presence of two more important economic cycles, besides the short-run business cycle described above. These are the structural cycle and the demographic cycle.

The business cycle lasts about 3-5 years—an acceleration of 3-5 years tends to mature and then turn into a softer period of 3-5 years. In policy we can think of business cycles as the time it takes to address *flow imbalances*, such as addressing a budget deficit or bouts of elevated inflation—this can typically be done in a period of 3-5 years.

Instead, a structural cycle can easily take one or two decades, or even three decades. Structural cycles are associated with *stock imbalances*, such as a mountain of debt, or an accumulation of external imbalances over the years. Structural imbalances often go together with the sense of fundamental competitiveness swings and the need for much deeper reforms to return the economy to a better and more sustainable shape. Structural reforms to change fundamental competitiveness, labor markets, or product and goods markets easily take a decade and it is often not until the following decade that the benefits become truly visible. Since politics is very short-run, with a horizon of the next election, deep structural reforms are politically very difficult and tend only to be done in times of distress. A budget deficit can be addressed in a few years; a debt problem takes two or three decades to resolve.

The third cycle is the demographic cycle. This takes one or two generations to play out—i.e. between 40-60 years. Aging is the demographic cycle of these times. Almost all advanced countries had a baby boom after WWII and that lowered dependency ratios until about 2000 (a period of 55 years). Then aging began to show in the demographic profile, and it is projected to last until about 2050 (another swing of around 50 years). These are huge forces in society and upon the economy, and if we don't prepare for them and take them into account, the economy will run into trouble. For instance, aging will naturally lead to slower growth. If the political system cannot accept this, then it may try to power through the creeping slowdown with ever more risky stimulus policies. And that causes the systemic buildup of debt in the ratchet that we already mentioned. Thus, the political system itself is driven by the aging challenge, and if we don't accept it as a force of nature, then countries will maintain unsound policies and economies will suffer.

This book argues that the effects of aging in the underlying macroeconomic developments and outlook are not so difficult to show. Democratically representative political systems have a difficult time with the new challenges that a slower-growing economy presents in terms of, for instance, distributional inequities, long-run environmental limits, long-run resource availabilities, etc. These challenges can lead to capture and inward turning to satisfy narrow interests. This is not good for a healthy society, nor for a healthy economy.

So, now we have a much richer context for fiscal and monetary counter-cyclical policies. Not only do policy makers need to consider the short-term business cycle (and not over-react); but they also need to think through, and spell out for the public, their views on structural underpinnings of the economy for the long run; and they need to address society with intuitive and equitable plans how to deal with naturally slowing economies and the challenges of aging, the environment, and resource use that will be with us for 50 years at a minimum.

The long run imperative for sustainable policies is so important that this book takes the view that long-run projections should be made systematically, and updated in the annual government budget, for a horizon of life-expectancy of the new generation. Since life expectancies are drifting toward 80, this takes us easily through 2100. It is the current new generation that is going to have to pay the bills that we leave behind.

Chapter 12—Money and Credit Policy

Monetary and fiscal policies are the two central instruments that monetary and fiscal authorities have at their disposal to manage the economic cycle. As we have said in the previous chapter, issues in managing the cycle sound intuitive in principle, but they are by no means easy in practice. Policy should avoid becoming pro-cyclical, because that magnifies volatility and uncertainty—the ups and downs in the economy that cause damage to growth and wellbeing. But pro-cyclical policies are quite common, partially because of *political interference*—Central Bank independence is recommended by most economists, but even that is subject to definitions and interpretations. Further, policy steps take time to achieve their effect, by when the cycle may have turned—one is often not sure *how fast* the policy action will transmit to the final objective, and *what dosage* is necessary to calibrate correctly the policy intervention.

A previous chairman of the Federal Reserve, Mr. Bernanke, noted that economic policy making is inherently difficult. He likened it to being a driver in a car and then you hear something rattling in the engine—something is going wrong. If this car is your economy, you can't simply park the car by the side of the road (stop the economy), open the hood, and take your time to figure out what is wrong. No, you have to address the problem *while the (economic) car keeps driving along the road.* Fixing the engine while you are driving on the road is not something for the meek.

The Federal Reserve, as the monetary authority of the US, has a so-called dual mandate: it needs to consider economic growth and inflation. Some central banks have a unique mandate—they may be focused on inflation only. If policy tools to support growth and keep inflation under control work in the same direction, then the situation may be manageable—say the FED lowers its policy interest rate to give a slow economy with low inflation a boost. But, sometimes supporting growth and managing inflation could require an opposing policy direction. If growth is weak but inflation high (stagflation), then lowering interest rates to support growth (a positive outcome) could unleash more inflation (a negative outcome), and vice versa. Thus, monetary policy, like everything else in economic policy making, is both a science and an art.

Modern economies are so complex, and there are so many policy objectives to achieve, that monetary policy can never be the *only* instrument to manage the cycle. Fiscal policy needs to do its part to manage the cycle. And structural policy needs to do its part to manage the underlying supply potential of the economy. Thus, policy challenges are always an interplay between different branches of the authorities coupled with different political and social sentiments. Further, there often tend to be different opinions how important a particular disturbance is, or how long this disturbance will last. Shocks to the economy that are of short duration are often best ignored; but other times shocks are so invasive and long-lasting that they can even change the underlying structure of the economy. All of these possible outcomes require different policy mixes. For instance, in 2020, is the coronavirus a big or a small shock to the economy? Are its effects temporary, and will they go away when we get the infection rate under control, or is this going to be a new normal with long-term structural implications? The answers to these questions matter and have implications for how one would want to use policy and avoid the risk of making results worse, rather than better.

About a hundred years ago, in the early 20th century, Irving Fisher developed a theory about how the quantity of money (M) and the speed or velocity at which this gets passed around in the economy (V) influences nominal GDP, either through prices (P) or quantities (Q)— $M*V = P*Q$. This became known as the quantity theory of money. It holds that if, for instance, the Federal Reserve buys government bonds in return for dollars (cash) (an expansion in the supply of money), then nominal GDP will speed up unless, for some reason, velocity drops because the private sector wants to hold this larger amount of cash as a cushion (the demand for money shifted up). Many papers were then written to understand better the demand for money, in a context of changing payment systems and money multipliers in the financial system, which both could influence the speed (V) at which the money stock (M), circulates through the economy. If the relationships in the quantity theory of money are fairly stable, then the Federal Reserve could help guide nominal output via control of the quantity of money that it issues (M).

Then things got complicated in the 1960s-1970s, when the demand for money became more complicated to predict, and even unstable in some respects. As a result, many industrial countries started gravitating away from controlling directly the stock of money, and towards managing the price of money, the representative interest rate. If one can aim for a relatively stable representative interest rate, then the demand for money could be unstable, but the policy interest rate of the Central Bank could then be used to stabilize this market for liquidity and credit, and that, in turn could ultimately stabilize developments in GDP. In this context, if prices are relatively well behaved and inflation stays tame around 2 percent a year, then monetary policy could help to support economic activity via an expansion of money and credit, originating at the source with a relaxation of Federal Reserve policies.

This gradual shift from direct control of the money supply to using indirect instruments (the policy interest rate) got further impetus when in 1971 president Nixon ended the Bretton Woods system of fixed parities between the world's most important currencies and the US dollar. President Nixon closed the so-called "gold window" and that meant that the value of the US dollar was no longer freely convertible into gold reserves that were kept on hand to back up the value of the US currency. Thus, monetary regimes were changing and that accelerated the development of using indirect instruments; it also ushered in a system of flexible exchange rates between important currencies in the world. The US dollar was taken off the gold standard and changed to a true fiat currency, controlled by Federal Reserve policies.

Then, as experience with the new monetary system increased and research became more comfortable how monetary policies, via control of the policy interest rate, was transmitted through the economy, it was found that good communication of the Central Bank regarding its monetary policy objectives could also contribute to stabilizing inflation and help to manage the economic cycle. This was possible if the central bank had "credibility" by which it is understood that the market place for money, credit, and interest responds predictably to the so-called "forward monetary policy guidance."[13] This, in turn, was

---

[13] On its website, the Federal Reserve explains forward guidance as "a tool that central banks use to provide communication to the public

combined with, or part of, a form of "inflation targeting" that could be relatively strict, with a narrow mandate of the monetary authorities to keep inflation "at or just below 2 percent a year" which is the objective of the European Central Bank (ECB), or a somewhat loser target of "around 2 percent a year" that, in practice, the Federal Reserve is using (deviations above and below are allowed as long as these are temporary and assessed to be relatively benign in the context of the shocks that are affecting the inflation path).

Most observers would say that monetary policy has become better over time at controlling inflation in the economy for goods and services (the traditional indicator of inflation). The models have become more elaborate and sophisticated. The amount of information that is available to read the market, and to use in the models, has grown. And Central Banks have learned from policy successes and mistakes. This development is also generally associated with stronger and more explicit recognition of Central Bank independence, which is seen to provide comfort that the monetary authorities cannot be easily pushed around by assertive politicians or special interest players who want to intervene and do themselves a short-term favor.

In fact, some observers are confident that controlling inflation has become so successful, and that the risks of a recurrence of high inflation is so small, that monetary policy can now focus on other objectives, such as financing the government more directly. This "Modern Monetary Theory" combines the experience of a gradually

about the likely future course of monetary policy. When central banks provide forward guidance, individuals and businesses will use this information in making decisions about spending and investments. Thus, forward guidance about future policy can influence financial and economic conditions today."

slowing economy (it would be nice to prevent this), and identifiable worthwhile investments that the government could do if it had the resources (such as improving infrastructure), with Federal Reserve financed deficit spending. In this hypothesis, the government could run sizeable deficits to implement the spending necessary, issue the bonds to raise the money, and the Federal Reserve would buy these bonds and exchange them for cash. In the end, you print dollar bills to finance government deficits and debt.

* * *

The constantly-moving disco ball of reality has many small mirrors attached to it that all shine in their own way. As we noted, on the republican side president Bush Jr and vice-president Cheney in the 2000s claimed that deficits do not matter. Now, the Modern Monetary Theory has acquired substantial political support from New Progressives in the Democratic Party (e.g. senator Bernie Sanders and representative Alexandra Ocasio-Cortez) who, by implication, also claim that deficits (and debt) do not matter. But, what is more, highly respected academic economists such as Larry Summers (Harvard University), who is principally worried about a secular stagnation, and Olivier Blanchard (ex-MIT; would like to increase the inflation rate target) and others, also are persuaded that high deficit spending is the way to go in the current environment; and a lot of this deficit spending can be financed by the Federal Reserve.[14]

---

[14]Mr. Blanchard says that with bond rates close to zero, replacing bonds with cash (dollar bills), which pay zero interest, nothing really changes in the economy if then the Federal Reserve monetizes the deficits and the debt, so we should not worry about it. Cash is a

Mr. Trump is also of the view that deficits (when these are the results of tax cuts) do not really matter. He has also put considerable pressure on the Federal Reserve to lower interest rates to increase the growth rate of the money supply to assist in stimulating the economy to 4 percent growth a year.

All these powerful groups are thus converging from very different angles on the notion that growth is too low, inflation is not a problem, and a monetary financed debt expansion from fiscal policy is the appropriate way to address the health and sustainability of the economy. In the long run, Irving Fisher is dead. With such consensus, what could possibly go wrong?

This book suggests that we also look at another mirror on the dynamic disco ball of reality. Because, this one does truly seem to shine a bit differently. It hypothesizes that low inflation for goods and services that show up in the consumer price index is the result of success—namely a combination of technology with globalization and aging.

The global economy has become a global *village* economy with the advances in connectivity, rapid-fire exchange of ideas, research, and news, and just-in-time-supply chains. Technology has made this progress possible. Globalization, meanwhile, has brought online 7 billion people living outside the US, Europe, and Japan. The iconic one is China, which rapidly has become the workshop of the world. The US, Europe, and Japan are high-income countries, with high prices and wages relative to the 7 billion people that have entered the competition with the

---

nominal instrument that pays no interest by design. A bond may *yield* around zero today, but this does not mean that its *interest* rate is also zero, as for cash, nor that its risk profile resembles anything like that of a dollar bill. So, this argument is somewhat controversial.

high-income countries and have access to the same technology as the high-income countries (capital and technology travel faster than people).

Research performed by staff of the International monetary Fund has found that the inequality *between* countries has lessened as a result of technology and globalization, but inequality *within* high-income countries has increased. Further, there is evidence that aging contributes to a slowdown of growth—elderly people do not consume as much or as frivolous as younger generations. High-income countries are in the vanguard of aging; emerging countries tend to have younger populations.

If globalization is a success, then the communicating vessels of two markets, one with high wages and prices, and another with low wages and prices, would put downward pressure on the high-income wages and prices and upward pressure on the low-income wages and prices, until a degree of convergence has taken place. On a global scale this convergence can take some time. Thus, it should be possible that *structurally low inflation for goods and services* in the high-income countries is the result of success in technology and globalization. Moreover, as high-income countries are aging, their saving would first tend to increase and their spending would tend to slow down (including as baby boomers prepare for retirement; especially if there is concern about the reliability of the social security system), causing a slowdown in the growth rate of the economy and potentially very low interest rates (in sync with Mr. Summers' secular stagnation).

If this is correct, then the *equilibrium* rate of inflation in high-income countries could drift down to zero or even slightly negative, at least for a while, while the rest of the world catches up. Also, the equilibrium interest rate in high-income countries could drift down to zero or even below (depending on how fast the real growth rate of the economy is coming down).

What happens in such environment if the Federal Reserve insists that inflation should not drop below 2 percent or so? This will induce the Federal Reserve to keep up a very expansionary monetary policy (relative to equilibrium), aiming to push up inflation above its dynamic equilibrium path. The policy authorities may be thinking that their efforts fit the pattern of aiming to close a negative output gap (after all CPI inflation is well behaved or even falling, so there must be a negative output gap). But from a more fundamental and structural standpoint, there may not be an output gap—we constantly, at least for a while, overestimate the potential growth rate of the economy and therefor mistakenly think that there is an output gap.

If technology and globalization continue to meet with success, this very expansionary policy will go against the grain of nature and prove only marginally successful if at all. Observers may be surprised for a long time that inflation does not react and jump back up. Japan has been trying to pump inflation for years without success. The specter of a "Japan scenario" is now also being brandied for Europe (second) and the US (third in line).

As the fiscal authorities are seduced by low borrowing rates and the Federal Reserve pumps in vast amounts of money stock, where is the missing inflation or, where does all this money go? It does not go into consumer goods spending, because the aging societies already have enough daily consumer goods and services and the 7 billion people brought online are happy to compete in the high-income countries both as labor and as suppliers in the global supply chains. Money could then find its way into other outlets, such as real estate and financial instruments—essentially inflation migrates from goods and services to asset markets. The prices from asset markets do not show up in the consumer price index.

Is this a problem? What is wrong with well-behaved consumer price inflation and rising asset price inflation? There are at least two problems.

One, not everyone owns assets so a very easy monetary policy is benefiting people who are capital rich and see their wealth inflating. It damages more moderately endowed people and families, for example if they have to pay exorbitant prices to find a house or apartment to live in. Thus, asset price inflation can easily widen inequality in the economy and we have no lack of information that this process is underway. High and rising inequality creates social unrest as citizens perceive an injustice.

Two, the policy authorities can be trapped (captured) into continuing or even intensifying the expansionary policies for political reasons. The wealthy, who mainly benefit, finance election campaigns and exercise influence to appoint favorite individuals to powerful positions, including the president, the secretary of the treasury, and the chairperson of the Federal Reserve (so much for FED independence...). Mr. Greenspan famously said that he does not favor stopping asset price inflation because he found this "difficult to measure," and hence one cannot say whether this is an equilibrium phenomenon or an aberration. He had no trouble measuring consumer price inflation and stopping it with strong contractionary policies, if that is what the FED would want to do. Mr. Bernanke, another highly-respected academic, repeated these arguments why the FED would not consider acting against asset price inflation. The fiscal authorities, meanwhile, saw no problem with the cost of borrowing going down to allow them to run ever larger deficits and accumulate large piles of debt.

But then another problem cropped up. The price of risk kept going down as monetary expansion kept being accommodative and as the government issued more and more government bonds.[15] Borrowing became so cheap that the entire financial industry was turned into financial engineering of leverage with the help of debt. Governments issued debt. Hostile takeover (private equity) funds issued debt. Hedge funds leveraged debt. Banks and other financial institutions increased leverage. And, households, too, leveraged up to borrow for everything, especially their education and their homes and, now, for their health. Asset price inflation accommodates leverage and is one of the engines of leverage. We all believe that our assets are good collateral, even if their prices reflect a bubble.

Bubbles burst, as they did during the dot-com collapse. Leverage kills, as WorldCom and Enron experienced in the light of their fraudulent accounting to inflate profits and understate debt exposures. Banks were next in the financial meltdown, beginning in the mortgage markets and with fancy engineered derivatives to hide risks that culminated into the Great Recession. Entire countries default too—Argentina is now at its ninth default in a row because of runaway deficit and debt financing, including in US dollars (of course, "this time is different," again...).

---

[15] Another problem with very low interest rates is that it permits poor investment projects that have almost no return, besides keeping zombie firms and banks in business. This is productivity reducing.

So, the policies of fiscal and monetary inflation of an economy that is slowing structurally, can create asset inflation and asset-type bubbles that pop as a shock of nature comes around. This shock of nature can be anything, including a coronavirus. The point is that the economy leverages onto splinter-thin margins with piles of debt. This pile of debt then becomes the tower of instability itself, ready to fall on all of us. The most important shocks in our era do not come from the real economy, but rather from financial markets.[16] Continuously heavily expansionary financial policies feed these financial market instabilities until they overwhelm. Even "macro- and microprudential" measures that were invented to prop up the towers of debt, have proven ineffective and too skimpy (indeed often not market based and thus distortionary in their own sense) to stop the consequences from overleveraging.

In the euro-zone, the northern countries, like Germany and the Netherlands, have consistently expressed their concern about unhinged financial markets and asset price inflation bringing with it financial instability. The southern countries have a great need for cheap financing of their very large deficits and to roll over their high debt, so they ask for the opposite—either finance our deficits or transfer income so that we can pay for it. It is not an easy or comfortable political and economic exercise to pilot all the countries within the

---

[16] Interestingly, the coronavirus shock started as a real economy shock, with both demand and supply disruptions. The policy response and developments in the economy with high leverage can also turn the coronavirus problems into a financial (after)shock. The full economic challenges following the coronavirus have not yet materialized.

euro-zone through this asymmetric problem and policy stance.

Depending on what little mirror of the dynamic disco ball of reality you are now on, the US, as the largest economy in the world and going full tilt for asset inflation, presents the most frightening specter. If the US were to become over-extended beyond a tipping point, a global melt down much bigger than the Great Recession could happen. From this vantage point, inflation has not disappeared, but only migrated. Structural challenges such as aging, globalization, and inequity, should be addressed with structural policies, not with endlessly expansionary financial policies that go against the grain of nature. Thus, the "consensus" that has formed, noted above, may have all its facts right, but does it draw the right conclusion?

Structural deflation is a concept that economists have difficulty with, and it even frightens them. Keynes talked about the concept of "downward wage and price rigidities." This implies that in the political economy, it is easier to cut real values with a bit of inflation than with a reduction in their own nominal value. If inflation is very low and you cannot cut nominal values, then a very painful and lengthy process may start that is intermediated through very high unemployment and many businesses going bankrupt (the economy will then adjust through volume, rather than prices). This process can feed upon itself through multipliers and result in a great depression, exactly as Keynes saw this in the 1930s. The problem was resolved with inflationary policies, including through war spending...

While Keynes focused on wages and prices in a world of very low inflation or even deflation, the above-mentioned Fisher studied financial markets and observed that during deflation, the real value of debt increases. So, inflation both facilitates adjustment of real values in labor and goods and services markets, and also helps to manage debt. Since debt is now the cocaine of the modern capitalist economy, with the entire political power structure built upon its success and management, is it likely that this political system will accept structural deflation as a natural equilibrating system for high wage and price economies?

Since debt is a stock adjustment problem, and stock adjustment problems are structural, resolving the debt problem will need many years to accomplish. Therefore, a structural long-term plan needs to be devised to gradually lower the debt in the future, while prices and wages in high-income and aging countries settle down at very low inflation. Separating countries with trade restrictions, immigration stops, and other discriminatory policies to reverse the effects of globalization and structural deflation is not optimal for the global economy, and eventually also not optimal for the US economy. Lower-income countries need time to catch up and the faster they are able and allowed to do this, the faster the global differences will lessen. Continuing to pump debt and monetary financing in high-income countries in such an environment is not sustainable, other than to absorb sudden shocks. At this moment, in 2020, there is no evidence that governments are devising long-term fiscal and monetary plans for the future.

Massive pumping of debt and money financing in high-income countries is also not healthy for emerging and poorer countries, because their governments are not strong enough to resist borrowing in "cheap" dollars. This is causing enormous spillovers from loose policy in the high-income countries to the low-income countries. When the US dollar conditions have even a minor hiccup, or the

US slows down in a recession, immediately all the emerging countries start popping with concatenated crises and defaults. The coronavirus effect is no exception. But even Reinhart and Rogoff now say that "this time is really different"!

Chapter 13—Macroeconomic Balance: Internal and External Equilibrium

In the previous chapters we have looked at the notion of structural policies to support potential real GDP growth, and cyclical policies to minimize the output gap. Within cyclical policies, we found monetary and fiscal policies as the two biggest levers that the authorities have to manage aggregate demand in the economy. Monetary policy should be aimed at maintaining moderate inflation and financial stability. We argued that there has been success in keeping consumer price inflation under control, but we are less certain that financial stability is under control—this problem looks like it is not fully on the radar screen. We still need to discuss fiscal policy, government debt, and the balance sheet of the public sector. We will dedicate section 4 of this book to this topic. Before we go there, however, it is worth touching upon the concept of macroeconomic balance as a policy objective. Policy needs to be sustainable, and therefore the concept of balance is important. Let us see what economists mean by this.

Let us say that you are the leader of a country and you are truly benevolent. You want the country to do well, raise the standard of living of the people, and make them feel at ease and at peace in their time. Since you are farsighted, you want them to be assured that the next generations also can enjoy this high-quality outcome. What does this mean in operational macroeconomic terms?

Internal balance. In macroeconomic terms, you would want to maintain relatively low unemployment and well-behaved inflation. You would want to keep an eye on distributional outcomes of your economy. This promotes general wellbeing. If you are already doing well as a country with a high standard of living, the headline growth rate of your economy may slow down a bit, but you would focus foremost on per-capita real GDP, not headline real GDP. This means that a slowdown of real GDP growth is OK, as long as this reflects slower population growth while maintaining a sense of equity among the people, a clean and sustainable environment, and a cushion of resources left for future generations.

The factors above are part of the *internal* equilibrium. They are observable within the domestic economy. Policy is geared towards steering these indicators within certain bands within a certain period of time and into the future. Reality is messy and there are shocks all the time that throw countries off course—automatic stabilizers of various sorts should be allowed to operate, and policy assistance should aim to address serious imbalances. Nature is never static, but resembles more a dynamic bouillabaisse that is constantly on the boil. You just never know what comes to the surface next.

In Table 2 below, we have summarized some indicators that give us a view on the evolution of the various aspects of internal balance. We can see in this table that nominal and real GDP growth have been fairly steady, with an uptick in nominal growth during the inflation years in the 1970s and early 1980s. Generally, growth in both variables has started slowing down, as demographic developments suggested that they would. We can see in the per capita real GDP line that the US has attained a high standard of living, within the top of the global list—this growth is also slowing down to around an average of just over 1 percent a year since the 2000.

Table 2. USA--Macroeconomic Internal Balance Indicators by Decade

	1950s	1960s	1970S	1980s	1990s	2000s	2010s	2020s Proj. 1/
Nominal GDP growth (%)	5.3	6.9	10.0	8.0	5.5	4.1	4.0	3.3
Real GDP growth (%)	3.8	4.5	3.2	3.1	3.2	2.0	2.3	1.3
Per-capita Real GDP e.o.p. (US$ 2012)	$17,293	$23,799	$29,808	$36,809	$45,272	$49,652	$57,961	$62,869
Per-Capita Real GDP growth (%)	2.1	3.3	2.3	2.2	2.1	0.9	1.6	0.9
Employment growth (%, persons)	1.1	1.9	2.4	1.7	1.3	0.5	1.2	0.4
Unemployment rate (% of LF)	4.5	4.8	6.2	7.3	5.8	5.5	6.2	5.7
GDP-deflator inflation (%)	1.4	2.3	6.5	4.7	2.2	2.1	1.7	2.0
CPI inflation (%)	2.1	2.3	7.1	5.6	3.0	2.6	1.8	...
Average increase in house prices (%)	...	...	11.8	5.4	3.3	4.5	2.9	...
Average increase in S&P500 (%)	20.8	8.7	7.5	18.2	19.0	1.2	14.2	...
Cyclically-adjusted price earnings (CAPE) 2/	14.6	20.7	12.7	11.5	25.3	26.7	25.6	...
Measure of income inequality (GINI) 3/	...	...	35.0	37.5	39.7	40.6	40.9	...
Life expectancy at birth 4/	69.0	70.2	72.0	74.5	75.9	77.5	78.8	...
Federal government fiscal balance (%GDP)	-0.4	-0.7	-1.9	-3.8	-2.1	-2.3	-4.8	-7.1
Federal government gross debt e.o.p. (%GDP)	55.1	35.9	31.6	50.8	58.2	82.2	105.8	142.3
Federal government debt held by the public e.o.p. (%GDP)	45.0	27.3	24.4	38.8	37.7	52.2	78.4	125.9
Federal government debt held by the FED e.o.p. (%GDP)	5.0	5.3	4.4	3.9	5.2	5.3	9.9	21.9
Memorandum items								
Misery index 5/	2.1	2.6	9.5	8.9	4.8	5.7	5.6	6.4
The debt trap 6/	...	-0.4	-0.1	0.6	0.2	1.2	1.0	2.8

1/ Projections by the author, central scenario.
2/ Source: Robert Shiller website.
3/ Source: Federal Reserve Bank of St Louis and World Bank. A higher number indicates increased inequality.
4/ Source: UN.
5/ Unemployment rate plus inflation rate minus real GDP growth rate; lower is better.
6/ Average increase in the Federal government gross debt ratio in 10-years divided by average real GDP growth rate in the decade; lower is better.

Employment growth is slowing down as well, likely dipping below an average of 1 percent a year as we move along. The unemployment rate is rising and will likely remain high, on average, for a while due to the shock of coronavirus in the economy. We noted that projecting a natural rate of unemployment of 5 percent going forward in the longer run is not a pessimistic assumption, compared with its historical average of 5.8 percent a year.

Price inflation has generally remained moderate, except for the 1970s and early 1980s that were marked by the effects of the oil crises. Price inflation around 2 percent a year continues to be a reasonable prospect. Asset price inflation is indicated by house price inflation that is generally higher than consumer price inflation (but also more volatile). We see a large cumulative runup particularly in equity prices. To some extent, that is precisely what we want, because companies that do well and are profitable should result in higher equity prices. But Robert Shiller from Yale University has long since pointed out that adjusted for inflation in corporate earnings, the price of equities has risen disproportionately, as shown in the cyclically-adjusted price-earnings ratio of the US stock market (this is Shiller's CAPE index). This means that for every unit of real profit, the price of equity assets has inflated well beyond what goods and services prices that these same companies produce would suggest. That is a form of asset price inflation.

Asset price inflation is only nice if you can get it. Can moderate income families in the US still find affordable housing or are they slowly being priced out of the market? Most families seem to be taking on more debt to buy their house and affordability indicators in the US are generally worsening, particularly in bigger cities, so this is a problem to discuss. Indeed, indicators of income inequality have worsened, sometimes back to the early 20th century, and that is leading to social and political stress. Can the success of the US economy be organized in such a way that it brings everyone along, or is the success increasingly meant to be enjoyed by a shrinking group of the happy few at the top only?[17] The GINI coefficient in the US is far higher (close to double) than that in Europe, which favors a more egalitarian society. Failed states with constant social and political stress and violence tend to have the highest GINI coefficients in the world, and they are marked by very little social cohesion.

We will look in part 4 of the book at fiscal policy, but here we give a preview of some indicators. The federal government budget balance is trending toward deeper deficits. Also, as we shall see, there was a pivot in the debt ratio around the time of president Reagan in the 1980s who started the policies of cutting taxes and allowing much larger deficits. Republican administrations have since broadly continued this strategy, notwithstanding the gradually rising need for government spending in a slowing economy and aging. Thus, cutting taxes not only sounds nice if you can benefit, but it also puts great pressure on expenditure cuts—it is a political strategy to keep government small in the areas that you don't favor (Mr. Reagan's administration called this the "starve the beast" fiscal policy strategy). Whether this is also the best strategy for the country as a whole and the sustainability of the macroeconomy is quite another matter, because some of the spending pressure are structural and follow naturally from slowing growth and aging. At least so far, the spending pressures have not been absorbed in higher

---

[17] And, does extremely loose monetary policy make this problem worse?

tax revenues, but rather in issuing more debt--i.e. the problem is being pushed to future generations.

The growing deficits have given rise to a growing debt to GDP ratio. The debt ratio cannot grow in an unlimited way, because that would lead to funding problems for the government. And the tradeoff between more debt to squeeze out an additional percentage point of extra real GDP growth is also getting worse. I call this the "Debt Trap" as in the memorandum item. This shows that for every extra percentage point of real GDP growth, the government has to issue more and more debt—this is the sense of an addiction to debt, or the cocaine of the modern capitalist economy. Meanwhile, the FED is buying more and more government paper through its extremely loose monetary policy. The FED balance sheet is booming.

The memorandum items also calculate the "misery index," which was used effectively by president Reagan in his bid to replace president Carter in the 1980 election campaign.[18] The misery index (that we use here) adds up the rate of inflation (bad) and the unemployment rate (bad), minus the real GDP growth rate (good). The higher this number, the worse the misery index. Since then, the misery index has been high in the 1970s, 1980s and 2000s, and it is climbing again fast at the present time in 2020.

External balance. The benevolent leader would also want to seek good numbers for the economy with

---

[18] The Misery Index was first developed by the economist Arthur Okun, who was the chairman of the Council of Economic Advisors for president Johnson in the late 1960s. Mr. Okun first defined the Index as the sum of inflation and unemployment. Later, more versions of the Index were formulated to bring in interest rates and the growth rate of real GDP. Here, we have calculated the Misery Index as inflation + unemployment - real GDP growth.

respect to its relations with the rest of the world—the external balance. In macroeconomic terms, this notion tends to gravitate to a smaller number of indicators. These include the current account of the balance of payments; a decent cushion of international reserves; a fairly stable but in any event well-calibrated exchange rate; and a sustainable net international investment position. External imbalances are not as easily observable to the general public, so it is not as much on the public's radar screen. But, external imbalances can influence the sustainability of internal equilibrium, so policy makers need to be aware of both internal and external balance for a healthy and sustainable economy.

Table 3. USA–Macroeconomic External Balance Indicators by Decade

	1950s	1960s	1970S	1980s	1990s	2000s	2010s
Current account balance (% GDP)	...	0.5	0.0	-1.7	-1.5	-4.5	-2.4
Official international reserves (months of imports)	...	...	3.8	3.6	1.9	1.1	1.7
Net International Investment Position (%GDP)	...	...	5.8	4.1	-5.5	-18.0	-36.7
Real Effective Exchang Rate e.o.p. (index 2010=100)	...	...	105.7	110.9	115.6	104.7	113.0

Sources: Federal Reserves Bank of St Louis; Bureau of Economic Analysis; World Bank; International Monetary Fund.

What the results of Table 3 suggest is that the US external balance has been steadily weakening since about the 1980s. This coincides with the views launched in the 1980s that government deficits and debt are no longer that important. The domestic economy has been pumped up with expansionary policies, perhaps as a leaning against the wind of a gradual decline in potential real GDP growth.

These expansionary policies have spilled over into the external balance, creating an external *im*balance. Like a balloon that has too much internal air pressure, and wherever the skin of the balloon is weakest, there we now see an aneurism. Or, high internal blood pressure causing over time a bulging of the blood vessels, until something ruptures somewhere.

The external current account of the balance of payments has steadily been eroded over time to result in sizeable deficits to GDP. This would be a wake-up call for any economy. But in the US, this is hardly discussed. And there is a partial reason that gives the US policy makers perhaps a false sense of security. That is, the US dollar is used around the world as the reserve currency and unit of account. This means in practical terms that the rest of the world has been willing to get paid in US dollars. Thus, the external deficit in the US can be paid for with dollars printed in the basement of the US Federal Reserve. No other country has this feature in its monetary system, and many observers wonder whether this aspect of the international system will hold if the US continuous to run up large and cumulative domestic and external imbalances.

This erosion in external cushions for the US is also visible in the international reserve position, which is the stock of foreign currency assets that the US holds to meet external payment needs. Import coverage has been steadily eroded. Here, again, one could say that the US needs less coverage in foreign exchange if it can pay for most imports in US dollars. If other countries had external numbers like the US, they would likely have to devalue or let the exchange rate of their domestic currency gradually depreciate to make foreign products more expensive and domestic products less expensive in international trade.

That would be the mechanism to restore competitiveness and turn around the external imbalances. But this process is largely absent in the US. So, the pressure from high domestic demand (pushing beyond potential real GDP on a steady basis) manifests itself in a steadily worsening external position.

The net international investment position signals that other countries are investing in the US more than US companies are investing in the rest of the world. This may in fact seem nice, because everyone wants to invest in the US, so to speak, but what it also means is that over time, income and returns on investment can flow abroad in ever larger potential amounts, whereas much less comes back in. Thus, while the interpretation of such numbers is not straightforward, the potential for a sudden reversal of such imbalances can cause a shock to the US economy. So far, foreigners have been willing to invest here (and willing to buy US government debt), but they have no obligation to continue to do so.

The real effective exchange rate (REER) is a measure of price competitiveness. The REER of the US has appreciated over time, but this process has been gradual. There are two types of potential pressures on the external balance of a country—the price effect and the income effect. If domestic prices in the same currency inflate faster than abroad, then price competitiveness deteriorates and exports could fall while imports go up. Further, if income in the domestic economy inflates faster than abroad relative to potential supply in each country, then the "excess demand" can spill over into added imports and lower exports. This is a second way to deteriorate the balance of goods and services with countries abroad. The US shows evidence that both these processes are underway. As long as the reserve currency status holds, the pressures are manageable. If and when this confidence in the US dollar wanes, then rapid and more difficult adjustments (shocks) can come. Some ministers of finance in other countries that faced similar large external imbalances have told the author over the years that "such a thing can never happen here." These then became "famous last words." For now, the US authorities seem confident that "this can never happen here."

Preliminary conclusions. What can we conclude from this panorama of internal and external macroeconomic balance indicators for the US? We could say that basic internal macroeconomic balance indicators show relatively good results in terms of continued real GDP growth, consumer price inflation and, to some extent, unemployment. But there is also evidence of growing inequities in the economy and, perhaps an underexamined interaction with monetary policy and asset prices. This deserves more attention. What is also striking is the steady erosion of the external cushions of the US economy. This is consistent with living beyond one's means and gradually eating all the reserves that had been built up. The US can live off its reserves a bit longer and use the reserve currency position of the US dollar for a while longer, but this is not a structural solution to the problem. Structural problems require structural solutions, they cannot be solved with cyclical policies, as seems to be attempted in the last few decades.

Part 4. The Public Finances and Fiscal Sustainability

Chapter 14—Federal Government Revenue, Expenditure, and Budget Balance

We have discussed structural policy to promote sustainable real GDP and monetary policy to control inflation and the financial conditions in the economy. Of the three-legged stool of government economic policy (structural, monetary, and fiscal policy), we now need to turn to fiscal policy in its important dimensions. Fiscal policy is in many ways the big enchilada, because this is where politics and economic management of the country meet in the most direct way. Monetary policy quickly gets technical, and has been granted a degree of independence. But anyone can run for public office and if you get elected, you carry a huge responsibility how to manage the finances of the country. How many wise and benevolent leaders do countries really have? The challenges of politics deserve our respect.

We are interested in fiscal policy because we want to develop a view on the future. What are the dynamics of the economy and what are the aspirations of the people. How do we use our knowledge about the interaction of these dynamics and aspirations, and experience from the past, to guide the economy in a good way for the future? Fiscal policy plays a crucial role because it is through the budget that countries express their preferences for spending and taxation. To help manage the future, it is necessary to understand the forces that are impacting on revenues and expenditures, so this is where we begin our fiscal analysis.

Given the structure of fiscal policy in the United States, we focus on the finances of the "federal government" first. The state and local governments also implement a substantial share of revenue and taxation, but because many of them have a balanced budget rule, their influence as a counter-cyclical instrument of policy is less pronounced than that of the federal government. We can look at the combination of the federal and state and local governments, in what is called the finances of the "general government," as necessary and as our investigation unfolds.

Federal government revenue. Revenue collected by the federal government (Table 4) is dominated by three taxes: personal income taxes (46 percent of total revenue), payroll charges (32 percent of total), and corporate income taxes (12 percent of total). Other smaller taxes are excises (a tax on consumption, 5 percent of total), estate taxes, import duties, and miscellaneous revenue (these three between 1-2 percent of total). Thus, federal taxes are dominated by levies on income. Import taxes, or taxes on wealth or consumption are small. State and local governments also levy income taxes, but for them taxes on property and sales are relatively more relevant sources of revenue.

Federal government taxes have averaged around 17 percent of GDP in the period 1962-2019, with a high of 19.8 percent of GDP in 2000 at the end of the Clinton administration and a low of 14.4 percent of GDP at the end of the Great Recession in 2010.

Table 4. USA--Federal Government Revenue (1962-2019)

	% GDP	Shares
Revenues	17.0%	100%
Personal income tax	7.8%	46%
Payroll charge	5.4%	32%
Corporate income tax	2.1%	12%
Excise tax	0.9%	5%
Estate and Gift taxes	0.2%	1%
Customs duties	0.2%	1%
Miscelaneous	0.4%	2%

Source: Congressional Budget Office.

If we consider taxes for the *general government* (federal, state, and local governments combined) then we get a revenue ratio of around 33 percent of GDP. It is worth noting that this is moderate in comparison with most other OECD countries. European countries have general tax ratios that are more than 10 percentage points of GDP higher than in the US, on average, with Scandinavian countries reaching up to 20 percentage points of GDP higher than the US (Figure 37). This difference, combined with that fact that European countries, including the Scandinavian ones, also are generating high standards of living and per-capita real GDP, suggests that the mantra of tax cuts as the key instrument necessary to generate economic wellbeing is false.

Figure 37: USA--OECD General Government Revenue (% GDP)

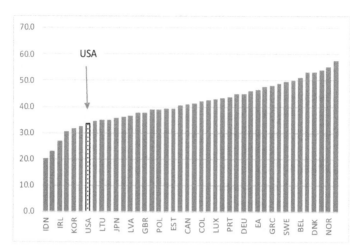

Source: OECD, data are for 2015.

Federal government expenditure. We can divide federal government expenditure in two important components: noninterest expenditures and interest on the federal debt (Table 5).

Table 5. USA--Federal Government Expenditures (1962-2019)

	% GDP			Shares		
	1962-2019	1962	2019	1962-2019	1962	2019
Total expenditures	20.1%	18.2%	20.8%	100.0%	100.0%	100.0%
Primary expenditures	18.2%	17.1%	19.0%	91%	93.6%	91.5%
Discretionary	8.8%	12.3%	6.2%	44%	67.5%	30.1%
Mandatory	10.5%	5.9%	14.0%	52%	32.5%	67.7%
Offseting Receipts	-1.2%	-1.2%	-1.3%	-5.7%	-6.4%	-6.3%
Net interest	1.9%	1.2%	1.8%	9.5%	6.4%	8.5%

Source: Congressional Budget Office.

The first component, or noninterest expenditures, is also known as primary expenditures. Primary expenditures may be discretionary (the government together with Congress determines every year in the budget spending bills how to allocate these resources), or mandatory (these expenditures are laid out in multiannual laws that determine how much and when to spend the resources). To change mandatory programs (entitlements) such as the social security system and Medicare requires special laws approved by Congress and the president. The president and his government thus have more influence over discretionary expenditure than over mandatory expenditure.[19]

The second component, or net interest, represents the interest rate paid on the gross debt outstanding, minus interest received by various on-budget and off-budget trust funds (thus, it reflects interest on the federal debt held by the public). The debt in 2019 was already very high, but interest rates have come down, which has helped to cushion the interest bill to 1.8 percent of GDP. The interest bill is sensitive to interest rates and, therefore to monetary policy set by the Federal Reserve. Mr. Trump is issuing large amounts of new federal debt with his yearly budgets, so this may be one reason why he is putting pressure on the federal reserve chairman to lower policy interest rates—to limit the damage to the public finances of this tide of red ink in the short run, while he is in office.

Within primary expenditures, *discretionary* spending comprises the defense budget and the

---

[19] For instance, Mr. Trump has re-allocated money from the military budget, which is a discretionary budget item, to building the border wall. He does not have authorization to re-allocate money from social security for such purposes, because social security falls under the mandatory programs.

nondefense budget. In 2019 both were over $0.6 trillion or $1.3 trillion combined (6.2 percent of GDP combined).

The *mandatory* programs comprise social security (retirement), Medicare and Medicaid (health care), income support programs such as unemployment insurance, child benefits, and nutrition, pensions for government and military retirees, veteran's affairs, and "other." Social security spending in 2019 was just over $1 trillion, Medicare about $0.8 trillion, and Medicaid over $0.4 trillion, with income support at $0.3 trillion. Total discretionary spending in 2019 added up to $3 trillion (14.0 percent of GDP).

Over time, and given how mandatory programs work, including their link to demographic developments, they have grown faster than discretionary expenditures. As a result, budgets are becoming less flexible, because an incremental share is taken up by mandatory programs. This is happening in virtually every country in the world. Mandatory programs can act well as automatic stabilizers to help manage the business cycle (e.g. unemployment spending automatically increases if the economy slows down, and falls when the economy speeds up—that is counter-cyclical), but they tend to put pressure on how to manage the financing of the budget—with taxes or with debt? Current trend in the US is: more debt.

After our introduction of the *structure* of revenues and expenditures, we can now look at a *time series* of revenue and expenditure to see how these have evolved over the years since 1950. 2020 is an unusual year in that it is afflicted by the effects of the coronavirus on the economy. This has triggered unprecedented new emergency expenditures and a decline in revenue because the economy has entered a recession. Data for 2020 reflect the author's preliminary (August 2020) projections.

Figure 38. USA: Federal Government Revenue and Primary Expenditure (% GDP)

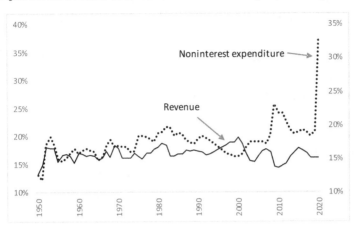

Source: Congressional Budget Office and Office of Budget and Management; author's projection for 2020.

When we study the evolution of the revenue and expenditure lines of Figure 38, we can see the interaction of the economic cycle and politics. Let us focus on the revenue line first. After the Second World War, revenues were restored from depressed levels to around 17 percent of GDP. Revenue cycled around this average for some time without too much variation—we can say that the volatility of the revenue ratio was relatively low. This changed beginning in the 1980s. President Reagan initiated what is known as the "Reagan revolution." This was marked on the foreign policy front by measures to put military pressure on the former Soviet Union—and, indeed, the former Soviet Union fell apart in the course of the 1980s, with the culmination in 1989 of the fall of the Berlin Wall and the reunification of Germany one year later in 1990. This was truly momentous in world politics.

On the economic front, Mr. Reagan initiated policies that became known as "Reaganomics" and may be summarized as "tax cuts and deregulation" and "starve the beast" (which meant engineering tax cuts and large deficits to force cuts in expenditure). Tax cuts and deregulation together with starve the beast became the mantra for the Republican Party and has been the centerpiece of republican presidential candidates ever since.[20] We can see the effects of the Reagan tax cuts combined with the weak cycle in Mr. Reagan's first term by the downturn in the revenue line in the 1980s.

When president Clinton was in office from January 1993-2001, he needed to clean up the budget situation after the first installment of Reaganomics, and used a combination of welfare reforms that generated savings for the budget, and tax increases, to bring the federal budget under control. President Clinton also benefited from the onset of the digital economy as computers were being introduced en masse in the economy, globalization was beginning to make its presence felt, and the US enjoyed a decade long upswing in productivity. Lastly, with a growing economy, increasing leverage in the private sector which boosted asset values and, hence, a base for tax revenue, public sector income further increased with the positive economic cycle. Revenue increased in percent of GDP during Mr. Clinton's term in office.

The revenue line took a new and very sharp turn downward in the early years of Mr. Bush's Jr. term in office. This was a second installment of tax cuts and deregulation with starve the beast attributes. Mr. Cheney launched the slogan that "deficits do not matter," and together with a short pause in activity that followed the

---

[20] As mentioned before, president George Bush Sr. made a slipup in the republican revolution by declaring "read my lips, no new taxes" and then increased taxes slightly anyway. He lost the election to president Clinton in 1992.

attack on the Twin Towers in New York City on September 11, 2001, revenue decline by 4½ percentage points of GDP. Mr. Bush Jr. used Mr. Clinton's excellent budget outcome to implement a large tax cut into a strong economy as a pro-cyclical fiscal policy device. This tax cut was accompanied with a campaign for sustained and deep deregulation of the economy, especially in the financial markets and the mortgage industry. This blew up in 2007-2009 and caused the Great Recession, leading to a sharp second downturn in tax revenue. These effects and the increased volatility in revenues are all visible in the time series record in Figure 38.

President Obama had to recover the economy after the Bush Jr. years from the mishaps with tax cuts and indiscriminate deregulation, but he did not focus his policies on large tax increases to do so. Instead, Mr. Obama injected a large special assistance package into the economy. Then over time, as the economy recovered, expenditure unwound and the tax revenues recovered as well. By the end of Mr. Obama's two terms in office, the economy was in good shape again, but the growth rate was not like it had been in the 1960s because of the altered demographic profile of the population—logically, potential real GDP was lower than a few decades earlier.

In turn, Mr. Trump won the election in November 2016 with the message that the US economy was a disaster with runaway spending and sky-high taxes, and over-regulation. The third full-bore implementation of Reaganomics soon manifested itself in yet another large tax cut, very large deficits to starve the beast, and a wide-reaching program of deregulation—this time focused in part on dismantling environmental policies and protections (including exiting the Paris Climate Accord), restricting and eventually stopping immigration, reversing policies under globalization, and alienating traditional US international partner countries. This strategy has now exploded with the arrival of the coronavirus, when the US economy is finding itself without reserves and cushions, and the only way to support counter-cyclical policies is to issue more debt. The revenue decline is once again plainly visible in the time series in Figure 38.

Thus, what we see in the record is an increase in tax revenue volatility with a string of three large structural tax cuts under republican administrations (Reagan, Bush Jr., and Trump). So far, two democratic presidents recovered from the effects of these policies (Clinton and Obama), and we will soon know whether a third change of the guard will then succeed once again to recover after Mr. Trump.

The structural legacy of these policies is an economy that continues to slow down on trend, because of demographic transition, but now has vastly more debt and much worse international relations than ever in post-war history. The tax cuts, deregulation, and starve the beast philosophy , now also complimented by anti-immigration policies, of the republican party may make for interesting identity politics, but there is evidence that it is mostly pro-cyclical and destroying US economic standing and leadership in the world.

We can also look at the historical *expenditure* record to develop a narrative of what happened, and to see how the cycle and politics have interacted in the post-war period until today. Here we note that expenditure was kept under control in the 1950s and 1960s, until the costs of the Vietnam war at the end of the 1960s and early 1970s caused the spending ratio to shift up. The first oil crisis led to a further spending boost, partly to support a flagging economy. In the early 1980s, we can clearly see a further shifting up of the expenditure ratio, which is related to Mr. Reagan's military buildup, which the Soviet Union could not keep up with. Then followed a long period through 2000 of the new world peace dividend of lower spending pressures, and Mr. Clinton's welfare reforms.

In early 2000, after the attack on the Twin Towers, Mr. Bush Jr. started two wars, one in Iraq and one in Afghanistan, that lifted expenditure once again to a higher plane. It is interesting that, by revealed preference under presidents Reagan and Bush Jr., starving the beast is reserved for mandatory programs (entitlements), and does not apply to (discretionary) military spending. Mr. Trump has done a third installment of increases in military spending, more recently. As noted, from 2009 spending temporarily ballooned to absorb the shock from the Great Recession after Mr. Bush Jr. Given the severity of the recession, few economists would advocate a large tax increase during such a downturn, even though surcharges on the rich and wealth taxes could have been introduced as less distorting technical adjustments.

In his two terms in office, Mr. Obama almost succeeded in unwinding the increases in primary expenditures from the Great Recession. His successor, Mr. Trump, has made little to no progress in cutting expenditure, instead opting to cut taxes into a recovery. The jump in expenditure from the coronavirus recession now underway in 2020 will have to be temporary and needs to be unwound diligently but carefully, once the worst effects of the coronavirus shock have been dealt with in the economy. Exactly how to do this, and how fast to do this, promises to be a major political challenge.

Figure 39 summarizes the evolution of fiscal policy in revenue and expenditure by showing the resulting federal government budget balance. The political events driving the results are as annotated. What is clearly visible are the difficult times in the 1970s with the two oil crises, followed by tax cuts and the military spending boom under Mr. Reagan that significantly increased the deficit. Part of this deficit was also the result of the deep recession that followed the policies to brake the back of inflation coming out of the two oil crises. These deficits were never really recovered under Mr. Reagan's second term or Mr. Bush Sr. one term in office through 1992.

Figure 39. USA: Federal Government Budget Balance 1950-2020 (% GDP)

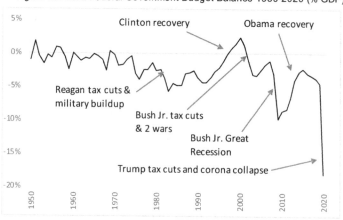

Source: CBO; and author's calculations.

Both the Clinton recovery and the Obama recovery into lower budget deficits are visible. These were the two efforts to bring the federal budget under control again, both undertaken by Democratic Party presidents. Mr. Bush Jr's two terms were particularly unfortunate, as is now very like also the case with Mr. Trump's term. Of course, the coronavirus is not a shock that Mr. Trump could predict, but to leave the country without any cushions for when a shock comes is a failure of policy and reflects the neglect under Mr. Trump of a sound rendering of fiscal policy (he is also trying to undermine monetary policy and external policy).

Economies are always subject to shocks—that is not a surprise. Only the timing of the shocks is a surprise, so spending all cushions in the economy as though shocks have been abolished is not advisable. The policies of tax cuts, indiscriminate deregulation, and starve the beast, lead to such outcomes and should be abandoned for a more sensible and analytical, and less ideological, approach.

Finally, the growing deficits shown above gradually turn into a structural problem for the US economy and the federal budget. That occurs because the almost-continuous series of deficits cumulate into a large stock of debt. Flow adjustments, to get the deficit down, can be done in a few years, as Messrs. Clinton and Obama have demonstrated. But these improvements are for naught if subsequent presidents then return to Reaganomics and spend all the gains again in structural tax cuts. The country needs to escape this trap. Figure 40 shows the evolution of the debt ratio.

The debt shown in Figure 40 reflects the federal government debt held by the public. It does not include the debt held within agencies and Trust Funds of various federal programs. It also does not reflect debt issued by state and local governments. Based on these historical data and the projection made though the end of calendar year 2020, the federal debt held by the public could grow to 101 percent of GDP.

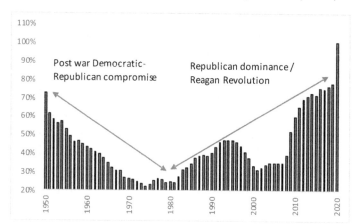

Figure 40. USA: Federal Government Debt Held by the Public (% GDP)

Source: CBO; and author's calulations.

According to the OECD, which presents internationally comparable data for *gross debt* for the *general government* (this includes the gross debt issued by the federal government and the states and local governments; Figure 41), this places the United States in place (5) from the top of the most indebted countries in the world, after Japan (1), Greece (2), Italy (3), and Portugal (4) (comparable data for 2015).

Figure 41: USA--OECD General Government Gross Debt (% GDP)

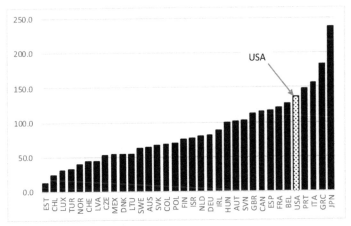

Source: OECD, data are for 2015.

Chapter 15—A Long-Run Central Projection for the Federal Public Finances

In the previous chapter we have analyzed the developments in the federal budget since 1950. We argued that policies and politics changed in 1980 with the advent of Reaganomics. In the 40-year period since 1980, there have been 4 republican presidents and 2 democratic ones (Reagan, Bush Sr., Bush Jr., and Trump—24 years in total) (Clinton and Obama—16 years in total). The dominance of republican politics seems to have normalized views on tax cuts, deregulation, and the notion that deficits and debt do not matter as much as we thought before (now complimented with resistance to immigration).

Earlier in the book, we have argued that demography and the composition of the population matter for economic growth, and that real GDP growth in the US, as in other countries undergoing similar processes, is slowing down and projected to slow down further in the future.

We can now combine the sentiments and constraints from politics, with the natural process of demographic transition and a slowing potential real growth rate in the economy, to see what a long-run central projection for the federal government finances could look like. It is important that the projections not be seen as a prediction, but rather as a scenario that can tell us in what direction the numbers are heading if we maintain policies broadly in place. The way we deal with uncertainty, as we have done before, is to calculate not only a central, but also a more optimistic (high growth) and less optimistic (low growth) scenario.

The range of outcomes, and possible economic consequences for the country, will tell us whether we must take extra precautions (covering risks on the downside) or whether we can feel somewhat relaxed about the risks around our central scenario. As always, it is important to spell out all assumptions that go into making the calculations, so that any interested person can reflect on these for him or herself. It is also important that we do not drive the exercise to what we would ideally like to see happen, but instead focus on what we believe is most likely to happen (the central scenario), as we investigate the data.

There is another aspect of scenario analysis that is worth noting, before we dig into the numbers. Even if we can develop confidence that the central, high, and low scenarios are numerically symmetrical (say the central scenario gives you a score of 10, the high one 12, and the low one 8), can we then say that the cone of possible outcomes is also symmetrical for the possible outcomes of wellbeing or satisfaction of the population? This book takes the view that it is not, because the psychological impact on the population is not symmetrical with respect to errors from the central scenario on the upside or the downside.

When we make "central scenarios" with maximum likelihood in macroeconomics, we are engaged in shaping and framing expectations. In the politics of a country as a whole, a substantial number of people transpose into their own behavior parts and elements of such expectations that may be developed out of the public debates about the economy, the budget, etc. When reality turns out different, such expectations are then disappointed. If the error is on the upside (reality is better than the central scenario), then these members of the public will be pleasantly surprised. If the error is on the downside, they will be unpleasantly surprised.

Even though, from a numerical point of view the error terms may be symmetrical around a central scenario, from a psychological point of view the error terms are not symmetrical. In almost all cases, the absolute value of the additional satisfaction that most people feel from being surprised on the upside by 1 unit of measurement is almost always *smaller* than the absolute value of the disappointment that they perceive from being surprised on the downside by 1 unit of measurement. This has to do with the sense of risk aversion that generates a utility function that is concave, which means in simplified terms that, as we take bigger risks we feel less extra satisfaction from an additional unit of good outcome.

We can translate these considerations into a very practical macroeconomic-political example. Let us say that a political party frames expectations that if you do t, d, and i (tax cuts, deregulation, and deficit irrelevance), then the growth rate of the country is going to take off. Now, this may be true or it may not be true. If it is true and many people have adopted these expectations, then the outcome is going to be satisfactory and nothing dramatic happens. If it is not true, because reality is even better, and many people have adopted these expectations, then those will find themselves with some extra margin and cushions at the end of the day, and that is easy to live with. If it is not true and the outcome is worse, but many had adopted these expectations, then not only will the government have borrowed against these expectations (deficits do not matter), but also individual households and businesses will most likely have borrowed against these expectations. Thus, in such a case, and at the end of the day, if there is a disappointment, both the public and the private sector will likely find themselves with an elevated *stock* of debt that may take years to unwind (during which the economic growth rate is certain to disappoint). Thus, the expectations that are generated in political discussions are important. The two "errors" in the above example are not "utility symmetric." The joy from the upside error is less than the pain from the downside error (in absolute terms).

These issues are also interesting when we study the psychology of language. Here, too, expectations are created that are often false, or at least not a good basis for decision making. Take for example the words "conservative" and "cautious." Many observers believe that republican party policies are "conservative" in the sense of being "cautious," because so many advocates of these policies are said to be "businessmen who know how to handle money." Generally, the public believes this. But it is false. Conservatism means that you are "careful with change"; you don't want to change too quickly. Sometimes, you could be so slow to adapt to new circumstances or changes in the economy that you wind up behind the curve of reality, and then you could lose a lot of money.

Conversely, democratic policies are sometimes labeled as "progressive" or "financially reckless" or even "revolutionary," as though this implies "more risk." But if reality changes and you don't adapt to it, then the risk lies in not adapting, as in being static or changing too slowly. If we study the figures of the previous chapter and note what policies have led to the biggest fiscal deficits and a mountain of debt, then the Republican Party wins hands down. The Republican Party may call this "conservative" but it cannot be called "cautious." Quite the contrary, in this context, the democratic presidents were cautious, the republic presidents were reckless. It is better that we do not believe on face value what politicians tell us. Let us always go to the numbers and check if reality corresponds with the stories. Quite frequently, reality stands in direct contrast from what we have been urged to believe.

Central projection for federal government revenues. There are many assumptions we can make regarding future revenues for the federal government. Revenues will vary with two main parameters: the cycle of GDP, and government policy. If we recall the past from the previous chapter and Figure 42 below, we see that overall revenue has averaged 17 percent of GDP over the period 1950-2019. This number has gone up very slightly in more recent decades to around 17.4 percent of GDP.

A key assumption we will make is that the political system again will have the tendency to keep it around 17.4 percent of GDP, as a central projection. Given political realities, it is possible that future democratic presidents would want gradually to increase the revenue ratio. We implicitly offset this over the long run by assuming also that the current policy advocated by republican presidents will continue to be in effect, i.e. they would want to lower the tax ratio again, as they have done since 1980. Volatility will continue in the future, but the underlying structural ratio of 17.4 percent is maintained here as a long-run average (the solid black line in Figure 42).[21]

---

[21] Part of the current tax cuts are supposed to expire, which could lead to a renewed increase in the revenue ratio. But this was also said after previous tax cuts, noticeably by president Bush Jr.. Revenues did in fact rebound under president Obama, but the next republican president then cut taxes again, with support of the American public. So, here, we do not count on *structurally* higher taxes in the future.

Figure 42. USA: Fed Govt Revenue and Primary Expenditure (1950-2100; % GDP)

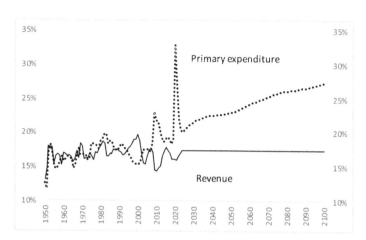

Source: CBO, OMB, projections by the author.

We can see in the figure that Mr. Trump lowered the tax ratio from over 17 percent of GDP in Mr. Obama's second term, to 16.2 percent of GDP in 2019. While there is a new discussion to lower payroll taxes to assist the economy in the difficult coronavirus recession, we assume that these plans will not be implemented for now, so that revenues stabilize around the lower level for a while, but then, as GDP growth normalizes, the revenue ratio is assumed to lift up again for cyclical reasons to 17.4 percent of GDP.

Central projection for federal government expenditures. Projecting primary expenditures is quite a bit more involved than projecting revenue. This occurs because within the expenditure envelope, there are mandatory programs that give their own dynamics to expenditure pressures. The political system may try to offset some of these automatic expenditure pressures in the budget in the future, but this is very difficult to do because the mandatory programs are big, they are growing over time, and they are tied in part to demographic developments that politics cannot stop.

The first step in projecting primary expenditures from 2020 onwards, is to take account of the response to the coronavirus recession (Table 6). There is much uncertainty still, so we have again made some assumptions that the readers hopefully will recognize as reasonable. First, we have added a line for discretionary spending in 2020, 2021, 2023, and 2024 that we call coronavirus relief spending. In 2020, the budgetary cost for coronavirus relief is assumed to be $2.5 trillion, in 2021 it is assumed to be $1.5 trillion, in 2022 it is assumed to be $ 500 billion, and in 2023 it is assumed to be $ 100 billion. The economy is assumed to return to more normal patterns in 2024, so we budget no additional coronavirus expenditures from then on. The total cumulative package of coronavirus relief is thus $4.6 trillion.[22] This additional debt from coronavirus relief spending adds up to the equivalent of 21.9 percent of GDP. The timing of this spending may change based on discussions in Congress, and the size of the cumulative assistance may be different. We are, in any event, assuming that there will be more financial assistance for the economy from the federal government in the short term.

---

[22] In the 2020 US Art IV Consultation, the IMF recommends additional stimulus spending of 10½ percent of GDP, after the package for fiscal year 2020. This book assumes 9.6 percent of GDP additional stimulus.

Table 6. Coronavirus Assumptions for the Federal Budget

	Coronavirus Relief Spending	
	$ billions	% GDP
2019	$0	0.0%
2020	$2,500	12.3%
2021	$1,500	7.0%
2022	$500	2.2%
2023	$100	0.4%
2024	$0	0.0%
Total	$4,600	

Source: author's assumptions.

As a second step, after considering this sudden discretionary additional spending over and above normal budgetary considerations and time-tables, we now need to turn to the recurring budgetary spending allocations and needs. A further assumption needs to be discussed here.

Above, we have related the projections for revenue to *actual* nominal GDP, because actual nominal GDP reflects the business cycle, and that is the basis for revenue collections in a baseline with current policies in place. But when we switch to expenditure pressures, we do not use actual nominal GDP, but rather *trend* nominal GDP, which we have calculated in a previous chapter. We do this, because expenditure decisions for ongoing outlays often reflect longer-run compromises between political parties that are not easy to change from year to year, even "discretionary" spending decisions have their own momentum. This momentum for spending often correlates better to trend growth than to actual year-on-year growth. All political systems in the world experience a certain momentum in spending, and therefore trend nominal GDP is a better scalar for recurrent primary expenditures as a base than actual nominal GDP.[23]

With this in mind, we now need to look at each expenditure item individually to see how we could project them in the baseline. We first look at discretionary expenditures, and then at mandatory expenditures, which each have their dynamic pattern from the past.

The first item in discretionary primary outlays is defense spending. This has gradually declined as a percentage of trend GDP from over 4 percent during the peak of the two wars in Iraq and Afghanistan, to just over 3 percent of trend GDP in recent years. For the future, we assume that the federal government will maintain the military budget at this percentage of trend GDP.

The second item in discretionary primary expenditures is nondefense spending (including on elementary and secondary education; housing; international affairs; justice; and certain highway programs). In recent years defense spending and nondefense spending have been roughly equal in proportion of total discretionary primary expenditure. For the future, we assume that the federal government will maintain nondefense spending also at just over 3 percent of GDP, as we did for military spending. The total discretionary primary spending components thus add up to 6.3 percent of trend GDP in the future, which is about

---

[23] The expenditure side also has some cyclical components in it, such as unemployment insurance and income support programs, but these respond in an *inverse* relationship to actual GDP, contrary to what happens with revenue, which always falls with a downturn and recovers in an upturn. Keeping spending on an even keel through downturns and expansions, thus with trend GDP, is recommended as good counter-cyclical policy.

equal to the rate of spending seen in recent years—we do not assume a major new expansion, nor major new savings from the discretionary federal budget primary expenditures in the future baseline outlook (Table 7).

Table 7. Overview of Central Scenario Primary Spending Assumptions (% GDP)

Annual Averages	Primary Expenditures		
	Total	Discretionary	Mandatory
1962-2019	17.8%	8.6%	9.2%
2000-2019	18.7%	7.1%	11.6%
2020-2100	24.3%	6.3%	18.1%

Annual Averages	Discretionary		Mandatory							
	Defense	Nondefense	Social Security	Medicare	Medicaid	Income Security	Federal Civilian and Military Retirement	Veterans' Programs	Other Programs	Receipts offset
1962-2019	4.9%	3.7%	4.0%	2.0%	0.9%	1.4%	0.9%	0.5%	0.8%	-1.2%
2000-2019	3.6%	3.5%	4.4%	3.1%	1.6%	1.8%	0.9%	0.4%	0.6%	-1.2%
2020-2100	3.1%	3.1%	6.0%	6.2%	3.3%	1.8%	0.8%	0.5%	0.6%	-1.3%

Sources: Congressional Budget Office; and author's projections.

The projections for the mandatory primary expenditure components are more involved, because these programs are driven by demographic developments and issues such as price inflation in healthcare. No-one has a crystal ball to see how these important parameters will evolve in the future, so different assumptions and approaches to financial programming of future budgetary needs are possible—these will produce somewhat different outcomes. The value of such long-run projections is not in pretending that one projection must necessarily be superior to another, but rather in discovering sensitivities of the outcome to variations in assumptions so that risks behind budgetary pressures can be better appreciated. If the public has advanced information about where the pressure points may lie in the future, then the political discourse around these issues can be better informed.

Social security. We project the baseline for social security by dividing past social security spending with the number of elderly dependents (>65) in the population. This gives us a scalar for social security spending per elderly dependent (social security reflects pensions for the elderly). We have numbers from the demographic profile through 2100 about how many elderly dependents there are going to be in the future. We also have assumed that the Federal Reserve will aim to keep inflation at around 2 percent a year (less than 2 percent in the current few years). The first two parameters that go into projecting the social security budget are thus the growth rate in the number of dependents and the annual inflation, or cost of living, adjustment that each pensioner is likely to get under current policies.

There is one other factor that we need to consider, and that is "cost drift." Cost drift occurs because workers work more years today than in the past, and new workers enter the social security system with higher salaries than in the past. Since social security benefits are determined by earnings history, new entrants into social security are "more expensive" than previous entrants and this translates into a gradual drift upward of average social security benefits over and above inflation or cost of living adjustment. In the past, this drift factor has been over 0.8 percentage points a year. For the future from 2020 onward, we assume in our projections that drift will continue at 0.62 percentage points a year. The total nominal inflation per capita for benefits in the future is thus 2.62 percent a year (inflation and drift).

What we see from these calculations is that in the future the spending on social security will increase as a share of GDP (Table 7). This reflects aging and drift, and this occurs in all countries. The Trustees of social security make such projections with greater detail than we do here, but our results fall well within the band of low and high outcomes that is presented in the Trustees' 2020 Report on Social Security.

There is one rule in the social security institution that we have ignored in the projection above. And that is that the federal government does not guarantee social security benefits. Thus, there is concern in the US that if the invested reserves run out, then the benefits will be cut to make cash in and outflows match (scaling down benefits to some 80 percent as a first step). In this book, we have ignored this rule because it may not be doable politically. The political party that will strenuously implement this rule may be expected to be voted out of office, and that threat will lead to further funding of the social security program. Indeed, if a political party holds that this view of concern about social security is mistaken and that their president will implement the sharp social security cuts, then it would be logical for that party to explain more explicitly to the public, as an early warning, that elderly people will receive less in the future.[24]

Medicare and Medicaid. Medicare is health care for the elderly and the disabled. Medicaid is healthcare for the poor. What holds for social security as underlying forces also holds in many respects for Medicare and Medicaid. The number of elderly, disabled, and poor, and inflation, are important drivers of future costs of the programs. Regarding inflation, here we are confronted not with

---

[24] The Trustees for Social Security have recently projected that the program will run out of investment reserves in 2035. The coronavirus recession may cut this horizon short; 15 years is not very long in any event, in the context of retirement.

consumer price inflation but with healthcare inflation. Healthcare inflation in the US has run higher for many years than consumer price inflation. As a result, the costs of Medicare and Medicaid are rising faster than those for social security. Above, we have suggested that the cost per beneficiary of social security could rise by 2.62 percent a year. For health inflation, we assume that the cost per beneficiary will rise by 3.39 percent a year. This causes the share of Medicare spending in GDP to overtake that of social security, and the average shares of Medicare and Medicaid in GDP to double over the projection interval through 2100 (Table 7).

Income support, civilian and military retirement, veterans' affairs, and other programs. The past statistical record for these programs suggest that they do not have a strong tendency to deviate significantly from the evolution of nominal GDP. As a result, the projections for these spending programs are, for now, benchmarked on nominal GDP growth. The big autonomous pressures in the budget thus come from social security and health care; strong pressures do not come from other programs (Table 7).

Receipts offset. There are charges and payments that various agencies receive when they provide services to the public. We have assumed that these elements of the budget also stabilize in the future, as they have done in the past. Therefore, we continue to project that receipts offset in the budget will be around 1.2 percent of GDP a year.

The interest bill. We have now made a projection for revenue and primary expenditure. Putting these together provides us with a projection for the primary balance of the federal budget (all spending included, except the interest bill on the debt). Thus, to get a view on the overall budget balance for the federal government, we need to develop a working assumption for the interest bill as well. The interest bill equals the stock of debt outstanding with the public, multiplied by the average implicit interest rate on the debt.[25] For guidance on interest rates, we can again look at the past, as shown in Table 8 and Figure 43.

Table 8. Implicit Interest Rate on Federal Debt held by the Public

	Nominal	Inflation 1/	Real
1950-2019	4.8%	3.2%	1.6%
2000-2009	4.7%	2.2%	2.4%
2010-2019	2.0%	1.7%	0.3%
2020-2100 Proj.	2.3%	2.0%	0.3%

Source: CBO, OMB, St Louis FED, and author's projections.
1/ Rate of change in the implicit GDP deflator.

---

[25] The Treasury of the federal government issues gross debt in the market place to finance the budget deficits and to top up cash reserves, fund student loans, etc., as necessary. A part of this debt is purchased by government agencies and trust funds of various kinds to invest their own reserves. The effective interest that the government pays on its debt is not the (gross) interest bill on the gross debt, but the (net) interest bill on that portion of the gross debt that is held by the public. Further, the debt is issued in different types of instruments and maturities, each of which have their own coupon interest rate. The "implicit" interest rate on the debt is the interest bill that results from the mix of different instruments, divided by the total outstanding stock of debt held by the public. The government pays attention to the volume of debt outstanding, and also to the mix of instruments (and interest rates) outstanding.

In the post-war period, implicit effective nominal interest rates on the debt held by the public averaged 4.8 percent a year. There was a large runup during the inflation years through the early 1980s, and then a steady decline. Nominal implicit effective interest rates fell significantly during the terms of Mr. Bush Jr. and Mr. Obama, but they have ticked up again under Mr. Trump. Part of this pattern reflected compensation for inflation, but interest rates in real terms, after we adjust for inflation, have dropped sharply in the previous decade to end at 0.6 percent in 2019. For the future, we assume low inflation in the next few years and 2 percent inflation thereafter, and 0.3 percent in effective real interest rates, which gives 2.3 percent average nominal implicit interest rates on the public debt held by the public. Note that in the few years immediately following 2019, the central scenario assumes that real interest rates will be below zero, but we do not consider this a sustainable condition for the longer run, especially since the amount of debt that needs to be placed is so large. Maintaining a (slightly positive) constant real interest rate in the future is again an artifice of the scenario building exercise. If the debt increases as is likely with this baseline scenario, then the interest rates are likely to go up as well. We have not modelled this feedback mechanism in the projections for now.

Figure 43. USA–Implicit Interest Rate on Debt held by the Public (%)

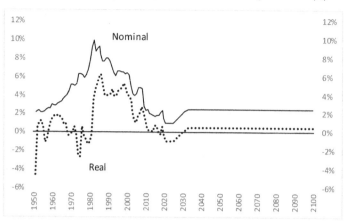

Source: CBO, OMB, calculations by the author.
Note: real i-rate equals nominal i-rate deflated by change in the implicit GDP deflator

Now that we have developed a possible path for the primary balance, and a working assumption for real interest rates, we can complete the projection for the overall balance and the stock of debt. To project the interest bill, we take the average debt stock for the current year, multiplied by the projected average implicit interest rates as derived above. The average debt stock is calculated as the sum of the debt at the end of the previous year plus one-half the projected primary deficit in the current year, plus one-half of a small amount of debt that is placed to keep cash reserves at an adequate level. The latter is called a stock-adjustment differential, which we have calculated as the average of the amounts that have been experienced in recent budget years. Having thus obtained a projection of the interest bill for the budget, we can add this amount to the primary balance to obtain the overall balance.

To track the buildup of debt, the overall balance for the current year is then added to the stock of debt at the end of the previous year—this gives a new stock of debt at the end of the current year. With the new debt at the end of the current year, we can then recursively repeat the calculation above to obtain the overall balance and the stock of debt for the following year, etc. for each year in the future through 2100. The results for the primary and overall balance are presented in Figure 44.

The results in Figure 44 show that on current policies and with the demographic developments described earlier, the federal budget balance will likely deteriorate on trend in the future. This is worsened by the coronavirus shock now underway, combined with a gradual slowing in underlying economic potential growth, a shift toward elderly people in society (aging), and high healthcare inflation costs. The primary balance is projected (mechanically) to deteriorate to -10 percent of GDP and the overall balance to -24 percent of GDP by 2100.

In reality, fiscal balances of this magnitude are not possible. The economy will react negatively to such large deficits, the cost of debt would not be constant, as we have assumed in the constant implicit interest rates, and the market would not want to absorb the enormous amount of debt that is implied by these budget dynamics. Indeed, on baseline, and as a mechanical calculation, the stock of debt held by the public would increase to 540 percent of GDP by 2100, as shown in figure 45 (an extension of Figure 40).

It deserves repeating that long-run central projections are not intended as predictions of what will happen, but rather indications of what direction these important macroeconomic variables will go in, if current

Figure 44. USA–Primary and Overall Federal Budget Balance (% GDP)

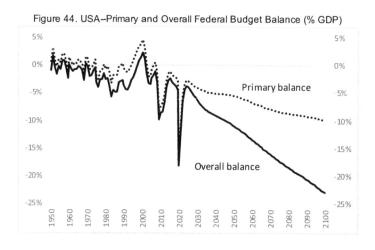

Source: CBO, OMB, projections by the author.

Figure 45. USA: Federal Government Debt Held by the Public (% GDP)

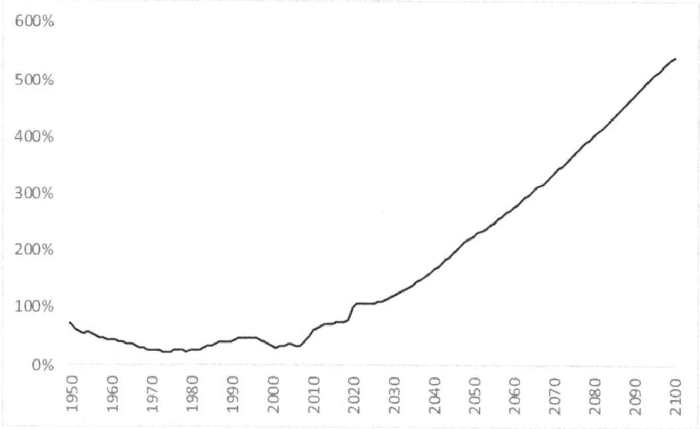

Source: CBO, OMB, projections by the author.

policies are not adapted to new underlying developments. In the short run, it is difficult to say whether certain fiscal policies are in some way sustainable. This becomes much more evident when the calculations are extended toward the long run.

The long run is in any event a better horizon, because that includes the plight of current young generations, and one assumes that the current population cares for the wellbeing and the outlook of its own offspring. The calculations, tables, and figures shown above suggest that US fiscal policy, as currently calibrated, is not sustainable in the long run (Appendix 7). In chapter 17, we will run various alternative scenarios to see how much adjustment in fiscal policy is necessary to make the federal budgetary outlook sustainable in the long run.

Appendix 7—Debt Sensitivity Analysis

Above, we have calculated through a central scenario. We wanted to see whether current fiscal policies interacting with slowing demographics and growth, and subject to the shock of coronavirus, produce a sustainable debt ratio in the long run. The conclusion is that they don't. The implication is that fiscal policy has to be strengthened so that the debt in the future becomes sustainable again, e.g. brought back to something like 60 percent of GDP or below.

Earlier, we had argued that growth and inflation could be higher or lower than in the baseline scenario. It is worth calculating through the high and low growth scenarios as well, to see if this makes any difference for the debt ratio and why. We show the numbers through 2050.

Appendix 7: USA--Debt held by the Public (% GDP)

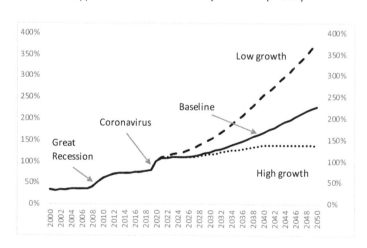

Source: Author's calculations.

The debt held by the public is projected to rise to over 200 percent of GDP by 2050 under the central scenario; it is projected to level off at nearly 150 percent under the high growth scenario; and rise to over 350 percent under the low growth scenario.

Thus, only in the high growth scenario is there a possibility that the debt will remain manageable in the long run. In the central and low growth scenarios, debt increases in relation to GDP which is unlikely to be sustainable. The key reason that the debt ratios are so different is because of the influence of growth on the costs of entitlement programs such as social security and health care.

An important index for entitlement programs is the consumer price index, which remains at 2 percent in these three scenarios. Especially the high growth scenario "eats away" at entitlement costs in relation to the growth of GDP. Further, real interest rates are kept very low for a while in all three calculations, which is unlikely to be the case if growth is high. In the high growth scenario more revenue is generated to pay for benefits and that allows for less debt placement, a lower interest bill (less snow-balling effect on the debt) etc. It is one reason why political systems are keen to "grow out of debt" in all countries. But there are no magical spigots to turn on growth.

We have noted before our skepticism that the high growth scenario might materialize, because it implies a concatenation of positive outcomes that is unlikely to occur. In fact, if Mr. Trump is successful in stopping or significantly slowing immigration, then the low growth scenario will become more likely than the central or high growth scenario.

The conclusion remains from a risk perspective that fiscal policy does not appear to be on a sustainable path and something has to give. Policies need to be set in motion to lower the debt ratio in the future. If this cannot be done, then, with these debt dynamics, it may only be a matter of time before the federal government needs to consider some form of debt restructuring in a non-market way.

Chapter 16—Three Cheers for the US Civil Service

In the previous chapter we presented a central scenario for the long-run US federal budget outlook. In most countries, such calculations take place in universities by professors that specialize in public finance, and in government offices and think tanks, to provide background information to the political system, and to investors. It is not so easy for the general public to understand what is going on and what the long-run budget outlook for their country is.

In the US, there are three institutions that publish regular reports on the long-run US federal budget outlook. These are the Congressional Budget Office (CBO), the US Treasury, and the Trustees of the institutions for social insurance. The reports they produce are referred to as "The Long-Term Budget Outlook" also referred to as the "extended baseline" by the CBO (updated once a year); the "Financial Report of the United States Government" (annual report audited by the General Accountability Office, GAO) by the Treasury Department; and "The Annual Reports of the Boards of Trustees of the [social security] Trust Funds" (updated once a year). Current and past reports can be found on the respective websites.

These reports are long and detailed, updated regularly, and they present a treasure of information for all the citizens who care to read them. There are few countries in the world that can match this level of transparency and detail of information about the government's long-run economic and financial outlook. No one is obliged to agree with all the information and all the assumptions that are in these reports, and, indeed, the reports raise questions, but that is how a vibrant democracy works.

In this chapter, we will compare some key findings of this book's long-run baseline projections and those of the government institutions for the US federal budget. We can see where the assumptions differ and where there are points of agreement. Since not one researcher or institution has a crystal ball to know what the future will bring, it is in the give and take of comparing numbers and discussing assumptions and policy steps that we make progress.

There is one striking question that we can ask upfront: why do US politicians ignore the helpful reports on long-run sustainability by their own technical staff? The CBO, the Treasury staff, and the Trustees have now for years been saying that the fiscal policies of the federal government are unsustainable, and that the problem is getting worse over time. The reports are addressed every year with formal accompanying letters and summaries to the president, the speaker of the House of Representatives, and the president of the Senate. The Secretary of the Treasury even says in every submittal letter of the "Financial Report" (FR) that he is "pleased" to present the *Financial Report of the United States Government* to these esteemed addressees. The FR then explains and says in black and white that policies are unsustainable, raising the question what the secretary of the Treasury is doing to clean up the mess that the US federal budget is in.

One hypothesis why this is happening, and how this hypocrisy can continue, is that the public is asleep at the wheel. The political system then simply orients itself to the next election and figures that it can always finagle a trick or a short-cut that kicks the can down the road. Only a cataclysmic crisis seems to wake up the people, by which time politicians then suddenly claim also to have *unique solutions that only they can deliver.* This may well be the warning bells announcing how a vibrant democracy is about to cease to exist. All empires in the past have succumbed to decadence.

* * *

After taking this deep breath, let us then carry on as best as possible and compare some numbers. What can we see? All macroeconomic fiscal analysis starts by assessing the assumptions about real GDP growth and inflation. After all, all macro-fiscal variables are scaled by, and have to be assessed relative to, nominal GDP.

Reality is dynamic and time does matter, so we need to know what vintage of the reports we are comparing. The latest reports from the Treasury and the Trustees are from slightly different dates and may thus have slightly different assumptions—we will try to infer common factors and highlight those where the reports may vary. What their versions from the beginning of 2020 have in common, however, is that they were written *before the coronavirus crisis* emerged.

The Congressional Budget Office also issued a 10-year budget outlook just before the coronavirus, and subsequently in March prepared preliminary updates only for 2020 and 2021 for the members of congress. Fortunately, in September, the CBO published a fuller update through 2030, including the effects on baseline of the coronavirus, and we can look at these numbers in comparison with the findings of this book.

In the official reports from early 2020 the starting year is 2019 and the horizon is 75-years through 2094. The Trustees reports on social insurance also present summary (actuarial) calculations for the *infinite horizon* for social insurance programs, and that turns out to make a big difference. One reason is that the US is still a relatively "young" country with a growing population through 2100—a lot of aging will still come after 2094. But we will not focus specifically on this important issue for now. In the Trustees report on social security we can see helpful tables with annual assumptions on real GDP growth, CPI inflation, growth in the GDP deflator, and nominal GDP. Table 9 below summarizes key assumptions from the authorities' reports, together with the assumptions for the same variables in this book.

Keeping in mind that the projections by the Treasury and the Trustees of social insurance were made *pre-coronavirus* crisis, we find that their assumptions on real GDP growth are consistently higher than the assumptions for the baseline scenario on real GDP growth used in this book. The central scenario for this book delivers a level of real GDP in 2100 that is 41 percent of the real GDP assumed by the authorities in early 2020 (Table 9).

Then, the September report, and considering the new information associated with the corona crisis, the CBO adjusts downward the decade outlook for real GDP in the direction of the central scenario of this book. For 2030, the CBO has the level of real GDP that is 3.4 percent higher than in the central scenario of this book, which falls well within the range of high and low real GDP that is reflected in the sensitivity scenarios discussed earlier.

Table 9. USA--Comparing Assumptions for the long-run scenarios

	CBO/FR/Trustees pre-corona	CBO 10-yr update post-corona 2/	this book post-corona Baseline	this book post-corona Low	this book post-corona High
Real GDP (chained $ billions)					
2019	19,073	19,073	19,073	19,073	19,073
2030	24,033	22,753	21,989	20,699	23,381
2100	94,487	...	56,688	32,614	97,980
Average annual %-change					
2020s	2.1	1.6	1.3	0.8	1.9
2030s	2.0	...	1.5	0.9	2.2
2020-2050	2.0	...	1.4	0.8	2.1
2050-2100 1/	2.0	...	1.3	0.6	2.0
%-change in the GDP deflator					
2020s	2.07	1.79	2.00	1.50	2.50
2030s	2.05	...	2.00	1.50	2.50
2020-2050	2.05	...	2.00	1.50	2.50
2050-2100 1/	2.05	...	2.00	1.50	2.50
Nominal GDP ($ billions)					
2019	21,428	21,220	21,428	21,428	21,428
2030	33,806	30,732	30,717	27,393	34,468
2100	550,137	...	316,712	122,381	813,439
Average annual %-change					
2020s	4.2	3.4	3.3	2.3	4.4
2030s	4.1		3.6	2.4	4.8
2020-2050	4.1		3.5	2.3	4.7
2050-2100 1/	4.1		3.3	2.1	4.5

Source: CBO; US Treasury/GAO; Trustees of Social Insurance; author's calculations.
1/ Treasury and Trustees reports end in 2094; growth rates for 2094-2100 are assumed constant at 2094 rates.
2/ CBO update to the budget outlook: 2020-2030, September 2020.

Interestingly, the authorities' pre-coronavirus central scenario assumptions for real GDP match almost exactly the post-coronavirus real GDP *high* scenario that was calculated for the sensitivity analysis in chapter 7 of this book (Figure 46—the US authorities central, and this book's high scenarios are virtually the same). The authorities' earlier projections thus now seem to be at the very high end of the possible outcomes through 2100 as envisioned in this book. This book explains why the very high-end scenario is unlikely to materialize, even though it is not impossible. This book also argues that with the policy decisions of Mr. Trump to limit or eliminate immigration, it may even be that the low growth scenario of this book becomes the more likely scenario. If that is the case, then the authorities' scenarios and the low-growth scenario calculated in this book would be very far apart indeed.

For fiscal analysis and projections, the evolution of nominal GDP is critical. Here we see that the implicit GDP deflators for the central scenarios that are used by the authorities and those used in this book are slightly different (by 0.05 percent growth a year). While this difference compounds over the years, we will for now consider it within the margins of error: the differences in our central scenario projections are not caused in a significant way by the different assumptions for GDP inflation. Thus, the different calculations for real GDP mainly drive the results for the central scenario nominal GDP.[26]

---

[26] Indeed, this book has lower potential real GDP growth rates than the authorities and the CBO.

Figure 46. USA: Comparison of Real GDP Scenarios (Chained $ billions)

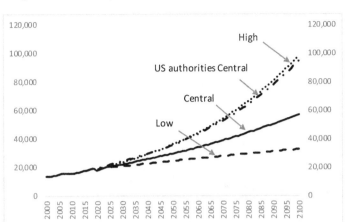

Source: Trustees report and author's calculations.

This book uses lower GDP inflation than official intermediate projections for the low growth scenario, and higher GDP inflation for the higher growth scenario. Thus, when considering nominal GDP, the authorities' central scenario lies within the band of the low-high range of the author's scenarios (Figure 47).

Figure 47. USA: Comparison of Nominal GDP Scenarios ($ billions)

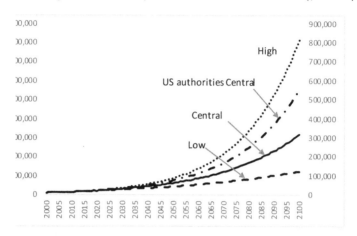

Source: Trustees report and author's calculations.

By 2100, in the authorities' central scenario, nominal GDP would amount to some $550 trillion. By 2100, the baseline or central scenario of this book yields a nominal GDP of $317 trillion. This difference does indeed impact the sustainability calculations of the long-run fiscal position, as we shall see.

It is worth recalling that even with what now seems to be a very optimistic assumption for long-run nominal GDP prior to the coronavirus crisis, the US federal civil service already had called the prevailing policy stance unsustainable. Thus, by downward shifting the growth outlook from the coronavirus setback, this situation will become further aggravated.

It is to be expected that the reports of the Trustees and the Treasury that will be published in early 2021 and include the corona crisis will show a major deterioration from the projections in their early 2020 versions, as the update of the CBO in September 2020 on the US longer-term outlook already foreshadows. The calculations in this book and those to be expected from the Trustees and the Treasury will likely come closer together.

Having compared the key assumptions on real growth, inflation, and nominal GDP, we can now turn to comparing the results from projecting the long-run outlook for the federal budget. Again, as best we can, we will use the reports of the Treasury and the Trustees from early 2020 as a composite report *pre-coronavirus*, and the update through 2030 by the CBO in September 2020 as a first official view *post-coronavirus*, and compare these respective numbers with the scenarios developed in this book, which are *post-coronavirus*.

Comparing projections for 2019-2050 for the budget begins with revenue (Table 10). This book assumes that revenue in the long run will gravitate to 17.4 percent of GDP. The CBO reports in its September long-term outlook that revenue is projected to be at 17.8 percent of GDP by 2030 and the reports from earlier in 2020 envisioned revenue to be at 18.5 percent by 2050, reflecting in part the expiry of some tax cuts in the law. As noted, this book does not assume that taxes will increase noticeably or permanently, beyond the cyclical recovery, because of the expiry of the tax cut measures, because there is no evidence that the US public will abandon Reaganomics. Over time, if Democratic governments raise the tax ratio, it is assumed that subsequent Republican administrations will lower the tax ratio again, as has been the political pattern since Mr. Reagan.[27]

---

[27] In the midst of the coronavirus pandemic, Mr. Trump is attempting to lower payroll taxes "to help the American people weather this crisis." If Mr. Trump succeeds (the payroll tax cut is now a deferral through early 2021), then the 17.4 percent of GDP revenue assumption in this book is too optimistic.

Table 10. USA--Comparing the Baseline/central Projections

	CBO/FR/Trustees pre-corona 1/	CBO 10-yr update post-corona 2/	this book post-corona
Revenue (% GDP)			
2019	16.1	16.3	16.2
2030	18.0	17.8	17.4
2050	18.5	...	17.4
Expenditure (% GDP)			
2019	20.7	21.0	20.8
2030	25.9	23.0	23.9
2050	30.4	...	28.4
Primary expenditure (% GDP)			
2019	18.9	19.2	19.0
2030	22.1	20.8	21.6
2050	21.5	...	23.0
Net interest (% GDP)			
2019	1.8	1.8	1.8
2030	3.8	2.2	2.3
2050	8.9	...	5.4
Primary balance (% GDP)			
2019	-2.8	-2.9	-2.8
2030	-4.1	-3.0	-4.2
2050	-3.0	...	-5.6
Overall balance (% GDP)			
2019	-4.6	-4.7	-4.6
2030	-7.9	-5.3	-6.5
2050	-11.9	...	-11.0
Debt held by the public (% GDP)			
2019	78.5	79.2	78.4
2030	101.0	108.9	120.3
2050	163.7	...	225.6

Source: CBO; US Treasury/GAO; Trustees of Social Insurance; author's calculations.
1/ Authorities' reports end in 2094; data through 2100 extended by the author.
2/ CBO update to the budget outlook: 2020-2030, September 2020.

On the expenditure side, total expenditure projections evolve to about 26 percent of GDP and 30 percent by 2030 and 2050, respectively, in the earlier scenarios pre-coronavirus. The later scenarios by the CBO and in this book have slightly lower expenditure ratios, but this hides a different composition within overall spending.

Primary expenditures in this book are higher, and the interest bill is lower than in the official earlier projections; the differences between the CBO update for 2020-2030 and this book are smaller. This reflects that with lower growth and recent events, most economists now assume lower average interest rates on the debt held by the public. Nevertheless, the growing primary deficits in this book, compared to the official projections, push up the stock of debt into more rapid compounding. By 2050, together with the lower growth outlook, the debt ratio in this book is higher than in the official projections, and the difference only grows after that. The official baseline projections of earlier this year could not foresee the emergency spending and growth slowdown brought on by the coronavirus crisis.

In the CBO update of September 2020, it is important to realize that this is a true baseline, which means that only the spending already legislated so far is included in the projections. Any further stimulus is not yet in these calculations. This book has another 9.5 percent of GDP in stimulus in the numbers (Table 6), so this is creating additional debt beyond the CBO's true baseline.

The bottom line is that the projections for this book paint a more difficult picture for the US budget in the long run than was hitherto assumed in official projections (Figures 48 & 49).

Even abstracting from the effects of the coronavirus, it is often the case that national projections

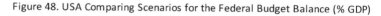

Figure 48. USA Comparing Scenarios for the Federal Budget Balance (% GDP)

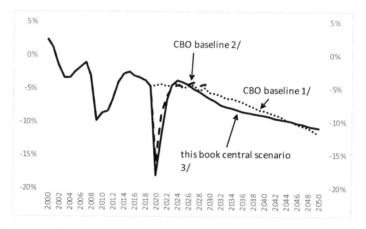

Source: CBO and author's calculations.
1/ CBO pre-coronavirus.
2/ CBO update September 2020.
3/ Includes preliminary effects of coronavirus.

Figure 49. USA Comparing Scenarios for the Debt held by the Public (% GDP)

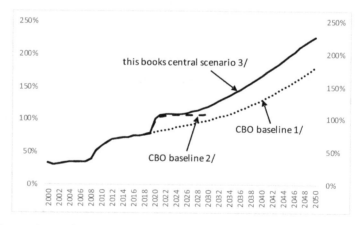

Source: CBO and author's calculations.
1/ CBO pre-coronavirus.
2/ CBO update September 2020.
3/ Includes preliminary effects of coronavirus.

are on the optimistic side—the author has seen this in many countries. There seems to be a political imperative to show that things in the future will work out all-right. Challenges may be difficult, but often a psychological effect creeps in that induces national authorities to leave out that essential safety margin of error that may come from future shocks that no-one can predict. Therefore, growth outlooks tends to be on the rosy side, and future fiscal pressures tend to get underestimated. The end result of this process in many economies is that policies have a bias toward accumulating debt, and the US economy is no exception to this finding.

As noted before, both the relatively optimistic projections by the US authorities, and the more somber projections in this book and in the CBOs update of September 2020 (including the coronavirus shock), point to an unsustainable long-term fiscal position. The author doffs his hat to the civil servants who perform these calculations every year and write down their concerns. Their work is important but mostly ignored by their masters.

It is remarkable that political systems do not reflect more deeply on the findings from their own staff in the public discussions on the budget. When politicians only follow what is popular and do not lead to inform the public about risks that need to be managed for future generations, then the people are on their own. In this context, the differences described above in the numbers from the civil service and in this book are mostly due to vintage effects, and do not reflect a fundamental difference in understanding the dynamics of the long-run position of the US federal budget.

Chapter 17—Simulations to Lower the Debt

In the previous two chapters we analyzed the deficit and debt dynamics of the federal. The conclusion was that fiscal policies as presently pursued are not sustainable—so something needs to be done. In this chapter we explore 4 different adjustment paths. What all the paths have in common is that we want to land the debt ratio at 60 percent of GDP by 2100. This number is not magical in any way. Perhaps we can sustain a healthy economy with 80 percent debt/GDP ratio, or 40 percent, but we need a number as an anchor for the concept of sustainability.[28]

To some extent, this exploration of possible ways of addressing the debt load now baked into the cake is a numbers game. There are an infinite number of paths that could get the US to a debt ratio of 60 percent of GDP by 2100, but we can't explore them all. So, our choice is to do numerical simulations that are anchored by our aspirational debt ratio in 2100, and that allow us to get some view on what is the influence on the path to this ratio from different revenue increases and expenditure cuts. Further consideration of policy options to implement such alternative paths in a realistic way comes in chapter 19.

Simulation 1—the primary balance gap (one-shot scenario). This first simulation asks a hypothetical

---

[28] Research suggests that as governments in high-income countries generate debt above 90 percent of GDP, the risk of debt stress increases. Debt ratios at 30 percent and below are now considered low. The 60 percent aspirational assumption we target here is not meant to be a hard number, but lies in between the 30-90 percent interval, leaving room for cyclical fluctuations.

question: if the president and congress had a magic wand, by how much should they adjust the primary balance (revenue minus noninterest expenditures) of the federal budget in one shot today, so that the debt ratio lands at 60 percent of GDP in 2100?

This question looks for *one policy measure* today that is *permanent*. We introduce the one-shot permanent reduction in primary spending in the central scenario. We assume (unrealistically) that everything else in the economy stays the same for now: no growth effect, and no effect on any of the revenue or other primary expenditure dynamics of any kind. Thus, this is truly just a numbers game to see how far away from a sustainable solution we are in today's dollars and percent of GDP. It is standard analysis in macroeconomics of debt sustainability first to stake out the size of the problem the country faces.

The answer: 8.1 percent of 2020 GDP.

If the budget outcome projected for 2020 could be permanently improved by 8.1 percent of GDP and nothing else changes in the economy, then the debt ratio would land on 60 percent of GDP by 2100. The central scenario had projected a primary deficit in 2020 of 16.8 percent of GDP and a debt ratio in 2100 of 545 percent of GDP. The first simulation would then project a primary deficit in 2020 of 8.7 percent of GDP and a debt ratio in 2100 of 60 percent of GDP. The debt ratio would peak at 93.6 percent of GDP in 2020 (Figure 50 and Table 11).

Figure 50. USA: Federal Government Debt Held by the Public–Simulation 1 (% GDP)

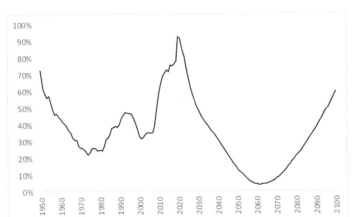

Source: CBO, OMB, projections by the author.
Note: Simulation 1 is one-shot permanent adjustment in 2020.

It is clear that simulation 1 is not possible in practice. The president and congress will not cut primary expenditure, or raise revenue, in one-shot and permanently by 8.1 percent of GDP. Such a large adjustment would throw the economy in a deep recession and create turmoil in the socio-economic conditions of the country. Lastly, it does not establish sustainability in a fundamental sense, because, as Figure 50 suggests, after the one-time adjustment, the aging of the economy and the gradual slowdown of potential real GDP would cause the primary balance to become negative in the long run and start increasing the debt ratio again. So, in 2100, the debt ratio would break through the 60 percent aspirational limit *from below* and continue to increase—that is inconsistent with a stable or falling debt ratio for long-run sustainability.

Table 11. USA--Summary of the Central Scenario and four Adjustment Simulations

	Revenue at the peak	Date	Primary Expenditure at the peak	Date	Cumulative adjustment	Debt/GDP ratio at the peak	Date	Debt/GDP ratio in 2100	Approaching from above or below?
Central Scenario	17.4%	2024-2100	36.6%	2020	0%	545.2%	2100	545.2%	...
Simulation 1: Fiscal Gap-- upfront one-shot adjustment	17.4%	2024-2100	24.9%	2020	8.1%	93.6%	2020	60.0%	Below
Simulation 2: 0.5 % GDP adjustment for 18 years	17.4%	2024-2100	32.4%	2020	8.7%	107.5%	2022	60.0%	Below
Simulation 3: 0.21 % GDP adjustment every year	17.4%	2024-2100	32.8%	2020	14.3%	150.4%	2047	60.0%	Above
Simulation 4: mix of revenue increases and spending cuts	21.3%	2042-2100	32.8%	2020	12.0%	126.4%	2040	60.0%	Above

Source: calculations by the author.

The implied revenue and primary expenditure from simulation 1 are shown in Figure 51. It shows revenue constant at 17.4 percent of GDP in the long run. Primary expenditure is now cut from a projected 32.9 percent in 2020 under the central projection to 24.9 percent of GDP in the one-shot adjustment scenario. The lowest point of primary expenditure would be reached in 2024 at 12.1 percent of GDP, which is comparable with the beginning of the time series in 1951. This further shows that this adjustment path is not realistic, because in 1951 there were scant entitlement programs and the population was much younger and dynamic on average than today. A sudden cut of the magnitude under simulation 1 is not realistic.

Figure 51. USA: Fed Govt Revenue and Primary Expenditure–Simulation 1 (% GDP)

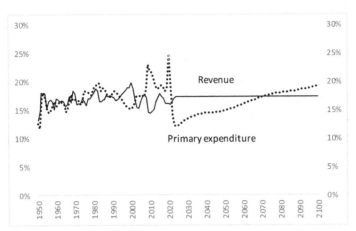

Source: CBO, OMB, projections by the author.
Note: Simulation 1 is one-shot permanent adjustment in 2020.

The reader may ask why the primary balance gap is useful at all, if it leads to answers that cannot possibly be implemented in the real world. The primary balance gap is useful in at least two dimensions—over time, and to compare with other countries. It provides perspective.

With regard to following the gap over time, the author has conducted similar calculations for the US federal government in 2006, towards the end of the Bush Jr./Cheney administration, concerned as he was about the "deficits do not matter" mantra. The primary balance gap at that time pointed to a shortfall of 6.5 percent of GDP. This seemed a very large number then (the Great Recession would explode shortly after), and it has only gotten bigger over time (the coronavirus crisis has exploded now). No-one expects that such a large sustainability gap can be resolved in a few years—this takes decades, so one needs to build buffers over time and strengthen the public finances. But the unsettling aspect is that the gap has gotten *worse*, not better, over time.

Since methodologies can make a difference in these numbers, it is good to compare the calculations made above with those of other authors. Professors Lawrence Kotlikoff and Alan Auerbach are well-known researchers into overlapping generations models, which provide a technique to study intergenerational aspects of fiscal policy and its sustainability (Appendix 8). In a paper published by Kotlikoff and Michel (2015), reflecting concern about the aftereffects of the Great Recession, these authors estimated the fiscal gap over an infinite horizon of $210 trillion, or the equivalent of 10.5 percent of GDP in permanent tax revenues.

This compares with the above calculations in this book of a gap of 8.1 percent of GDP in 2020 over an 80-year horizon until 2100. If the above calculations of this book had been extended to the infinite horizon, the gap would have become larger. This comparison brings up two recurrent themes that research in this area keeps producing: (1) as we extend the time horizon to compute the fiscal gap for a system that is not sustainable, the gap becomes bigger, and, (2) if we postpone addressing this fiscal gap, then the eventual need for new measures also gets bigger. In other words, fiscal gaps do not go away by themselves—you can't "grow out of them."

With regard to international comparison, the European Commission produces a fiscal sustainability report and/or a debt sustainability monitor every year, in which it calculates long-run primary balance gaps for each of the 28 EU member countries. In its latest report of January 2020, it finds that its so-called "S2" indicator is on average 2.4 percent of GDP, with a high for Romania of 8.8

percent of GDP and Luxembourg of 8.6 percent of GDP.[29] The US authorities report that their fiscal gap is around 4 percent of GDP (this assumes that social benefits are cut when reserves in the Trust Funds run out; maintaining social benefits would make the fiscal gap larger). Any number above 6 percent of GDP is labeled by the EU commission as "high risk" for long-term fiscal sustainability. These calculations are not exactly comparable to those for the US or those by Kotlikoff and colleagues, but they do give ranges of magnitude. The numbers for the US federal budget come in high in virtually all variations of this research, and that is worrisome.[30]

Simulation 2—constant annual cuts of 0.5 percent of GDP in primary expenditures (gradual scenario). Fiscal adjustment has a speed limit. What do we mean by that? In the above findings, the political system will not and cannot adjust the fiscal deficit by 8.1 percent of GDP in one shot, and politicians are right not to do this. Doing so would cause such a large decline in aggregate demand that GDP would decline even faster than the debt. That would not reduce the debt/GDP ratio, but increase it. So, if a political system wants to reduce its debt, what is the appropriate speed at which to address this problem—how

---

[29] The EU Commission defines the S2 indicator as measuring the budgetary adjustment that would ensure sustainable public finances in the long term. Specifically, this indicator shows the upfront adjustment to the current primary balance that is required to stabilize the debt-to-GDP ratio over the infinite horizon, including any additional expenditure arising from an aging population.

[30] It would be helpful if the International Monetary Fund could adopt one sensible methodology and report on the fiscal gap for every country in its annual Article IV Consultations.

fast should the government try to reduce the deficit, or strengthen the surplus, without killing off growth in real GDP?

The speed of adjustment in fiscal accounts depends on the quality of the measures and the cyclical position and dynamics of the economy. Empirical findings suggest that moderate permanent measures are better than large (and sudden) one-time spending or revenue adjustments. One reason is that permanent measures compound over time and that can produce a more gradual but ultimately powerful adjustment. Further, it also tends to be the case that if the budget balance needs to be strengthened, often a cut in expenditure can be maintained longer than an increase in revenue.[31] Distributional effects must always be considered.

If taxes need to be increased, governments need to consider raising taxes on inelastic tax bases, such as real property (and wealth), instead of income. And if income taxes need to be increased, taxing labor income tends to be easier than taxing capital income. Capital income and investment decisions are more elastic than labor income; but, again, some balance is necessary because of distributional effects. If a country has systematic external imbalances (domestic demand is always higher than domestic supply), then consumption taxes such as a value-added tax, tend to be more powerful than taxes on income

---

[31] The recently departed economist Alberto Alesina is known for his work on the political economy of budget adjustments. His research found that the initial conditions before fiscal adjustment is undertaken matter (say, just after a fiscal crisis strong fiscal adjustment tends to be more feasible). His findings also suggested that expenditure-based adjustments are often more durable and efficient than tax-based adjustments. Further, credibility of the adjustment effort is key; and this depends in part on the quality of the measures undertaken.

and entrepreneurship (but again, watch distributional issues).

If a government wants to strengthen the fiscal balance by 1 percent of GDP, and the economy experiences a negative shock during the process, then revenues will decline and the measures will not bring in what was expected. If the deficit can be financed, it is best to let automatic stabilizers function, rather than doubling up on additional measures. Automatic stabilizers reflect the cycle and prevent that policy measures become very pro-cyclical.

There seems to be a rule of thumb when it comes to the speed of adjusting the budget balance. In the author's experience of working with governments to manage the budget, it tends to be that if an *emerging country* adjusts its budget balance at a pace greater than around 2 percent of GDP a year, then the negative effect on GDP could become bigger than the savings that would be generated to keep the debt down. Thus, adjusting by more than 2 percent of GDP, other things being equal, should be avoided if financing conditions allow it. It may be better to adjust two years in a row by 1 percent of GDP, than 2 percent of GDP in one shot.[32]

For *high-income* countries, this speed limit seems to be lower. Few high-income countries can sustain annual adjustments in their budget that exceed 1 percent of GDP. In the EU, countries that had budget deficits above the medium-term objective were routinely advised/requested by the EU Commission to reduce their deficits by 0.5

---

[32] These rules of thumb are based on general practical operational experience from 33 years at the IMF. Mr. Alesina found that even some fiscal contractions could be *expansionary* for growth effects, but that depends on specific circumstances combined with very capable political leadership.

percent a year until the budget pressures were resolved. Few governments managed even to deliver 0.25 percent of GDP adjustment a year... At the other extreme of this spectrum, Greece adjusted by over 4 percent a year for the first 4 years of its euro-crisis from 2010-2014. This is an extraordinary adjustment effort that left the economy into a deep recession (the effect on GDP was stronger than the containment in the amount of debt). The cardinal problem for Greece was that allowing a more moderate pace of adjustment would have required even larger financing flows, and those were not at hand. This was a case where the financing constraint forced an adjustment that went far beyond the notion of a "speed limit" of fiscal adjustment—the unmovable wall turned the unstoppable ship.

With this background in mind, and considering that there is also a speed limit of fiscal adjustment in the US economy, for simulation 2 we ask the question: if we adjust the fiscal deficit by 0.5 percent of GDP in permanent measures each year, how long would it take before we bend the debt/GDP ratio down to 60 percent of GDP by 2100?

Answer: 18 years of annual permanent cuts of 0.5 percent of GDP, from 2020 through 2037 (8.7 percent of GDP cumulatively).

Figures 52 and 53 show the results. The debt will continue to increase for 2 years to 107.5 percent of GDP in 2022, while the gradual but steady fiscal adjustment is taking place. Going more slowly requires more time to bend the debt ratio down. As before, this scenario is not a resolution to the problem of sustainability either, because at the end of the sample period, the debt ratio again

crosses the 60 percent aspirational target from below, and
it will continue to increase after this, in violation of the
notion of long run sustainability.

Figure 52. USA: Federal Government Debt Held by the Public–Simulation 2 (% GDP)

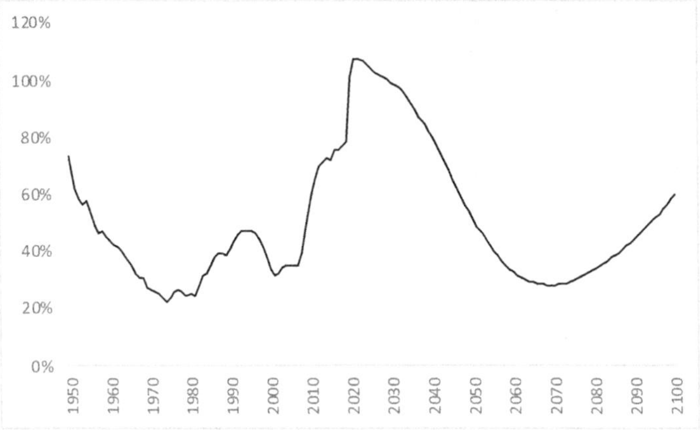

Source: CBO, OMB, projections by the author.
Note: Simulation 2 is 0.5 % GDP permanent adjustment in 2020-2037.

Figure 53 shows that adjustment of 0.5 percent of
GDP a year will gradually lower primary expenditures to
13.8 percent of GDP by 2037. After this date, the pressures
from an aging population and healthcare cost inflation
take over again and the level of primary expenditures
starts going up once more. It is not realistic to assume that
primary expenditures can be reduced progressively to such
a low number, so simulation 2 is not technically and
politically realistic either. What this number crunching is
showing, however, is that being more gradual, subject to
the fiscal adjustment speed limit, takes more time to get
the debt down.

Do countries have the intestinal fortitude to lower their public expenditure for 18 years in a row? One doubts this. It also brings home the enormity of the task ahead. Perhaps this is the reason that almost no US politician wants to talk about the long-run sustainability of the federal budget, because it is strategically more convenient to kick the can down the road. Millennials and generation Z and alpha, beware!

Figure 53. USA: Fed Govt Revenue and Primary Expenditure–Simulation 2 (% GDP)

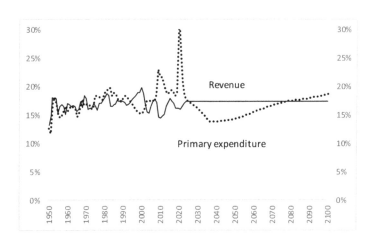

Source: CBO, OMB, projections by the author.
Note: Simulation 2 is 0.5 % GDP permanent adjustment in 2020-2037.

Simulation 3—Equal annual fiscal adjustment until 2100 (very gradual scenario). Simulation 2 provided different insights than simulation 1, but it still did not produce a satisfactory solution that we can consider realistic. Neither was it necessarily designed that way—we are investigating sensitivities. In that vein, let us now ask a follow up question for a new simulation 3: if the political system can only work in a very gradual way and is willing to commit to 2100 to get the debt down to 60 percent of GDP, how much would the need for equal annual expenditure cuts be, relative to the baseline?

Answer: 0.18 percent of GDP every year until 2100 (14.3 percent of GDP cumulatively).

Since this is the very gradual adjustment scenario, which means that the cumulative measures very gradually build strength, the turnaround in the debt ratio from its peak does not take place until 2047, nearly 3 decades from today. The debt ratio would then peak at 150.4 percent of GDP. It is interesting to note in Figure 54 that by 2100 the debt ratio crosses the aspirational limit of 60 percent of GDP from above, and that it would continue to decline afterwards. This occurs because the cumulation of equal annual measures builds strength over time. The fiscal balance will thus also build strength over time. In this case, the cumulative effect of the annual measures is larger than the effects of aging on fiscal costs and the gradual slowing of the economy over time. In this technical sense, the scenario is sustainable.

Figure 54. USA: Federal Government Debt Held by the Public–Simulation 3 (% GDP)

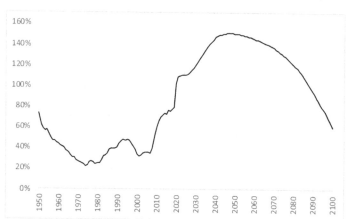

Source: CBO, OMB, projections by the author.
Note: Simulation 3 is 0.18 % GDP annual permanent adjustment in 2020-2100.

Figure 55 shows the implications of simulation 3 for revenue and primary spending. Since the measures are modelled as annual primary expenditure cuts, the primary expenditure line slowly declines until 2100, to end at 13 percent of GDP. This is once again unrealistic, because aging automatically imparts an upward pressure on spending in the future. It is not possible to adjust only through the expenditure side, even if it is very gradual. This simulation may be the Republican's dream (only spending cuts, no revenue measures; and everything very gradual), but the distributional effects of this simulation would be so draconian that it renders this solution to the problem unrealistic from a socio-economic, and therefore, political point of view. Expenditure austerity until 2100 is just not in the cards.

Figure 55. USA: Fed Govt Revenue and Primary Expenditure–Simulation 3 (% GDP)

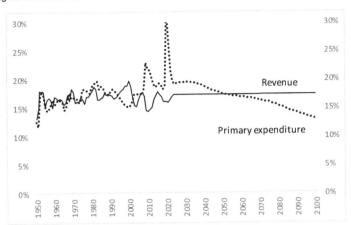

Source: CBO, OMB, projections by the author.
Note: Simulation 3 is 0.18 % GDP annual permanent adjustment in 2020-2100.

Simulation 4—A Mix of Revenue increases and Expenditure Cuts (compromise scenario).

This simulation recognizes that the solution to America's debt problem cannot come only from the expenditure side. There is a need for higher taxes as well. The Republican dream of tax cuts, deregulation, and deficit irrelevance is not consistent with socio-economic sustainability.

This brings us to the question of how much adjustment should be obtained from the revenue side and how much from the expenditure side? This is of course where the political fights will take place.

Answer: one option is 0.10 percent of GDP annually in primary expenditure cuts through 2100, combined with 0.17 percent of GDP in revenue increases for 23 years through 2042.

This answer is only one option; the distribution between expenditure and revenue measures needs to reflect political compromise. In this sense, simulation 4 is for demonstration purposes only and functions as an example. It opts to distribute the burden of adjustment as 1/3rd revenue (cumulative measures of 3.9 percentage points of GDP) and 2/3rds primary expenditure (cumulative measures of 8.1 percentage points of GDP). Figure 56 first shows the resulting debt ratio.

The debt ratio peaks at 127 percent of GDP in 2040; some 2 decades from today. The debt ratio crosses the aspirational limit of 60 percent of GDP in 2100 from above. So, the trajectory is sustainable from a technical point of view. We see that the measures build strength over time, so the devil is once again in the details.

Figure 56. USA: Federal Government Debt Held by the Public–Simulation 4 (% GDP)

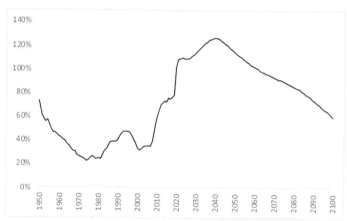

Source: CBO, OMB, projections by the author.
Note: Simulation 4 is 1/3rd revenue and 2/3rd expenditure measures.

Figure 57 shows the implications for revenue and
primary expenditure. We see the effects of permanent
revenues measures of 0.17 percent each year for 23 years
until 2042. There are no further tax increases after the tax
ratio reaches 21.3 percent of GDP, or 5.1 percentage
points of GDP higher than in 2019 (3.9 percentage points
in measures plus 1.2 percentage points in cyclical recovery
in the revenue ratio). Expenditures are cut by 0.10 percent
of GDP every year until 2100. This is "leaning against the
wind" of continuous aging and the effects of economic
slowdown as population growth diminishes through the
analysis horizon in the central scenario. The cumulative
cuts in primary expenditure then add up to 8.1 percent of
GDP, which is double the adjustment obtained from the
revenue side measures.

Figure 57. USA: Fed Govt Revenue and Primary Expenditure–Simulation 4 (% GDP)

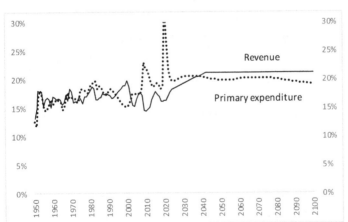

Source: CBO, OMB, projections by the author.
Note: Simulation 4 is 1/3rd revenue and 2/3rd expenditure measures.

Whether this expenditure containment is doable is not at all certain, because the expenditure ratio will decline over time even though the fiscal accounts are subject to aging and slower growth effects. In this scenario, even though we call on help from the revenue side, there is a need for quite steep structural cuts in primary expenditure over time. If this proves politically impossible, then revenue contributions will have to be increased to maintain the same objective to bring the debt ratio down to our aspirational anchor of 60 percent of GDP by 2100. In this compromise simulation, the US federal budget will run a primary surplus from 2039 onward.

Some conclusions from these Simulations.

- The US federal government has a big debt problem.
- There are no easy solutions.
- If the country postpones a solution, the problem will get bigger for the next generations.
- The problem cannot be solved in one shot—that is too large a burden on the economy.
- There is a speed limit to fiscal adjustment beyond which growth would be too adversely affected. The political system needs to discuss this speed limit, but it is probably between 0.5 and 1 percent of GDP a year.
- The problem cannot be resolved by expenditure cuts alone.
- The Republican mantra since Reagan has to go— taxes need to go up and deficits do matter.
- Further analysis is needed as to how much federal debt the market can absorb at the peak, and whether there may be a financing constraint beyond a certain level of debt.

- The economy can become non-linear and adverse when debt ratios reach beyond a tipping point of confidence in the economic soundness of the federal budget and the debt. We assume in the above that the US does not want to use the default option.
- Even in the midst of the coronavirus crisis, where extra spending is needed, the political system needs to discuss a compromise how to pilot the public finances back to sustainability after the corona crisis lessons. The citizens should not be given a one-way ticket to more spending and higher debt, but also a view of revenue increases and expenditure cuts after the crisis—the return ticket to lower debt ratios. The policy decisions need to be intertemporal, to protect future generations.
- Resolving the problem and assuring confidence anchors can take multiple decades—it is a big challenge for the country and the US political system.

Appendix 8—Intergenerational Accounting and the Fiscal Gap

Wikipedia, in May 2020, describes the fiscal gap as follows:

The fiscal gap is a measure of a government's total indebtedness proposed by economists Laurence Kotlikoff and Alan Auerbach, who define it as the difference between the present value of all of government's projected financial obligations, including future expenditures, including servicing outstanding official federal debt, and the present value of all projected future tax and other receipts, including income accruing from the government's current ownership of financial assets. According to Kotlikoff and Auerbach, the "fiscal gap" accounting method can be used to calculate the percentage of necessary tax increases or spending reductions needed to close the fiscal gap in the long-run.

Generational accounting, an accounting method closely related to the fiscal gap, has been proposed by the same authors as a measure of the future burden of closing the fiscal gap. The "generational accounting" assumes that current taxpayers are neither asked to pay more in taxes nor receive less in transfer payments than current policy suggests and that successive younger generations' lifetime tax payments net of transfer payments received rise in proportion to their labor earnings.

According to Kotlikoff and Auerbach, "fiscal gap accounting" and "generational accounting" reports have been done for roughly 40 developed and developing countries either by their treasury departments, finance ministries, or central banks, or by the IMF, the World Bank, or other international agencies, or by academics and think tanks.

The U.S. fiscal gap. Fiscal gap accounting is not new to the U.S. government. The Social Security Trustees and Medicare Trustees have been presenting such calculations for their own systems for years in their annual reports. And generational accounting has been included in the President's Budget on three occasions.

Based on calculations using the 2012 Alternative Fiscal Scenario long-term projections by the Congressional Budget Office, some estimate that the U.S. fiscal gap stands to be $222 trillion – more than 13 times larger than the reported U.S. National Debt. According to the same estimates, the gap grew $11 trillion from 2011 to 2012. Eliminating the entire U.S. fiscal gap through revenue alone would require a permanent 64%[33] increase in all federal taxes. Alternatively, closing the gap through spending reductions alone would require a permanent 40% cut in all federal purchases and transfer payments.

---

[33] Note: 64% of 17 percent of GDP = 10.9 percent of GDP.

Appendix 9—How about the Inflation Tax?

Observers from different backgrounds with concern for the finances of the Federal Government are wondering how the unsustainable fiscal and debt situation will be resolved. The phenomenon of very low interest rates is a conundrum and gives rise to worries that monetary policy has lost power, while it provides incentives to use even more debt—will this blow up at some point? It would be ideal if the political system could agree on a long-term fiscal plan back to sustainability, and then implement this with appropriate diligence and discipline. But, who has confidence that political actors can do this? In a polarized world, agreeing who pays what has not proven easy. Thus, and almost as a residual after exhausting all alternatives, some say that in the end the FED will inflate away part of the debt. That is seen as the "easy and most likely solution—inflation."

One wonders if it is really so straightforward.

The FED has already been trying to inflate the economy, and so far it has led to asset inflation, zombification of entities, and increasingly troubling inequality, not CPI inflation and lower real debt.

Once, and if inflation starts increasing in such a world, where there is an enormous amount of liquidity already, how high would inflation go, and how does the FED keep this under control? When the liquidity fuel in the economy catches fire, that may not be easy to stop. What happens with "low" interest rates then?

Proponents of the inflation tax say that after WWII, many countries, including the US, burnt off debt with the inflation tax. However, that required a complimentary dose of financial repression. Can this be done in modern financial markets? The computing power today is vastly bigger than in 1950, the political sentiments are much different (and less patriotic), and financial capital has become extra-ordinarily mobile in the global village.

The Treasury now issues TIPS (Treasury Inflation Protected Securities) which are indexed to inflation. The demand for fixed nominal instruments will drop like a stone the minute that financial markets get wind of the inflation tax and financing possibilities for the Treasury through traditional instruments could then seize up.

In the 1950s most people were young and did not count on a social security system for a fixed income pension. Now we have the boomers retiring and they vote. If the Treasury inflates away their fixed income social benefits, the political system will hear their voice. And the income and wealth distribution effects are not only relevant for retirees, but for all people on moderate (non-indexed) incomes and fixed contracts, who are already seeing their fortunes slipping relative to the wealthy and those with high (and indexed) incomes.

More inflation will accelerate inequality through asset wealth effects, and that is unlikely to be sustainable. Lastly, globalization and technology have contributed to low CPI inflation and this book argues that this may be structural for now. Is the US willing to close itself off from open global trade and finance, and jettison the dollar standard, to be able to engineer domestic inflation? A nominal boost to GDP may result in a further widening trade deficit, without much higher inflation. Japan has been trying for years during aging to lift inflation without success. In sum, the distortions needed to levy a significant inflation tax could damage the economy. It is not straightforward to "inflate" ourselves out of this debt problem.

Chapter 18—The US Federal Government Balance Sheet

We have noted in the previous chapters that the US civil service keeps alerting the country that fiscal policy is on an unsustainable path, and that the political system seems to keep ignoring these warnings. Over time, the situation has only gotten worse. We also speculated that the public is asleep at the wheel—it does not force the political system to confront this serious issue. In turn, the political system does not have the leadership qualities to explain to the public what is going on and what the country can do about it. How can such a sad situation be improved or nudged in the right direction?

Nature is an equilibrating machine, and when something is unsustainable, it will stop. Nature has no empathy, does not talk to us in fine English, and has no mercy for anyone or anything when a crisis comes. In this sense, crises are cleansing mechanisms that weed out those who cannot adapt, are ideological instead of flexible, or have no ability to think forward. Nature does not ask whether we like this or not.

So, the trick seems to be to think forward, take seriously and in an open-minded way what we see, and adapt policies to improve resilience and sustainability. Communication is also important, and this is where a government balance sheet may help.

Some say that accounting is boring. This is nonsense. For a good example why accounting is not boring, have a look at "The reckoning" by Jacob Soll. This is a book about the history of accounting that explains that progress in modern society depended on our ability to develop systems that inform policy makers, society, and businesses, what is going on.

An accounting system is an instrument or tool to help us recognize what is going on. Every business owner or shop keeper knows what a balance sheet is, because this tells them whether the business has a positive net worth, and thus is solvent and therefore viable. They also learn, sometimes intuitively, how to look forward and test what they believe they see against a notion of what will happen to their net worth under certain circumstances and with certain policies for the future. That is where accounting helps us to make visible what is happening, or even what may happen under certain circumstances and assumptions. Our scenario analysis earlier of the future possible fortunes of the federal budget are just such exercises.

A balance sheet records all assets and liabilities that an entity has. The difference between what we own and what we owe is net worth. If net worth is negative, that spells trouble because the entity is insolvent. If net worth is positive and growing over time, then something is going right and the existential strength of the entity is being safeguarded. Political systems have now laid down laws to oblige private sector enterprises to write down an honest and audited balance sheet, because this is to the benefit of the stakeholders in these private sector entities. For entities that make promises about the future, say a pension fund or a life insurance company, the balance sheet needs to contain an estimate of what the cost of these promises for the future is and then show that the entity has assets to meet these costs in the future when the promises fall due. If private entities do not follow these rules, there may be penalties under law. Would it not be wonderful if the politicians also write down such a balance sheet for the government itself, and cost the promises that politicians make to the citizens, to see if the state has enough resources in the future to meet all these obligations?

Well, there is a surprise: the US federal government civil service does calculate a balance sheet for the US federal government, and it does present summary statistics of what the net balance for the future of political promises is (another cheer for the civil service). This chapter takes a look at how this accounting exercise is done and what information the results provide us.

Table 12 presents the statement of operating results for the US federal government since 1994. These results are available annually, but we show the numbers for every 5th year only. The line revenue is very close to revenue in the budget. The line net cost is often larger than the line expenditures in the budget. This is so because the budget is recorded on a cash basis, when the government actually pays for fiscal operations, whereas the statement of operating results records on an accrual basis, which means that a cost is recorded when it is incurred, not when it is paid (which may be later). It is often the case that the government incurs costs that do not have a short-term cash counterpart, such as adjustments in future benefits for civil servants or military pensions. These commitments do not have a short-run cash component, but they do increase liabilities of the government, so they need to be recorded on an accrual basis.

Table 12. USA--Operating Result of the US Federal Government

	1994	2000	2005	2010	2015	2019	2020 1/
	($ billions)						
Revenue	1,386.1	2,044.8	2,189.8	2,216.5	3,339.1	3,622.6	3,366.7
Net cost	1,515.7	2,005.2	2,950.0	4,296.8	3,858.8	5,067.7	7,399.9
Net operating cost	**-129.6**	**39.6**	**-760.2**	**-2,080.3**	**-519.7**	**-1,445.1**	**-4,033.2**
Memorandum item: budget balance	-203.2	236.2	-318.3	-1,294.4	-442.0	-984.4	-3,698.5
	(Percent of GDP)						
Revenue	19.0	19.9	16.8	14.8	18.3	16.9	16.5
Net cost	20.8	19.6	22.6	28.7	21.2	23.7	36.3
Net operating cost	**-1.8**	**0.4**	**-5.8**	**-13.9**	**-2.9**	**-6.7**	**-19.8**
Memorandum item: budget balance	-2.8	2.3	-2.4	-8.6	-2.4	-4.6	-18.1
Nominal GDP ($ billions)	7,287	10,252	13,037	14,992	18,225	21,428	20,387

Source: the 2019 Financial Report of the US Federal Government, and author's calculations.
1/ 2020 projections are by the author.

As we see from comparing the memorandum item "budget balance" with the line "net operating cost," then it follows that the accrual deficits tend to be bigger than the (modified cash) budget balance. That a more complete measure of the fiscal outcome of the federal government has even bigger deficits than commonly reported outcome is not ready knowledge for many in the public. The US fiscal operations have been running accrual deficits over a trillion dollars for years, even though it may seem that the budget deficit had been reduced to below a trillion dollars for a number of years. The balance that really counts is the net operating costs, not the budget balance. So, this lack of familiarity with cash and accrual accounting would be useful to clear up. An increasing number of countries record the budget on an accrual basis, and the US should start doing this as well.

After this note on the operating balance versus the budget deficit, now we can turn to the balance sheet of the US federal government. What we see here is that assets have been less than liabilities for as far back as the numbers go. And the shortfall, which is a negative net worth, is getting worse over time. If a company were to do this, it would be declared bankrupt. The assets do not include valuation of heritage assets (such as monuments or places of historical cultural value) or legacy assets such as the national parks. These assets are not for sale and cannot be used to pay the bills on time, so their value is excluded from the balance sheet. The liability side is dominated by debt in the hands of the public, and post-employment commitments for civil servants and the military staff.

Table 13. USA--Balance Sheet of the US Federal Government

	1994	2000	2005	2010	2015	2019	2020 1/
				($ billions)			
Assets	1,350.9	911.5	1,447.9	2,883.8	3,229.8	3,992.0	4,147.3
Liabilities	5,357.1	6,856.9	9,914.8	16,356.6	21,451.7	26,944.8	31,358.9
Net worth	-4,006.2	-5,945.4	-8,466.9	-13,472.8	-18,221.9	-22,952.8	-27,211.6
				(Percent of GDP)			
Assets	18.5	8.9	11.1	19.2	17.7	18.6	20.3
Liabilities	73.5	66.9	76.1	109.1	117.7	125.7	153.8
Net worth	-55.0	-58.0	-64.9	-89.9	-100.0	-107.1	-133.5
Memorandum items							
Nominal GDP ($ billions)	7,287	10,252	13,037	14,992	18,225	21,428	20,387

Source: the 2019 Financial Report of the US Federal Government, and author's calculations.
1/ 2020 projections are by the author.

A helpful feature from the operating result and the balance sheet is that the net operating result is virtually identical to the drop in net worth. The budget balance is not equal to the deterioration in net worth, and is therefore an incomplete and misleading indicator for how well or poorly the public finances are doing. The financial statements in the Fiscal Report of the US federal government explain in detail what other (relatively small) effects operate on the net worth, such as valuation changes or data revisions. They also explain the variation in cash at hand by the Treasury to pay the bills on time—the cash flow statement. So, accrual statements tell a complete story, which the budget does not. The civil service once again delivers all this information, but it does not seem to be utilized fully by the political system.

To a corporation, a *negative* net worth of over 100 percent of GDP, and steadily getting worse, would be a nightmare; and it should be thus with the US federal government net worth for the US citizens as well. But no-one seems to care and the deficits just keep piling up without any sensible plan from the federal administration or congress to do anything about it.

The balance sheet above is not complete, because it gives no indication of the size of promises that have been made to the public for the future under the social insurance programs. It is possible that the reason the actuarial shortfalls in the social insurance programs are not included is because the government does not recognize these shortfalls as a liability. By law, if the social insurance programs run out of money, then benefits need to be cut to be in line with expenditures, and thus, technically, there would not be a future deficit. This book assumes that this stance will be politically difficult to sustain when the social insurance programs run out of money. As noted, private companies that make promises for the future are required by law to include in their balance sheets estimates of what these promises are worth and how the private enterprises intend to pay when the promises fall due. The government could also start to integrate an estimate of the value of future promises in the financial accounts. This process is partially underway, but not much discussed.

Based on projections of fiscal operations in the future, as we have done in the central scenario above, we can project the primary balance of the government into the future. These primary balances can in turn be discounted back to the present, using assumptions on the average interest on the debt that the government has to pay. Calculating "net present values" of amounts that come due in the future is standard practice for pension funds and insurance companies, and this can also be done for the government.

In the financial accounts presented in the Financial Report of the US federal government, the civil service also presents estimates of two complementary solvency related indicators. One is the net present value of the primary balances in the central scenario for 75 years into the future. This does not include the future deficits in social security because these would be resolved by automatic expenditure cut, as per law. The other, and separate estimate, is the net present value, or actuarial value, of the social insurance programs, assuming that the expenditure cuts do not automatically occur. The official reports provide assumptions about real GDP growth rates, how wages are expected to evolve, the level of average interest rates, the inflow of new retirees, and a host of other relevant parameters, so the basics of these calculations are well understood. Around 2019, the civil ⁓⁓ds that the net present value of future costs is ⁓⁓illion. We can use this information ⁓⁓balance sheet" of the US

⁓nce sheet reflects not only ⁓ies from the past, as Table 13

above shows, but also includes estimates of the net present value (NPV) of future primary balances. An intertemporal net worth that includes effects from the past and from promises for the future is helpful and more complete than the backward-looking traditional accounting balance sheet described above.

Table 14 presents the intertemporal balance sheet of the US federal government. Let us ignore 2020 just for now, because these are the new estimates that come out of this book, and are not exactly comparable with the previous years (2011-2019), that use numbers presented in the Fiscal Report of the US federal Government. Based on FR numbers, the information is already noteworthy. The regular net worth by 2019 is *negative* $23 trillion (-107 percent of GDP). If we add the NPV of the forward-looking dynamic part of the budget (this is the NPV of projected future primary balances), then we find an intertemporal net worth of *negative* $72 trillion (-336 percent of GDP). If the Treasury staff had computed a time horizon that goes beyond 75 years, the shortfall in net worth would have been bigger.

Then if we add in the NPV of the social security system, the net worth would be even deeper negative.

Table 14. USA--Intertemporal Balance Sheet of the US Federal Government

	2011	2015	2016	2017	2018	2019	2020 1/
				($ billions)			
Assets	2,707.3	3,229.8	3,480.7	3,534.8	3,836.7	3,992.0	4,147.3
Liabilities	17,492.7	21,451.7	23,896.9	22,831.6	25,357.4	26,944.8	31,358.9
Net worth	-14,785.4	-18,221.9	-20,416.2	-19,296.8	-21,520.7	-22,952.8	-27,211.6
NPV of future primary deficits 2/	-6,400.0	-4,100.0	-16,200.0	-10,600.0	-46,200.0	-49,000.0	-215,020.4
Intertemporal net worth	-21,185.4	-22,321.9	-36,616.2	-29,896.8	-67,720.7	-71,952.8	-242,232.0
				(Percent of GDP)			
Assets	17.4	17.7	18.6	18.1	18.6	18.6	20.3
Liabilities	112.5	117.7	127.7	117.0	123.2	125.7	153.8
Net worth	-95.1	-100.0	-109.1	-98.9	-104.6	-107.1	-133.5
NPV of future primary deficits 2/	-41.2	-22.5	-86.6	-54.3	-224.5	-228.7	-1,054.7
Intertemporal net worth	-136.3	-122.5	-195.7	-153.2	-329.1	-335.8	-1,188.2
Memorandum items							
Nominal GDP ($ billions)	15,543	18,225	18,715	19,519	20,580	21,428	20,387

Source: the 2019 Financial Report of the US Federal Government, and author's calculations.
1/ 2020 projections are by the author.
2/ Net present value of a stream of future primary balances until 2094; number for 2020 is by the author through 2100

Specialists in overlapping intergenerational general equilibrium models, such as professor Kotlikoff and colleagues, argue that an infinite horizon model gives the only true picture of the intertemporal shortfall, and in 2011 they came up with numbers that were at that time already some 12 times the size of GDP (a shortfall of -1,200 percent of GDP). In 2020, Table 14 presents numbers calculated in this book, including the shock from coronavirus. One may not agree with all the assumptions that this book employs, but the numbers will certainly shift significantly from the results in 2019. Owing to the large coronavirus expenditures started in 2020, this book projects a net operating result (deficit) of $4 trillion (Table 12) and a net worth of *negative* $27 trillion (-134 percent of GDP). The NPV of forward primary balances through 2100 is estimated at $215 trillion (-1,055 percent of GDP), so that the intertemporal net worth of the federal government at end 2020 would stand at *negative* $242 trillion (-1,188 percent of GDP). If the author had used an infinite horizon model, these numbers would have become deeper negative.

"Solving" the problem of the negative intertemporal net worth means different things for different people. The problem can in any event not be solved in the short run or even in the medium run. This is going to take many decades of steady effort. We note in a previous chapter that it would take 8.1 percent of GDP in upfront (2020) fiscal measures to get the debt down to 60 percent of GDP by 2100 (other things being equal). If the problem takes a gradual approach, which it certainly will, then the cumulative effort must be bigger. Thus, instead of saying that we need to *solve* the problem, let us say that at least we need to start *acknowledging and managing* the problem, to progress toward sustainability, no matter how long this ultimate goal may seem to be in the future.

For instance, can the Secretary of the Treasury respond to the excellent work of his civil servants by indicating a possible quantified path forward that would start to address the problem? Then we have a basis for public discussion that society can use to find a solution. Many issues will then come to the surface and need to be discussed, but that is what healthy democracies do. Healthy democracies do not adopt the approach of pretending that the problem does not exist or will go away by itself (after the next election...). A teenager in Sweden by the name of Greta Thunberg has grasped this challenge intuitively, and she is concerned about her generation's future. The Secretary of the Treasury in the US has not encouraged or started a dialogue about it and ask society for help to begin solving it.

Chapter 19—Policy Considerations

The US economy is in a difficult position, with the coronavirus in full vigor after a weak response by the federal government. The states are essentially on their own, and this has become official policy. Further, because fiscal policy had been pro-cyclical during the previous years of the Trump administration, the federal government had no cushions to absorb the blow from coronavirus in 2020. The only remedy is: more debt. Monetary and credit policy has also been troubled as it has been put to work to protect asset prices at all cost, thereby materially boosting inequalities in US society and allowing the multiplication of zombie entities. Debt has truly become the cocaine of modern capitalist society, and it will destroy capitalism as we know it. It is no joke to read that we need to rescue capitalism from the "capitalists." Adam Smith, who was a professor of moral philosophy, must be spinning in his grave.

We do not have to become Dr. Pangloss in Voltaire's Candide to see the sunny side in every crisis, but there is something to it in asking that society rise to the occasion when Mother Nature lets us know that she is always in charge, not us, as is now again the case with the coronavirus crisis. Let us have a discussion to do some difficult things that we were unable to do when times were better, so that the new attention and energy that the coronavirus crisis has unleashed is not going to waste. We will have to do these difficult things when society is down on its luck, which is yet again pro-cyclical in many ways. It seems from history that societies that are successful tend to enter into a kind of stupor, or laziness, or a species of decadence, as was noted before. It seems to be in our psychology that we only pay attention when there is a real threat, and we are not very good at steadying ourselves for the long-run when things are going well. What are some of the policy considerations that we need to keep in mind to build a better economy when we come to the end of this crisis?

* * *

In terms of demographics, let us welcome a smaller footprint on this planet. This is difficult and cannot be enforced, for humanitarian reasons (no wars, no one-child policies, no coercion of any kind), but the shrinking populations in high-income countries should not be feared—instead this trend should be welcomed. We should aim for quality of life, not quantity of people in our countries that may make us feel powerful. With regard to other countries that have faster growing populations, it is important to avoid discriminating against them, but instead to help them reach higher income levels also. This will automatically slow down their populations as well. This is good for humanity, the quality of all life on earth, and for the sustainability of the earth's resources on which we depend.

Globalization and technology should not be stopped but rather encouraged and protected. Globalization and specialization in supply chains is a much better way to start leveling off inequalities and poverty on a global scale then hoping for foreign aid or international income transfers. One doubts that rich countries have it in them to support poorer countries with income and wealth transfers—it is better to let poor countries fully participate in the uplifting force of a well-organized rules-based international system that seeks to optimize the use of our resources in the liberal economic sense of the word, not in the modern nativist sense of the world.

In the realm of managing the domestic real economy, fiscal, and monetary and credit policies, let us vote for politicians who have something interesting to say about the long-run, instead of focusing on the next election. We need to demand as an electorate that our politicians tell us how we are going to address the enormous intertemporal inconsistencies that are obvious to students of this matter, including the civil servants of the ministries (and have been for years). Saying thank you to the civil servants and professors and all others who analyze these issues, without doing anything about it, should disqualify anyone from being in government—just vote them out of office. The public has to lead because politicians won't, or may not be able to.

Governments should pay more attention to long-run sustainability and resilience issues in macroeconomics compared to what they have been doing thus far. Peripheral vision needs to be expanded both to the global context of our economic activities (we now live in a global village) and also to the intertemporal dimension (what sort of economy do we leave for our grandchildren). Continue with structural reforms, especially those focused on improving harsh transparency and exposing corruption.

When we make projections, let us accept that growth is slowing down and will slow down further in countries that already have very high incomes. Don't overestimate future growth rates, because that misaligns expectations, causes debt ratchets, and allows politicians to hide behind generalities and avoid the real issues.

* * *

On the fiscal front, budgets need to be recalibrated for slower future growth. The Secretary of the Treasury needs to include in every budget a view of the very long-run fiscal outlook and a presentation of the intertemporal US federal government balance sheet. The aspirational objective of fiscal policy needs to move away from the annual cash budget deficit to the accrual intertemporal net worth of the public sector. The Secretary of the Treasury needs to say something credible in the budget, on paper, about what the government is doing to determine long-run fiscal policy and why. If he or she is unable or unwilling to do so, let us ask the president to find another Secretary of the Treasury as fast as possible.

Specifically, with regard to the coronavirus, one key issue is that we don't know how long this will last, but countercyclical support for the economy is still needed. Full transparency and monitoring who gets what is essential. Independent Inspectors General are essential. Frequent reporting to Congress and the public in a transparent manner is essential. If the executive branch of government resists this, vote them out of office.

All countercyclical measures need to be quantified and placed in an intertemporal fiscal scenario. The public needs to be told by how much taxes will need to increase and expenditures will need to be cut to keep the long-run fiscal outlook credible and sound. The public should not be sent into the future with a one-way ticket of unending deficits with no return ticket attached. Give a return ticket also, and explain how much this will cost.

In framing the very long-run fiscal outlook, observe a speed limit for structural fiscal adjustment and let automatic stabilizers function around this path for short-term blips, if financing conditions allow it. This causes the need to discuss a tradeoff in the speed of bringing the deficit into a surplus in the future against how much new debt the market is willing to absorb at reasonable interest rates. Modern Monetary Policy will not rescue the budget with endless very low interest rates. All of this will need to be spelled out transparently in the Secretary of the Treasury's very long-run fiscal plan so that this can be discussed and so that all can assist him or her in finding the best solution.

If governments provide very long-run fiscal scenarios and policy steps to bring the intertemporal net worth position into sustainability, there will not be a need for debt forgiveness or debt restructuring. Thus, official debt restructuring is not needed and should be avoided. Financial repression should also be avoided. The inflation tax should also be avoided. Longer-run inflation around 2 percent a year at the macro level provides enough lubricant for the real economy to affect adjustments in relative prices.

* * *

Revenue measures. How fast can revenues be increased without unduly restraining the economy? This requires an investigation into price and income elasticities, and the incentives that are currently embedded in the US tax system.

If used well, this crisis may be an opportunity to restructure the tax system. Tax progressivity needs to be increased and taxes on high income, wealth, and inheritance need to go up. The tax wedge, which means taxes as a percentage of labor costs, may need to be (temporarily) reduced to help a speedy return to full employment. Permanent corporate income tax cuts need to be replaced by temporary investment incentives, such as accelerated depreciation allowances. Green taxes need to be used to raise new revenue and to assist shifting to a healthier environment and economy—including carbon taxes, congestion charges, and other higher charges against environment destruction (the Trump government is doing the opposite). The Federal Government should introduce a VAT, possibly with partial sharing with the states.[34] Further, the US federal government spends around 7 percent of GDP annually on tax expenditures (including for interest deductibility). These should be examined for cuts, especially those that originate in interest cost deductions for companies and households, because they are a subsidy for debt accumulation. Some tax expenditures are also highly regressive and worsen inequality. Fixing multinational corporate tax avoidance is also essential.

The US general government has an enormous potential to raise revenue in an economically responsible and least-distorting way. Needless to say, these revenue measures need to be introduced gradually and in full transparency. The mantra of "tax cuts and deficits do not matter" needs to be abandoned as this has led to troubling growth and inequality effects and large debts.

* * *

Expenditure measures. The social safety net for the US population needs to be strengthened. It is a human right to have access to health care. The US *health care system* is more aptly called a *health care business*, and it is

---

[34] The IMF estimates that a 5 percent VAT would yield around 1.5 percent of GDP in new federal revenues.

the most expensive in the world (around 5-7 percent of GDP more expensive than in Europe), and it does not deliver the best health outcomes in the world (US life expectancy is trailing, and even stagnating). The inhumane treatment of poor citizens needs to stop. Many families in the US are one sickness away from bankruptcy. Income support and unemployment policies can be made into more robust anti-cyclical instruments, but there is no reason why such programs could not come with conditionality, in the direction of Denmark's Flexicurity policies.

For a country that is so keen on private corporate dynamism and initiative, there appears to be a large amount of corporate pork in US budgets. This should be reviewed and appropriately curtailed. The "heads you lose, and tails I win" mentality in US business and especially in the financial sector, which benefits enormously from tax-payer financed free insurance protection when a financial crisis comes, needs to be cut back through higher paid-up (first tier) capital instead of undecipherable risk-weighted capital requirements.[35] The financial industry needs to have much more direct skin in the game when they leverage up entire societies. Remuneration and governance in US corporations also require attention. For instance, instead of extending performance bonuses benchmarked on (short-term) equity prices, these should be shifted to benchmarked on much broader and longer-

---

[35] The author was helping to manage a crisis once in a country where the banking system had lost its entire capital base. He was visited by gentlemen from renowned global investment banks who proceeded to explain that they could engineer synthetic capital for the banks so that even the Basle Committee rules would allow this. This meeting was troubling considering that investment bankers were selling these services all over the world.

term performance indicators, such as sustainable return on capital. Equity prices can be goosed and manipulated and put on short-term steroids far too easily with debt leverage, and that is precisely what is happening with the use of debt as the cocaine of the modern capitalist society.

*   *   *

Monetary policy. As noted in a previous chapter, monetary policy has become hostage to the asset and debt world. Monetary policy is now used as a prop for the equity markets, and to allow higher leveraging of ever thinner margins. This is causing asset inflation, accelerated inequalities, a false sense of financing room for politicians, and steady progress in the zombification of the economy. It is unsustainable as the financial markets have now become the tower of instability in the economy, overwhelming the real economy. Policy now prioritizes Wall Street over Main Street. Hyman Minsky has become rightly famous for his work on instability emanating from financial markets.

Asset price inflation needs to acquire a different role in monetary policy, and consumer price inflation may even have to be tolerated at low levels for a while as globalization and technological progress brings the other 7 billion people in the world online and into the modern high-income economy. As monetary policy becomes more firmly oriented to long-run stability, there will be many bankruptcies. These should proceed as efficiently as possible, but without simple restructuring of old balance sheets, whereby pension liabilities etc. are jettisoned in favor of continuing with the same old structure. In bankruptcy, resources need to be reallocated to more efficient means and under better management, instead of merely an alleviation of some selected liabilities.

Needless to say, none of these are easy policy steps and nothing is simple to manage and implement. What is needed is a re-orientation of the compass, while respecting that all of these issues are complex and require reflection. Society should no longer postpone these discussions.

Chapter 20-- Preliminary Conclusions

- US population growth is favorable compared with many trading partners. This continues to make the US economy relatively attractive.
- The US population is slowing and aging, just like in other industrial countries. Immigration has maintained population growth positive for now.
- If immigration is stopped, potential real GDP growth will decline further.
- US potential real GDP growth is around 1½ percent a year (see Appendix 9 for some fiscal implications).
- We cannot solve structural problems (growth, competitiveness, environmental decay) with cyclical policies (fiscal deficits or money printing).
- Structural economic policy is about potential real GDP growth.
- Fiscal and monetary policies are cyclical policies for managing demand and minimizing the output gap.
- Technology, globalization, and aging are structurally lowering US consumer price (CPI) inflation.
- But inflation has not disappeared; it has migrated to asset prices.
- Pumping money while equilibrium CPI inflation is low leads to higher risks of financial instability.
- Government debt has become the political-economy cocaine of our days. We need ever larger doses of it to feel happy.
- It would appear that politics has deteriorated to the sense that if you don't want to do structural reform, and you don't want to pay for what you

want, then you can always kick the can down the road and issue debt.

- Debt is the vehicle to transfer our problems to the next generation.
- Targeting macroeconomic policy for the next *election* is a fool's game, like a dog chasing its own tail. Eventually, the economy exhausts itself and it will fall down. The policy horizon should be indexed to life expectancy—at least 80 years into the future to protect the new generation. Infinity (*Aeternitatis*) is even better.
- The US civil service has been saying for years that fiscal policy is unsustainable. Why are politicians going in the opposite direction?
- The Reagan mantra of tax cuts, deficits do not matter, and blind deregulation needs to go. It has caused a debt ratchet for the country, caused an increase in inequality, and set the US back in the world pecking order.
- Mr. Trump has put the capstone on this four-decade slide, with procyclical policies that exhausted all fiscal and monetary cushions. The effects of the coronavirus shock are made worse by our own behavior, and the absence of policy cushions.
- One wonders if independence of the Central Bank is only an illusion.
- Monetary policy should not be the put for equity markets. Main street is still important.
- If the president and the secretary of the treasury have nothing credible to say (and do) about long-term sustainability of our economy, let us look for their replacement.

- Economic policies should be built to last beyond the next election, because...
- ...the next generations will have to pay the bills that we leave behind.

Appendix 10—Two Helpful Equations

Leonhard Euler (1707-1783) was a Swiss mathematician who developed equations for motion. We can use these equations to assess the dynamics of debt/GDP ratios. This is helpful if we want to make a sustainable macroeconomy, which includes a condition that the debt ratio does not rise indefinitely. Here are two insightful economic applications of Mr. Euler's work.

The first one asks: what is the relationship between debt and GDP so that we know whether certain fiscal policy decisions cause the debt ratio to increase, stay the same, or decrease? Let:

$$D = B/Y \qquad (1)$$

Where D is the ratio of debt to GDP; B represents the stock of debt (or "bonds" outstanding); and Y is the symbol for nominal GDP. Then, using total differentiation, we can express the rate of change in the debt ratio as:

$$\dot{d} = \frac{\partial D}{\partial t} * \frac{1}{D} \qquad (2)$$

Using the chain rule we can write this as:

$$\dot{d} = \frac{\partial B}{\partial t} * \frac{1}{B} * \frac{1}{Y} - B * \frac{\partial Y}{\partial t} * \frac{1}{Y^2} \qquad (3)$$

Which is equal to:

$$\dot{d} = \frac{\partial B}{\partial t} * \frac{1}{B} * \frac{1}{Y} - D * \frac{\partial Y}{\partial t} * \frac{1}{Y} \qquad (4)$$

Now, the rate of change in the amount of bonds outstanding is equivalent to the budget deficit. The deficit can be written as the sum of the interest bill on the amount of bonds outstanding (i*B) minus the budget primary balance (PB), which reflects all revenue minus noninterest expenditure. Further, and equivalent to equation (1), we can express the rate of change in nominal GDP as:

$$\dot{y} = \frac{\partial Y}{\partial t} * \frac{1}{Y} \qquad (5)$$

Thus:

$$\dot{d} = (i*B - PB) * \frac{1}{Y} - D*\dot{y} \qquad (6)$$

This can be rewritten in an economically useful way:

$$\boxed{\dot{d} = (i - \dot{y}) * D - (PB/Y)} \qquad (7)$$

This equation says that the debt ratio will change according to the difference between the interest rate on the debt and the rate of GDP growth (the interest-growth differential), multiplied by the debt ratio, minus the primary balance in percent of GDP. If the interest rate on de debt is higher than the growth rate of GDP (i-y>0), then a primary surplus is necessary to stabilize or lower the debt ratio. If the interest rate on the debt is less than the growth rate of GDP (i-y<0), then the US can permit a primary deficit up to a certain size and still stabilize the debt ratio.

There is a second helpful implication from the equations above. Since, in equation (6), the term (i*B − PB) is equal to the budget deficit, we can rewrite the equation as follows:

$$\dot{d} = (Def/Y) - D*\dot{y} \qquad (8)$$

This means that the rate of change in the debt ratio is equal to the deficit in percent of GDP minus the debt ratio to GDP multiplied by the growth rate of GDP. We can now ask the question: if fiscal policy can stabilize the deficit as a percent of GDP at a level of x percent, and if structural and monetary policy can stabilize nominal economic growth at y percent, will de debt ratio stabilize at some point? To stabilize the debt ratio means that $\dot{d}$ = 0. Thus, we can rewrite equation (8) as:

$$(Def/Y) = D*\dot{y} \qquad (9)$$

This gives us in turn, that:

$$\boxed{D = (Def/Y)/\dot{y}} \qquad (10)$$

Equation (10) implies that debt dynamics are asymptotic if the deficit and the growth rate can be stabilized: the debt ratio will approach in the limit a fixed value given by the ratio of the deficit in percent of GDP and the nominal growth rate. Thus, if the deficit stabilizes at 3 percent of GDP, and GDP growth remains at 5 percent a year (say 3 percent real and 2 percent inflation), then the debt will gravitate to a ratio of 3/5 = 60 percent of GDP.

This is the idea behind the European Maastricht criteria for deficit and debt management, which seek to limit the debt ratio at or below 60 percent of GDP. It is based on a deficit policy ceiling of 3 percent of GDP and a target for nominal GDP growth of 5 percent.

Equations (7) and (10) can be calculated quickly and are useful in fiscal analysis as benchmarks for policy insights. For instance, in chapter 15 we calculated a long-run baseline average implicit real (nominal) interest rate on the debt of 0.5 (2.5) percent. In chapter 9 we projected real (nominal) growth to be around 1.5 (3.5) percent a year on average. This means that for the

US, the condition i-y = - 1 percent; i.e. the interest-growth differential of equation (7) is favorable, on average. This is unusual in international comparison and the US may hope that this continues in the future.

Similarly, if we aim the debt ratio at 60 percent of GDP as we did in the adjustment scenario simulations, and nominal GDP growth is around 3.5 percent a year on average, then the US should aim at overall deficits below 2.1 percent of GDP a year (2.1/3.5 = 0.60) (equation (10)). This is again favorable in international comparison, given that other high-income countries tend to have lower nominal average growth rates than the US.

References

Alesina, Alberto and Silvia Ardagna: Tales of Fiscal Adjustment. June 1998.

Armstrong, Robert: Companies are dangerously drunk on debt. The Financial Times. May 6, 2020.

Blanchard, Olivier and Jean Pisani-Ferry: Monetization: Do Not Panic. VOX CEPR Policy Portal. 10 April 2020.

Board of Trustees of the Federal Old-Age and Survivors Insurance and Federal Disability Insurance Trust Funds: 2020 Annual Report of the Board of Trustees of the Federal Old-Age and Survivors Insurance and Federal Disability Insurance Trust Funds. April 22, 2020.

Board of Trustees of the Federal Hospital Insurance and Federal Supplementary Medical Insurance Trust Funds: 2020 Annual Report of the Boards of Trustees of the Federal Hospital Insurance and Federal Supplementary Medical Insurance Trust Funds. April 22, 2020.

Buiter, Willem: The Problem With MMT. Project Syndicate. May 4, 2020.

CBO. The 2019 Long-Term Budget Outlook. June 2019.

CBO. CBO's January 2020 report The Budget and Economic Outlook: 2020 to 2030. www.cbo.gov/publication/56020.

CBO. CBO's January 2020 report The Budget and Economic Outlook. Key projections in its extended baseline 2020-2050. www.cbo.gov/publication/56020.

CBO. CBO's March 2020 report Baseline Budget Projections as of March 6, 2020. www.cbo.gov/publication/56268.

CBO. Interim Economic Projections for 2020 and 2021. May 2020. www.cbo.gov/publication/56351

CBO. Swagel, Phillip. CBO's Current Projections of Output, Employment, and Interest Rates and a Preliminary Look at Federal Deficits for 2020 and 2021. CBO Blog. April 24, 2020.

CBO. Swagel, Phillip L, Director. CBO's Current Economic Projections and a Preliminary Look at Federal Deficits and Debt for 2020 and 2021. CBO—A Presentation to the House Budget Committee. April 27, 2020.

CBO. An Update to the Budget Outlook: 2020-2030. September 2020.

Corkery, Michael and David Gelles: Robots Welcome to Take Over as Pandemic Accelerates Automation. New York Times. April 10, 2020.

Dallari, Pietro, Nicolas End, Fedor Miryugin, Alexander Tieman, Seyed Reza Mousefi: Pouring Oil on Fire: Interest Deductibility and Corporate Debt. International Tax and Finance. https://doi.org/10.1007/s10797-020-09604-7, 13 May 2020.

Douthart, Ross: The Decadent Society; How We Became the Victims of Our Own Success. 2020.

The Economist: What would Keynes do? The Pandemic will leave the rich world deep in debt, and force some hard choices. April 23rd 2020 edition.

The Economist: The Pandemic has sent Public Debt Rocketing Across the World. May 5, 2020.

Eppsteiner, Harris, Jason Furman, and Wilson Powell II: Adjusted for Aging, the US Employment Rate Continued to Rise Above Its Pre-Recession Level in 2018. PIIE—Peterson Institute for International Economics, January 11, 2019.

EU Commission: Debt Sustainability Monitor 2019. Institutional Paper 120, January 2020

Federal Reserve Bank of St. Luis. Web page. A key source for many data in this book.

Fisher, Irving: The Purchasing Power of Money. 1911.

Friedman, Milton and Anna Schwartz: A Monetary History of the United States 1867-1960. 1963.

Friedman, Thomas: Is Trump Challenging Mother Nature to a Duel? New York Times. May 20, 2020.

Foroohar, Rana: "We may be heading towards a post-dollar world. The Financial Times. May 31, 2020.

GAO, US Government Accountability Office: Financial Audit: FY 2019 and FY 2018 Consolidated Financial Statements of the US Government, February 27, 2020.

Goldfeld, Stephen: The Case of the Missing Money. Brookings Papers on Economic Activity, 3:1976

Gordon, Robert: The Rise and Fall of American Growth. 2016.

Harford, Tim: Why we fail to prepare for disasters. FT Magazine Coronavirus. April 16, 2020.

Heller, Peter S.: Who Will Pay? IMF book. 2003.

International Monetary Fund: Fiscal Policies for the Recovery from COVID-19. Blog. May 6, 2020.

International Monetary Fund: World Economic Outlook. Various annual issues.

International Monetary Fund: Fiscal Monitor. Various annual issues.

International Monetary Fund: Global Stability Report. Various annual issues.

International Monetary Fund: United States 2020 Article IV Consultation—Press Release; Staff Report; and Statement by the Executive Director for the United States. August 2020.

Isaacs, Julia B.: Spending on Children and the Elderly. Brookings report. November 5, 2009.

Jackson, Gavin: book reviews of "Slowdown" and "Fully Grown"—Why slower growth may be no bad thing. Economics books. The Financial Times. April 9 2020.

Kaeble, Danielle and Mary Cowhig: Correctional Populations in the United States, 2016. BJS—Bulletin of Justice Statistics, April 2018.

Kay, John: Other People's Money; The Real Business of Finance. 2015.

Keynes, Maynard: The General Theory of Employment, Interest, and Money. 1936.

Kotlikoff, Laurence J. and Adam N. Michel: Closing America's Enormous Fiscal Gap: Who Will Pay? Mercatus Working Paper, George Mason University, June 2015.

Mackenzie, Michael: Opinion—The Long View, Central Banks are storing up problems in fight to shield credit. The Financial Times, May 2, 2020.

Micklewait, John and Adrian Woolridge: The Virus Should Wake up the West. Bloomberg, Politics & Policy. April 12, 2020.

Minsky, Hyman: John Maynard Keynes. 1975.

Morrissey, Monique: Kids vs. Seniors, an Urban Myth. Working Economics Blog. Economic Policy Institute. April 18, 2013.

Paulson, Henry M. Jr.: 7 Principles for a post-coronavirus economy. The Washington Post, April 10, 2020.

Paulson, Henry M. Jf.: The Future of the Dollar. The Financial Times. May 19, 2020.

Politifact: Average Government Spending on Each Elderly Person and on Each Child.

Reinhart, Carmen and Kenneth Rogoff: This Time Is Different: Eight Centuries of Financial Folly. 2009.

Roach, Stephen: A return to 1970s stagflation is only a broken supply chain away. The Financial Times. May 6, 2020.

Sandbu, Martin: Move the financial system away from the false security of debt. The Financial Times. May 7, 2020.

Sandbu, Martin: Seize the opportunity of Covid-19 to restructure taxes. The Financial Times. May 11, 2020.

Shiller, Robert: Irrational Exuberance. 2000.

Soll, Jacob: The Reckoning; Financial Accountability and the Rise and Fall of Nations. 2014.

Spinoza, Baruch: Complete Works. 2002.

Summers, Larry: U.S. Economic Prospects: Secular Stagnation, Hysteresis, and the Zero Lower Bound. Business Economics, Vol. 49, No. 2. 2014.

Tett, Gillian: Investors should ask who will buy all of this new US government debt. Opinion US Treasury Bonds. The Financial Times. April 9, 2020.

Tett, Gillian: US stock market rally confuses liquidity with solvency. The Financial Times. April 30, 2020.

Tett, Gillian: Is it safe to go to the shops, see a friend or get on a plane? The Financial Times. May 8, 2020.

United Nations Population Division. 2019 Revision of World Population Prospects. https://population.un.org/wpp/Download/Standard/Population/

US Government, Department of the Treasury: Financial Report of the United States Government. February 27, 2020.

US Bureau of Labor Statistics. www.bls.gov

Voltaire: Candide. 1759.

Vollrath, Dietrich: Fully Grown; Why a Stagnant Economy is a sign of Success. The University of Chicago Press. 2020.

Wolf, Martin: The Shifts and the Shocks; What we have Learned and Still have to Learn from the Financial Crisis. 2014.

Wolf, Martin: How to escape the trap of excessive debt. The Financial Times. May 5, 2020.

World Population Review 2020: Gini Coefficient by Country 2020.

Data Annex

This Annex presents the data behind key variables, Figures, Tables, and Appendices that have been used throughout this book. The most important data sources have been:

Bureau of Economic Analysis
Bureau of Labor Statistics
Congressional Budget Office
Federal Reserve Bank of St. Louis
General Accountability Office
International Monetary Fund
OECD
Office of Management and Budget
The Trustees of Social Insurance
UN population division
US Census Bureau
US Department of the Treasury
World Bank

Annex Table 1: Population (Central Scenario)							
	thousands	%-ch		thousands	%-ch		thousands	%-ch
1950	158,804							
1951	160,872	1.3	2001	284,608	1.0	2051	380,599	0.3
1952	163,266	1.5	2002	287,279	0.9	2052	381,776	0.3
1953	165,910	1.6	2003	289,816	0.9	2053	382,955	0.3
1954	168,736	1.7	2004	292,355	0.9	2054	384,140	0.3
1955	171,685	1.7	2005	294,994	0.9	2055	385,335	0.3
1956	174,705	1.8	2006	297,759	0.9	2056	386,542	0.3
1957	177,751	1.7	2007	300,608	1.0	2057	387,763	0.3
1958	180,788	1.7	2008	303,486	1.0	2058	388,995	0.3
1959	183,786	1.7	2009	306,308	0.9	2059	390,240	0.3
1960	186,721	1.6	2010	309,011	0.9	2060	391,495	0.3
1961	189,570	1.5	2011	311,584	0.8	2061	392,760	0.3
1962	192,314	1.4	2012	314,044	0.8	2062	394,033	0.3
1963	194,932	1.4	2013	316,401	0.8	2063	395,313	0.3
1964	197,408	1.3	2014	318,673	0.7	2064	396,595	0.3
1965	199,734	1.2	2015	320,878	0.7	2065	397,876	0.3
1966	201,896	1.1	2016	323,016	0.7	2066	399,155	0.3
1967	203,905	1.0	2017	325,085	0.6	2067	400,429	0.3
1968	205,806	0.9	2018	327,096	0.6	2068	401,693	0.3
1969	207,659	0.9	2019	329,065	0.6	2069	402,943	0.3
1970	209,513	0.9	2020	331,003	0.6	2070	404,174	0.3
1971	211,384	0.9	2021	332,915	0.6	2071	405,385	0.3
1972	213,270	0.9	2022	334,805	0.6	2072	406,573	0.3
1973	215,179	0.9	2023	336,679	0.6	2073	407,738	0.3
1974	217,115	0.9	2024	338,543	0.6	2074	408,878	0.3
1975	219,081	0.9	2025	340,400	0.5	2075	409,993	0.3
1976	221,086	0.9	2026	342,252	0.5	2076	411,082	0.3
1977	223,136	0.9	2027	344,101	0.5	2077	412,145	0.3
1978	225,223	0.9	2028	345,948	0.5	2078	413,184	0.3
1979	227,339	0.9	2029	347,795	0.5	2079	414,200	0.2
1980	229,476	0.9	2030	349,642	0.5	2080	415,197	0.2
1981	231,636	0.9	2031	351,490	0.5	2081	416,176	0.2
1982	233,822	0.9	2032	353,335	0.5	2082	417,137	0.2
1983	236,030	0.9	2033	355,163	0.5	2083	418,082	0.2
1984	238,257	0.9	2034	356,953	0.5	2084	419,015	0.2
1985	240,500	0.9	2035	358,691	0.5	2085	419,937	0.2
1986	242,763	0.9	2036	360,372	0.5	2086	420,851	0.2
1987	245,053	0.9	2037	361,998	0.5	2087	421,758	0.2
1988	247,372	0.9	2038	363,570	0.4	2088	422,661	0.2
1989	249,726	1.0	2039	365,094	0.4	2089	423,564	0.2
1990	252,120	1.0	2040	366,572	0.4	2090	424,470	0.2
1991	254,539	1.0	2041	368,006	0.4	2091	425,381	0.2
1992	256,991	1.0	2042	369,397	0.4	2092	426,297	0.2
1993	259,532	1.0	2043	370,746	0.4	2093	427,220	0.2
1994	262,241	1.0	2044	372,060	0.4	2094	428,148	0.2
1995	265,164	1.1	2045	373,343	0.3	2095	429,082	0.2
1996	268,335	1.2	2046	374,598	0.3	2096	430,022	0.2
1997	271,714	1.3	2047	375,828	0.3	2097	430,968	0.2
1998	275,175	1.3	2048	377,037	0.3	2098	431,921	0.2
1999	278,548	1.2	2049	378,233	0.3	2099	432,883	0.2
2000	281,711	1.1	2050	379,419	0.3	2100	433,854	0.2

Annex Table 2: Young population <16 (Central Scenario)								
	thousands	%-ch		thousands	%-ch		thousands	%-ch
1950	42,596							
1951	44,300	4.0	2001	61,445	0.5	2051	62,878	0.1
1952	45,850	3.5	2002	61,568	0.2	2052	62,910	0.1
1953	47,363	3.3	2003	61,506	-0.1	2053	62,942	0.1
1954	48,879	3.2	2004	61,506	0.0	2054	62,974	0.1
1955	50,410	3.1	2005	61,598	0.1	2055	63,006	0.1
1956	51,872	2.9	2006	61,721	0.2	2056	63,122	0.2
1957	53,273	2.7	2007	61,968	0.4	2057	63,238	0.2
1958	54,711	2.7	2008	62,216	0.4	2058	63,355	0.2
1959	56,024	2.4	2009	62,403	0.3	2059	63,471	0.2
1960	57,307	2.3	2010	62,435	0.1	2060	63,586	0.2
1961	58,395	1.9	2011	62,373	-0.1	2061	63,747	0.3
1962	59,213	1.4	2012	62,186	-0.3	2062	63,908	0.3
1963	59,746	0.9	2013	61,999	-0.3	2063	64,070	0.3
1964	60,045	0.5	2014	61,813	-0.3	2064	64,232	0.3
1965	60,056	0.0	2015	61,685	-0.2	2065	64,390	0.2
1966	59,936	-0.2	2016	61,510	-0.3	2066	64,526	0.2
1967	59,816	-0.2	2017	61,336	-0.3	2067	64,661	0.2
1968	59,577	-0.4	2018	61,162	-0.3	2068	64,797	0.2
1969	59,338	-0.4	2019	60,989	-0.3	2069	64,933	0.2
1970	58,868	-0.8	2020	60,811	-0.3	2070	65,067	0.2
1971	58,162	-1.2	2021	60,629	-0.3	2071	65,135	0.1
1972	57,289	-1.5	2022	60,507	-0.2	2072	65,203	0.1
1973	56,315	-1.7	2023	60,386	-0.2	2073	65,272	0.1
1974	55,583	-1.3	2024	60,265	-0.2	2074	65,340	0.1
1975	54,781	-1.4	2025	60,246	0.0	2075	65,408	0.1
1976	54,069	-1.3	2026	60,366	0.2	2076	65,443	0.1
1977	53,421	-1.2	2027	60,548	0.3	2077	65,479	0.1
1978	52,779	-1.2	2028	60,729	0.3	2078	65,515	0.1
1979	52,252	-1.0	2029	60,911	0.3	2079	65,550	0.1
1980	52,030	-0.4	2030	61,126	0.4	2080	65,586	0.1
1981	51,873	-0.3	2031	61,377	0.4	2081	65,639	0.1
1982	51,770	-0.2	2032	61,628	0.4	2082	65,692	0.1
1983	51,718	-0.1	2033	61,881	0.4	2083	65,745	0.1
1984	51,770	0.1	2034	62,135	0.4	2084	65,799	0.1
1985	51,949	0.3	2035	62,379	0.4	2085	65,852	0.1
1986	52,209	0.5	2036	62,566	0.3	2086	65,947	0.1
1987	52,679	0.9	2037	62,754	0.3	2087	66,042	0.1
1988	53,311	1.2	2038	62,817	0.1	2088	66,137	0.1
1989	53,951	1.2	2039	62,880	0.1	2089	66,233	0.1
1990	54,646	1.3	2040	62,933	0.1	2090	66,327	0.1
1991	55,356	1.3	2041	62,933	0.0	2091	66,447	0.2
1992	56,076	1.3	2042	62,932	0.0	2092	66,568	0.2
1993	56,805	1.3	2043	62,932	0.0	2093	66,689	0.2
1994	57,543	1.3	2044	62,931	0.0	2094	66,809	0.2
1995	58,376	1.4	2045	62,931	0.0	2095	66,928	0.2
1996	59,077	1.2	2046	62,914	0.0	2096	67,039	0.2
1997	59,668	1.0	2047	62,897	0.0	2097	67,149	0.2
1998	60,145	0.8	2048	62,880	0.0	2098	67,259	0.2
1999	60,626	0.8	2049	62,863	0.0	2099	67,370	0.2
2000	61,139	0.8	2050	62,846	0.0	2100	67,479	0.2

Annex Table 3: Working-Age Population (16-64) (Central Scenario)								
	thousands	%-ch		thousands	%-ch		thousands	%-ch
1950	103,166							
1951	103,126	0.0	2001	188,139	1.2	2051	232,145	0.2
1952	103,565	0.4	2002	190,373	1.2	2052	232,434	0.1
1953	104,295	0.7	2003	192,652	1.2	2053	232,716	0.1
1954	105,192	0.9	2004	194,871	1.2	2054	232,996	0.1
1955	106,192	1.0	2005	197,077	1.1	2055	233,283	0.1
1956	107,342	1.1	2006	199,283	1.1	2056	233,395	0.0
1957	108,601	1.2	2007	201,334	1.0	2057	233,509	0.0
1958	109,802	1.1	2008	203,143	0.9	2058	233,533	0.0
1959	111,129	1.2	2009	204,825	0.8	2059	233,556	0.0
1960	112,393	1.1	2010	206,461	0.8	2060	233,552	0.0
1961	113,762	1.2	2011	207,933	0.7	2061	233,618	0.0
1962	115,305	1.4	2012	209,341	0.7	2062	233,777	0.1
1963	117,017	1.5	2013	210,524	0.6	2063	234,028	0.1
1964	118,831	1.6	2014	211,491	0.5	2064	234,273	0.1
1965	120,782	1.6	2015	212,208	0.3	2065	234,517	0.1
1966	122,668	1.6	2016	212,876	0.3	2066	234,770	0.1
1967	124,372	1.4	2017	213,514	0.3	2067	235,010	0.1
1968	126,059	1.4	2018	214,142	0.3	2068	235,232	0.1
1969	127,707	1.3	2019	214,678	0.3	2069	235,532	0.1
1970	129,588	1.5	2020	215,143	0.2	2070	235,755	0.1
1971	131,702	1.6	2021	215,586	0.2	2071	235,967	0.1
1972	133,965	1.7	2022	215,953	0.2	2072	236,148	0.1
1973	136,363	1.8	2023	216,256	0.1	2073	236,403	0.1
1974	138,536	1.6	2024	216,499	0.1	2074	236,732	0.1
1975	140,791	1.6	2025	216,670	0.1	2075	236,905	0.1
1976	142,968	1.5	2026	216,752	0.0	2076	237,204	0.1
1977	145,089	1.5	2027	216,856	0.0	2077	237,581	0.2
1978	147,202	1.5	2028	217,054	0.1	2078	238,039	0.2
1979	149,215	1.4	2029	217,356	0.1	2079	238,582	0.2
1980	150,927	1.1	2030	217,674	0.1	2080	239,027	0.2
1981	152,633	1.1	2031	218,067	0.2	2081	239,454	0.2
1982	154,353	1.1	2032	218,580	0.2	2082	239,918	0.2
1983	156,087	1.1	2033	219,204	0.3	2083	240,364	0.2
1984	157,782	1.1	2034	219,778	0.3	2084	240,907	0.2
1985	159,374	1.0	2035	220,266	0.2	2085	241,391	0.2
1986	160,881	0.9	2036	220,848	0.3	2086	241,758	0.2
1987	162,167	0.8	2037	221,516	0.3	2087	242,117	0.1
1988	163,311	0.7	2038	222,404	0.4	2088	242,471	0.1
1989	164,471	0.7	2039	223,316	0.4	2089	242,822	0.1
1990	165,637	0.7	2040	224,297	0.4	2090	243,088	0.1
1991	166,868	0.7	2041	225,256	0.4	2091	243,304	0.1
1992	168,212	0.8	2042	226,168	0.4	2092	243,522	0.1
1993	169,665	0.9	2043	227,036	0.4	2093	243,742	0.1
1994	171,338	1.0	2044	227,866	0.4	2094	244,082	0.1
1995	173,211	1.1	2045	228,634	0.3	2095	244,389	0.1
1996	175,480	1.3	2046	229,333	0.3	2096	244,630	0.1
1997	178,032	1.5	2047	230,003	0.3	2097	244,874	0.1
1998	180,778	1.5	2048	230,649	0.3	2098	245,122	0.1
1999	183,430	1.5	2049	231,193	0.2	2099	245,375	0.1
2000	185,826	1.3	2050	231,759	0.2	2100	245,767	0.2

Annex Table 4: Elderly Population >64 (Central Scenario)								
	thousands	%-ch		thousands	%-ch		thousands	%-ch
1950	13,043							
1951	13,447	3.1	2001	35,023	0.8	2051	85,577	0.9
1952	13,851	3.0	2002	35,339	0.9	2052	86,432	1.0
1953	14,252	2.9	2003	35,657	0.9	2053	87,297	1.0
1954	14,665	2.9	2004	35,978	0.9	2054	88,170	1.0
1955	15,084	2.9	2005	36,319	0.9	2055	89,045	1.0
1956	15,491	2.7	2006	36,755	1.2	2056	90,025	1.1
1957	15,878	2.5	2007	37,306	1.5	2057	91,015	1.1
1958	16,275	2.5	2008	38,127	2.2	2058	92,107	1.2
1959	16,633	2.2	2009	39,080	2.5	2059	93,213	1.2
1960	17,021	2.3	2010	40,115	2.6	2060	94,356	1.2
1961	17,412	2.3	2011	41,279	2.9	2061	95,394	1.1
1962	17,795	2.2	2012	42,517	3.0	2062	96,348	1.0
1963	18,169	2.1	2013	43,877	3.2	2063	97,215	0.9
1964	18,533	2.0	2014	45,369	3.4	2064	98,090	0.9
1965	18,896	2.0	2015	46,986	3.6	2065	98,968	0.9
1966	19,293	2.1	2016	48,630	3.5	2066	99,859	0.9
1967	19,717	2.2	2017	50,235	3.3	2067	100,758	0.9
1968	20,170	2.3	2018	51,792	3.1	2068	101,665	0.9
1969	20,614	2.2	2019	53,398	3.1	2069	102,478	0.8
1970	21,058	2.2	2020	55,049	3.1	2070	103,353	0.9
1971	21,521	2.2	2021	56,700	3.0	2071	104,283	0.9
1972	22,016	2.3	2022	58,345	2.9	2072	105,221	0.9
1973	22,500	2.2	2023	60,037	2.9	2073	106,063	0.8
1974	22,995	2.2	2024	61,778	2.9	2074	106,806	0.7
1975	23,508	2.2	2025	63,483	2.8	2075	107,680	0.8
1976	24,049	2.3	2026	65,134	2.6	2076	108,434	0.7
1977	24,626	2.4	2027	66,697	2.4	2077	109,084	0.6
1978	25,242	2.5	2028	68,164	2.2	2078	109,630	0.5
1979	25,873	2.5	2029	69,528	2.0	2079	110,068	0.4
1980	26,520	2.5	2030	70,842	1.9	2080	110,585	0.5
1981	27,129	2.3	2031	72,046	1.7	2081	111,082	0.4
1982	27,699	2.1	2032	73,127	1.5	2082	111,527	0.4
1983	28,225	1.9	2033	74,077	1.3	2083	111,973	0.4
1984	28,705	1.7	2034	75,040	1.3	2084	112,309	0.3
1985	29,177	1.6	2035	76,045	1.3	2085	112,695	0.3
1986	29,673	1.7	2036	76,958	1.2	2086	113,146	0.4
1987	30,207	1.8	2037	77,727	1.0	2087	113,599	0.4
1988	30,750	1.8	2038	78,349	0.8	2088	114,053	0.4
1989	31,304	1.8	2039	78,898	0.7	2089	114,509	0.4
1990	31,837	1.7	2040	79,342	0.6	2090	115,054	0.5
1991	32,315	1.5	2041	79,818	0.6	2091	115,630	0.5
1992	32,703	1.2	2042	80,297	0.6	2092	116,208	0.5
1993	33,062	1.1	2043	80,778	0.6	2093	116,789	0.5
1994	33,360	0.9	2044	81,263	0.6	2094	117,256	0.4
1995	33,576	0.6	2045	81,778	0.6	2095	117,765	0.4
1996	33,778	0.6	2046	82,351	0.7	2096	118,353	0.5
1997	34,014	0.7	2047	82,927	0.7	2097	118,945	0.5
1998	34,252	0.7	2048	83,508	0.7	2098	119,540	0.5
1999	34,492	0.7	2049	84,176	0.8	2099	120,138	0.5
2000	34,745	0.7	2050	84,813	0.8	2100	120,608	0.4

Annex Table 5: Employment (Central Scenario)								
	thousands	%-ch		thousands	%-ch		thousands	%-ch
1950	58,892							
1951	59,967	1.8	2001	136,939	0.0	2051	182,087	0.4
1952	60,272	0.5	2002	136,481	-0.3	2052	182,773	0.4
1953	61,206	1.5	2003	137,729	0.9	2053	183,461	0.4
1954	60,107	-1.8	2004	139,240	1.1	2054	184,152	0.4
1955	62,131	3.4	2005	141,710	1.8	2055	184,850	0.4
1956	63,792	2.7	2006	144,418	1.9	2056	185,507	0.4
1957	64,065	0.4	2007	146,050	1.1	2057	186,171	0.4
1958	63,043	-1.6	2008	145,373	-0.5	2058	186,842	0.4
1959	64,629	2.5	2009	139,894	-3.8	2059	187,520	0.4
1960	65,785	1.8	2010	139,077	-0.6	2060	188,206	0.4
1961	65,744	-0.1	2011	139,885	0.6	2061	188,870	0.4
1962	66,702	1.5	2012	142,475	1.9	2062	189,540	0.4
1963	67,760	1.6	2013	143,941	1.0	2063	190,214	0.4
1964	69,301	2.3	2014	146,319	1.7	2064	190,889	0.4
1965	71,070	2.6	2015	148,845	1.7	2065	191,565	0.4
1966	72,878	2.5	2016	151,439	1.7	2066	192,254	0.4
1967	74,376	2.1	2017	153,334	1.3	2067	192,940	0.4
1968	75,913	2.1	2018	155,760	1.6	2068	193,620	0.4
1969	77,875	2.6	2019	157,529	1.1	2069	194,293	0.3
1970	78,669	1.0	2020	148,420	-5.8	2070	194,956	0.3
1971	79,355	0.9	2021	153,688	3.5	2071	195,644	0.4
1972	82,135	3.5	2022	156,343	1.7	2072	196,321	0.3
1973	85,051	3.6	2023	158,058	1.1	2073	196,984	0.3
1974	86,803	2.1	2024	159,772	1.1	2074	197,633	0.3
1975	85,830	-1.1	2025	160,743	0.6	2075	198,268	0.3
1976	88,753	3.4	2026	161,469	0.5	2076	198,907	0.3
1977	92,017	3.7	2027	162,155	0.4	2077	199,531	0.3
1978	96,046	4.4	2028	162,836	0.4	2078	200,142	0.3
1979	98,825	2.9	2029	163,814	0.6	2079	200,740	0.3
1980	99,303	0.5	2030	164,774	0.6	2080	201,327	0.3
1981	100,400	1.1	2031	165,714	0.6	2081	201,893	0.3
1982	99,529	-0.9	2032	166,652	0.6	2082	202,449	0.3
1983	100,822	1.3	2033	167,579	0.6	2083	202,996	0.3
1984	105,003	4.1	2034	168,485	0.5	2084	203,536	0.3
1985	107,154	2.0	2035	169,367	0.5	2085	204,071	0.3
1986	109,601	2.3	2036	170,249	0.5	2086	204,577	0.2
1987	112,439	2.6	2037	171,099	0.5	2087	205,078	0.2
1988	114,974	2.3	2038	171,991	0.5	2088	205,578	0.2
1989	117,327	2.0	2039	172,855	0.5	2089	206,077	0.2
1990	118,796	1.3	2040	173,699	0.5	2090	206,579	0.2
1991	117,713	-0.9	2041	174,549	0.5	2091	207,070	0.2
1992	118,488	0.7	2042	175,373	0.5	2092	207,563	0.2
1993	120,259	1.5	2043	176,175	0.5	2093	208,060	0.2
1994	123,071	2.3	2044	176,957	0.4	2094	208,560	0.2
1995	124,908	1.5	2045	177,721	0.4	2095	209,065	0.2
1996	126,720	1.5	2046	178,479	0.4	2096	209,578	0.2
1997	129,572	2.3	2047	179,222	0.4	2097	210,096	0.2
1998	131,476	1.5	2048	179,955	0.4	2098	210,617	0.2
1999	133,501	1.5	2049	180,679	0.4	2099	211,143	0.2
2000	136,901	2.5	2050	181,399	0.4	2100	211,676	0.3

Annex Table 6: Unemployment (Central Scenario)								
	thousands	%-LF		thousands	%-LF		thousands	%-LF
1950	3,230	5.2						
1951	2,050	3.3	2001	6,830	4.8	2051	9,584	5.0
1952	1,880	3.0	2002	8,375	5.8	2052	9,620	5.0
1953	1,850	2.9	2003	8,770	6.0	2053	9,656	5.0
1954	3,566	5.6	2004	8,140	5.5	2054	9,692	5.0
1955	2,834	4.4	2005	7,579	5.1	2055	9,729	5.0
1956	2,745	4.1	2006	6,991	4.6	2056	9,764	5.0
1957	2,877	4.3	2007	7,073	4.6	2057	9,798	5.0
1958	4,627	6.8	2008	8,948	5.8	2058	9,834	5.0
1959	3,731	5.5	2009	14,295	9.3	2059	9,869	5.0
1960	3,874	5.6	2010	14,808	9.6	2060	9,906	5.0
1961	4,706	6.7	2011	13,739	8.9	2061	9,941	5.0
1962	3,918	5.5	2012	12,499	8.1	2062	9,976	5.0
1963	4,053	5.6	2013	11,457	7.4	2063	10,011	5.0
1964	3,776	5.2	2014	9,602	6.2	2064	10,047	5.0
1965	3,354	4.5	2015	8,294	5.3	2065	10,082	5.0
1966	2,867	3.8	2016	7,757	4.9	2066	10,119	5.0
1967	2,972	3.8	2017	6,979	4.4	2067	10,155	5.0
1968	2,797	3.6	2018	6,308	3.9	2068	10,191	5.0
1969	2,830	3.5	2019	5,989	3.7	2069	10,226	5.0
1970	4,127	5.0	2020	13,393	8.3	2070	10,261	5.0
1971	5,022	6.0	2021	10,850	6.6	2071	10,297	5.0
1972	4,876	5.6	2022	10,146	6.1	2072	10,333	5.0
1973	4,359	4.9	2023	9,366	5.6	2073	10,368	5.0
1974	5,173	5.6	2024	8,576	5.1	2074	10,402	5.0
1975	7,940	8.5	2025	8,460	5.0	2075	10,435	5.0
1976	7,398	7.7	2026	8,498	5.0	2076	10,469	5.0
1977	6,967	7.0	2027	8,534	5.0	2077	10,502	5.0
1978	6,187	6.1	2028	8,570	5.0	2078	10,534	5.0
1979	6,135	5.8	2029	8,622	5.0	2079	10,565	5.0
1980	7,671	7.2	2030	8,672	5.0	2080	10,596	5.0
1981	8,276	7.6	2031	8,722	5.0	2081	10,626	5.0
1982	10,715	9.7	2032	8,771	5.0	2082	10,655	5.0
1983	10,694	9.6	2033	8,820	5.0	2083	10,684	5.0
1984	8,529	7.5	2034	8,868	5.0	2084	10,712	5.0
1985	8,313	7.2	2035	8,914	5.0	2085	10,741	5.0
1986	8,245	7.0	2036	8,960	5.0	2086	10,767	5.0
1987	7,414	6.2	2037	9,005	5.0	2087	10,794	5.0
1988	6,697	5.5	2038	9,052	5.0	2088	10,820	5.0
1989	6,524	5.3	2039	9,098	5.0	2089	10,846	5.0
1990	7,061	5.6	2040	9,142	5.0	2090	10,873	5.0
1991	8,640	6.8	2041	9,187	5.0	2091	10,898	5.0
1992	9,611	7.5	2042	9,230	5.0	2092	10,924	5.0
1993	8,927	6.9	2043	9,272	5.0	2093	10,951	5.0
1994	7,976	6.1	2044	9,314	5.0	2094	10,977	5.0
1995	7,407	5.6	2045	9,354	5.0	2095	11,003	5.0
1996	7,231	5.4	2046	9,394	5.0	2096	11,030	5.0
1997	6,729	4.9	2047	9,433	5.0	2097	11,058	5.0
1998	6,204	4.5	2048	9,471	5.0	2098	11,085	5.0
1999	5,879	4.2	2049	9,509	5.0	2099	11,113	5.0
2000	5,685	4.0	2050	9,547	5.0	2100	11,141	5.0

Annex Table 7: Real GDP (2012 Chained $ billions)(Central Scenario)							
	$ billions	% ch		$ billions	% ch		$ billions	% ch
1950	2,289.5							
1951	2,473.8	8.0	2001	13,262.1	1.0	2051	29,947.1	1.4
1952	2,574.9	4.1	2002	13,493.1	1.7	2052	30,360.6	1.4
1953	2,695.6	4.7	2003	13,879.1	2.9	2053	30,779.6	1.4
1954	2,680.0	-0.6	2004	14,406.4	3.8	2054	31,204.5	1.4
1955	2,871.2	7.1	2005	14,912.5	3.5	2055	31,636.0	1.4
1956	2,932.4	2.1	2006	15,338.3	2.9	2056	32,065.8	1.4
1957	2,994.1	2.1	2007	15,626.0	1.9	2057	32,502.4	1.4
1958	2,972.0	-0.7	2008	15,604.7	-0.1	2058	32,945.8	1.4
1959	3,178.2	6.9	2009	15,208.8	-2.5	2059	33,396.1	1.4
1960	3,260.0	2.6	2010	15,598.8	2.6	2060	33,853.3	1.4
1961	3,343.5	2.6	2011	15,840.7	1.6	2061	34,312.7	1.4
1962	3,548.4	6.1	2012	16,197.0	2.2	2062	34,778.7	1.4
1963	3,702.9	4.4	2013	16,495.4	1.8	2063	35,251.3	1.4
1964	3,916.3	5.8	2014	16,912.0	2.5	2064	35,730.1	1.4
1965	4,170.7	6.5	2015	17,403.8	2.9	2065	36,215.3	1.4
1966	4,445.9	6.6	2016	17,688.9	1.6	2066	36,708.9	1.4
1967	4,567.8	2.7	2017	18,108.1	2.4	2067	37,208.3	1.4
1968	4,792.3	4.9	2018	18,638.2	2.9	2068	37,713.0	1.4
1969	4,942.1	3.1	2019	19,073.1	2.3	2069	38,222.3	1.4
1970	4,951.3	0.2	2020	17,790.6	-6.7	2070	38,736.3	1.3
1971	5,114.3	3.3	2021	18,569.3	4.4	2071	39,261.9	1.4
1972	5,383.3	5.3	2022	19,268.0	3.8	2072	39,791.6	1.3
1973	5,687.2	5.6	2023	19,674.1	2.1	2073	40,325.3	1.3
1974	5,656.5	-0.5	2024	20,086.3	2.1	2074	40,862.7	1.3
1975	5,644.8	-0.2	2025	20,410.5	1.6	2075	41,404.0	1.3
1976	5,949.0	5.4	2026	20,707.7	1.5	2076	41,952.8	1.3
1977	6,224.1	4.6	2027	21,003.6	1.4	2077	42,505.3	1.3
1978	6,568.6	5.5	2028	21,302.8	1.4	2078	43,061.7	1.3
1979	6,776.6	3.2	2029	21,645.0	1.6	2079	43,622.3	1.3
1980	6,759.2	-0.3	2030	21,989.5	1.6	2080	44,187.3	1.3
1981	6,930.7	2.5	2031	22,336.1	1.6	2081	44,754.6	1.3
1982	6,805.8	-1.8	2032	22,687.1	1.6	2082	45,326.7	1.3
1983	7,117.7	4.6	2033	23,041.5	1.6	2083	45,903.8	1.3
1984	7,632.8	7.2	2034	23,397.7	1.5	2084	46,486.2	1.3
1985	7,951.1	4.2	2035	23,755.4	1.5	2085	47,074.4	1.3
1986	8,226.4	3.5	2036	24,117.9	1.5	2086	47,662.9	1.3
1987	8,511.0	3.5	2037	24,480.8	1.5	2087	48,257.6	1.2
1988	8,866.5	4.2	2038	24,854.4	1.5	2088	48,858.9	1.2
1989	9,192.1	3.7	2039	25,229.1	1.5	2089	49,467.4	1.2
1990	9,365.5	1.9	2040	25,605.8	1.5	2090	50,083.8	1.2
1991	9,355.4	-0.1	2041	25,988.4	1.5	2091	50,704.6	1.2
1992	9,684.9	3.5	2042	26,372.3	1.5	2092	51,333.7	1.2
1993	9,951.5	2.8	2043	26,757.8	1.5	2093	51,971.1	1.2
1994	10,352.4	4.0	2044	27,145.3	1.4	2094	52,617.0	1.2
1995	10,630.3	2.7	2045	27,535.2	1.4	2095	53,271.8	1.2
1996	11,031.3	3.8	2046	27,929.1	1.4	2096	53,936.7	1.2
1997	11,521.9	4.4	2047	28,325.9	1.4	2097	54,610.5	1.2
1998	12,038.3	4.5	2048	28,726.0	1.4	2098	55,293.5	1.3
1999	12,610.5	4.8	2049	29,130.1	1.4	2099	55,986.0	1.3
2000	13,131.0	4.1	2050	29,538.5	1.4	2100	56,688.5	1.3

Annex Table 8: Nominal GDP (Central Scenario)								
	$ billions	% ch		$ billions	% ch		$ billions	% ch
1950	299.8							
1951	346.9	15.7	2001	10,581.8	3.2	2051	63,403.8	3.4
1952	367.3	5.9	2002	10,936.4	3.4	2052	65,564.9	3.4
1953	389.2	6.0	2003	11,458.2	4.8	2053	67,799.1	3.4
1954	390.5	0.3	2004	12,213.7	6.6	2054	70,109.9	3.4
1955	425.5	8.9	2005	13,036.6	6.7	2055	72,500.8	3.4
1956	449.4	5.6	2006	13,814.6	6.0	2056	74,955.7	3.4
1957	474.0	5.5	2007	14,451.9	4.6	2057	77,495.7	3.4
1958	481.2	1.5	2008	14,712.8	1.8	2058	80,124.0	3.4
1959	521.7	8.4	2009	14,448.9	-1.8	2059	82,843.4	3.4
1960	542.4	4.0	2010	14,992.1	3.8	2060	85,657.2	3.4
1961	562.2	3.7	2011	15,542.6	3.7	2061	88,555.8	3.4
1962	603.9	7.4	2012	16,197.0	4.2	2062	91,553.7	3.4
1963	637.5	5.6	2013	16,784.9	3.6	2063	94,653.7	3.4
1964	684.5	7.4	2014	17,527.3	4.4	2064	97,858.2	3.4
1965	742.3	8.4	2015	18,224.8	4.0	2065	101,170.8	3.4
1966	813.4	9.6	2016	18,715.0	2.7	2066	104,600.8	3.4
1967	860.0	5.7	2017	19,519.4	4.3	2067	108,144.2	3.4
1968	940.7	9.4	2018	20,580.2	5.4	2068	111,803.2	3.4
1969	1,017.6	8.2	2019	21,427.7	4.1	2069	115,579.6	3.4
1970	1,073.3	5.5	2020	20,386.6	-4.9	2070	119,476.5	3.4
1971	1,164.9	8.5	2021	21,704.6	6.5	2071	123,519.5	3.4
1972	1,279.1	9.8	2022	22,971.6	5.8	2072	127,689.8	3.4
1973	1,425.4	11.4	2023	23,924.9	4.1	2073	131,990.3	3.4
1974	1,545.2	8.4	2024	24,914.7	4.1	2074	136,424.5	3.4
1975	1,684.9	9.0	2025	25,823.2	3.6	2075	140,996.1	3.4
1976	1,873.4	11.2	2026	26,723.2	3.5	2076	145,722.2	3.4
1977	2,081.8	11.1	2027	27,647.1	3.5	2077	150,594.2	3.3
1978	2,351.6	13.0	2028	28,601.8	3.5	2078	155,616.9	3.3
1979	2,627.3	11.7	2029	29,642.5	3.6	2079	160,795.5	3.3
1980	2,857.3	8.8	2030	30,716.5	3.6	2080	166,135.8	3.3
1981	3,207.0	12.2	2031	31,824.7	3.6	2081	171,634.3	3.3
1982	3,343.8	4.3	2032	32,971.4	3.6	2082	177,304.7	3.3
1983	3,634.0	8.7	2033	34,156.2	3.6	2083	183,153.2	3.3
1984	4,037.6	11.1	2034	35,377.9	3.6	2084	189,186.6	3.3
1985	4,339.0	7.5	2035	36,637.0	3.6	2085	195,412.0	3.3
1986	4,579.6	5.5	2036	37,940.0	3.6	2086	201,812.1	3.3
1987	4,855.2	6.0	2037	39,281.1	3.5	2087	208,416.6	3.3
1988	5,236.4	7.9	2038	40,678.3	3.6	2088	215,233.8	3.3
1989	5,641.6	7.7	2039	42,117.3	3.5	2089	222,272.7	3.3
1990	5,963.1	5.7	2040	43,601.1	3.5	2090	229,543.3	3.3
1991	6,158.1	3.3	2041	45,137.6	3.5	2091	237,036.5	3.3
1992	6,520.3	5.9	2042	46,720.4	3.5	2092	244,776.9	3.3
1993	6,858.6	5.2	2043	48,351.5	3.5	2093	252,772.7	3.3
1994	7,287.2	6.3	2044	50,032.7	3.5	2094	261,032.5	3.3
1995	7,639.7	4.8	2045	51,766.3	3.5	2095	269,566.6	3.3
1996	8,073.1	5.7	2046	53,557.0	3.5	2096	278,389.6	3.3
1997	8,577.6	6.2	2047	55,404.3	3.4	2097	287,504.8	3.3
1998	9,062.8	5.7	2048	57,310.7	3.4	2098	296,922.5	3.3
1999	9,630.7	6.3	2049	59,279.1	3.4	2099	306,653.7	3.3
2000	10,252.3	6.5	2050	61,312.6	3.4	2100	316,711.7	3.3

Annex Table 9: Implicit GDP Deflator (Central Scenario)						
	Index, 2012	% ch		Index, 2012	% ch		Index, 2012	% ch
1950	13.1							
1951	14.0	7.1	2001	79.8	2.2	2051	211.7	2.0
1952	14.3	1.7	2002	81.1	1.6	2052	216.0	2.0
1953	14.4	1.2	2003	82.6	1.9	2053	220.3	2.0
1954	14.6	0.9	2004	84.8	2.7	2054	224.7	2.0
1955	14.8	1.7	2005	87.4	3.1	2055	229.2	2.0
1956	15.3	3.4	2006	90.1	3.0	2056	233.8	2.0
1957	15.8	3.3	2007	92.5	2.7	2057	238.4	2.0
1958	16.2	2.3	2008	94.3	1.9	2058	243.2	2.0
1959	16.4	1.4	2009	95.0	0.8	2059	248.1	2.0
1960	16.6	1.4	2010	96.1	1.2	2060	253.0	2.0
1961	16.8	1.1	2011	98.1	2.1	2061	258.1	2.0
1962	17.0	1.2	2012	100.0	1.9	2062	263.2	2.0
1963	17.2	1.1	2013	101.8	1.8	2063	268.5	2.0
1964	17.5	1.5	2014	103.6	1.9	2064	273.9	2.0
1965	17.8	1.8	2015	104.7	1.0	2065	279.4	2.0
1966	18.3	2.8	2016	105.8	1.0	2066	284.9	2.0
1967	18.8	2.9	2017	107.8	1.9	2067	290.6	2.0
1968	19.6	4.3	2018	110.4	2.4	2068	296.5	2.0
1969	20.6	4.9	2019	112.3	1.7	2069	302.4	2.0
1970	21.7	5.3	2020	114.6	2.0	2070	308.4	2.0
1971	22.8	5.1	2021	116.9	2.0	2071	314.6	2.0
1972	23.8	4.3	2022	119.2	2.0	2072	320.9	2.0
1973	25.1	5.5	2023	121.6	2.0	2073	327.3	2.0
1974	27.3	9.0	2024	124.0	2.0	2074	333.9	2.0
1975	29.8	9.3	2025	126.5	2.0	2075	340.5	2.0
1976	31.5	5.5	2026	129.0	2.0	2076	347.3	2.0
1977	33.4	6.2	2027	131.6	2.0	2077	354.3	2.0
1978	35.8	7.0	2028	134.3	2.0	2078	361.4	2.0
1979	38.8	8.3	2029	136.9	2.0	2079	368.6	2.0
1980	42.3	9.0	2030	139.7	2.0	2080	376.0	2.0
1981	46.3	9.5	2031	142.5	2.0	2081	383.5	2.0
1982	49.1	6.2	2032	145.3	2.0	2082	391.2	2.0
1983	51.1	3.9	2033	148.2	2.0	2083	399.0	2.0
1984	52.9	3.6	2034	151.2	2.0	2084	407.0	2.0
1985	54.6	3.2	2035	154.2	2.0	2085	415.1	2.0
1986	55.7	2.0	2036	157.3	2.0	2086	423.4	2.0
1987	57.0	2.5	2037	160.5	2.0	2087	431.9	2.0
1988	59.1	3.5	2038	163.7	2.0	2088	440.5	2.0
1989	61.4	3.9	2039	166.9	2.0	2089	449.3	2.0
1990	63.7	3.7	2040	170.3	2.0	2090	458.3	2.0
1991	65.8	3.4	2041	173.7	2.0	2091	467.5	2.0
1992	67.3	2.3	2042	177.2	2.0	2092	476.8	2.0
1993	68.9	2.4	2043	180.7	2.0	2093	486.4	2.0
1994	70.4	2.1	2044	184.3	2.0	2094	496.1	2.0
1995	71.9	2.1	2045	188.0	2.0	2095	506.0	2.0
1996	73.2	1.8	2046	191.8	2.0	2096	516.1	2.0
1997	74.4	1.7	2047	195.6	2.0	2097	526.5	2.0
1998	75.3	1.1	2048	199.5	2.0	2098	537.0	2.0
1999	76.4	1.4	2049	203.5	2.0	2099	547.7	2.0
2000	78.1	2.2	2050	207.6	2.0	2100	558.7	2.0

Annex Table 10: Federal Government Revenue (Central Scenario)							
	$ billions	% GDP		$ billions	% GDP		$ billions	% GDP
1950	39.4	13.2						
1951	51.6	14.9	2001	1,991.1	18.8	2051	11,032.3	17.4
1952	66.2	18.0	2002	1,853.1	16.9	2052	11,408.3	17.4
1953	69.6	17.9	2003	1,782.3	15.6	2053	11,797.0	17.4
1954	69.7	17.8	2004	1,880.1	15.4	2054	12,199.1	17.4
1955	65.5	15.4	2005	2,153.6	16.5	2055	12,615.1	17.4
1956	74.6	16.6	2006	2,406.9	17.4	2056	13,042.3	17.4
1957	80.0	16.9	2007	2,568.0	17.8	2057	13,484.3	17.4
1958	79.6	16.5	2008	2,524.0	17.2	2058	13,941.6	17.4
1959	79.2	15.2	2009	2,105.0	14.6	2059	14,414.7	17.4
1960	92.5	17.1	2010	2,162.7	14.4	2060	14,904.3	17.4
1961	94.4	16.8	2011	2,303.5	14.8	2061	15,408.7	17.4
1962	99.7	16.5	2012	2,450.0	15.1	2062	15,930.3	17.4
1963	106.6	16.7	2013	2,775.1	16.5	2063	16,469.7	17.4
1964	112.6	16.5	2014	3,021.5	17.2	2064	17,027.3	17.4
1965	116.8	15.7	2015	3,249.9	17.8	2065	17,603.7	17.4
1966	130.8	16.1	2016	3,268.0	17.5	2066	18,200.5	17.4
1967	148.8	17.3	2017	3,316.2	17.0	2067	18,817.1	17.4
1968	153.0	16.3	2018	3,329.9	16.2	2068	19,453.8	17.4
1969	186.9	18.4	2019	3,462.2	16.2	2069	20,110.8	17.4
1970	192.8	18.0	2020	3,294.0	16.2	2070	20,788.9	17.4
1971	187.1	16.1	2021	3,472.7	16.0	2071	21,492.4	17.4
1972	207.3	16.2	2022	3,790.3	16.5	2072	22,218.0	17.4
1973	230.8	16.2	2023	4,067.2	17.0	2073	22,966.3	17.4
1974	263.2	17.0	2024	4,335.2	17.4	2074	23,737.9	17.4
1975	279.1	16.6	2025	4,493.2	17.4	2075	24,533.3	17.4
1976	298.1	15.9	2026	4,649.8	17.4	2076	25,355.7	17.4
1977	355.6	17.1	2027	4,810.6	17.4	2077	26,203.4	17.4
1978	399.6	17.0	2028	4,976.7	17.4	2078	27,077.3	17.4
1979	463.3	17.6	2029	5,157.8	17.4	2079	27,978.4	17.4
1980	517.1	18.1	2030	5,344.7	17.4	2080	28,907.6	17.4
1981	599.3	18.7	2031	5,537.5	17.4	2081	29,864.4	17.4
1982	617.8	18.5	2032	5,737.0	17.4	2082	30,851.0	17.4
1983	600.6	16.5	2033	5,943.2	17.4	2083	31,868.7	17.4
1984	666.4	16.5	2034	6,155.8	17.4	2084	32,918.5	17.4
1985	734.0	16.9	2035	6,374.8	17.4	2085	34,001.7	17.4
1986	769.2	16.8	2036	6,601.6	17.4	2086	35,115.3	17.4
1987	854.3	17.6	2037	6,834.9	17.4	2087	36,264.5	17.4
1988	909.2	17.4	2038	7,078.0	17.4	2088	37,450.7	17.4
1989	991.1	17.6	2039	7,328.4	17.4	2089	38,675.4	17.4
1990	1,032.0	17.3	2040	7,586.6	17.4	2090	39,940.5	17.4
1991	1,055.0	17.1	2041	7,853.9	17.4	2091	41,244.4	17.4
1992	1,091.2	16.7	2042	8,129.4	17.4	2092	42,591.2	17.4
1993	1,154.3	16.8	2043	8,413.2	17.4	2093	43,982.5	17.4
1994	1,258.6	17.3	2044	8,705.7	17.4	2094	45,419.7	17.4
1995	1,351.8	17.7	2045	9,007.3	17.4	2095	46,904.6	17.4
1996	1,453.1	18.0	2046	9,318.9	17.4	2096	48,439.8	17.4
1997	1,579.2	18.4	2047	9,640.3	17.4	2097	50,025.8	17.4
1998	1,721.7	19.0	2048	9,972.1	17.4	2098	51,664.5	17.4
1999	1,827.5	19.0	2049	10,314.6	17.4	2099	53,357.7	17.4
2000	2,025.2	19.8	2050	10,668.4	17.4	2100	55,107.8	17.4

	Annex Table 11: Federal Government Primary Expenditure (Central Scenario)							
	$ billions	% GDP		$ billions	% GDP		$ billions	% GDP
1950	37.8	12.6						
1951	40.8	11.8	2001	1,656.7	15.7	2051	14,623.8	23.1
1952	63.0	17.1	2002	1,839.9	16.8	2052	15,193.4	23.2
1953	70.9	18.2	2003	2,006.8	17.5	2053	15,785.3	23.3
1954	66.0	16.9	2004	2,132.6	17.5	2054	16,400.3	23.4
1955	63.6	14.9	2005	2,288.0	17.6	2055	17,038.6	23.5
1956	65.6	14.6	2006	2,428.4	17.6	2056	17,715.4	23.6
1957	71.2	15.0	2007	2,491.6	17.2	2057	18,419.2	23.8
1958	76.8	16.0	2008	2,729.8	18.6	2058	19,164.8	23.9
1959	86.3	16.6	2009	3,330.8	23.1	2059	19,941.0	24.1
1960	85.2	15.7	2010	3,260.9	21.8	2060	20,753.0	24.2
1961	91.0	16.2	2011	3,373.1	21.7	2061	21,579.3	24.4
1962	99.9	16.5	2012	3,306.2	20.4	2062	22,422.9	24.5
1963	103.6	16.2	2013	3,234.0	19.3	2063	23,283.3	24.6
1964	110.3	16.1	2014	3,277.3	18.7	2064	24,177.1	24.7
1965	109.6	14.8	2015	3,468.7	19.0	2065	25,104.8	24.8
1966	125.1	15.4	2016	3,612.6	19.3	2066	26,069.1	24.9
1967	147.2	17.1	2017	3,719.1	19.1	2067	27,070.9	25.0
1968	167.0	17.8	2018	3,784.1	18.4	2068	28,111.6	25.1
1969	170.9	16.8	2019	4,071.0	19.0	2069	29,171.5	25.2
1970	181.3	16.9	2020	6,715.1	32.9	2070	30,283.4	25.3
1971	195.3	16.8	2021	5,884.4	27.1	2071	31,448.2	25.5
1972	215.2	16.8	2022	5,077.6	22.1	2072	32,658.0	25.6
1973	228.4	16.0	2023	4,884.7	20.4	2073	33,889.9	25.7
1974	247.9	16.0	2024	5,019.2	20.1	2074	35,142.7	25.8
1975	309.1	18.3	2025	5,262.3	20.4	2075	36,473.4	25.9
1976	345.1	18.4	2026	5,513.3	20.6	2076	37,821.5	26.0
1977	379.3	18.2	2027	5,781.7	20.9	2077	39,190.6	26.0
1978	423.3	18.0	2028	6,058.4	21.2	2078	40,579.5	26.1
1979	461.4	17.6	2029	6,339.4	21.4	2079	41,986.5	26.1
1980	538.4	18.8	2030	6,628.4	21.6	2080	43,464.3	26.2
1981	609.5	19.0	2031	6,921.8	21.7	2081	44,987.7	26.2
1982	660.7	19.8	2032	7,218.2	21.9	2082	46,547.5	26.3
1983	718.6	19.8	2033	7,516.9	22.0	2083	48,161.6	26.3
1984	740.7	18.3	2034	7,827.8	22.1	2084	49,795.4	26.3
1985	816.9	18.8	2035	8,153.6	22.3	2085	51,501.7	26.4
1986	854.4	18.7	2036	8,484.7	22.4	2086	53,289.6	26.4
1987	865.4	17.8	2037	8,817.1	22.4	2087	55,140.3	26.5
1988	912.6	17.4	2038	9,149.5	22.5	2088	57,056.4	26.5
1989	974.8	17.3	2039	9,487.9	22.5	2089	59,039.8	26.6
1990	1,068.6	17.9	2040	9,829.2	22.5	2090	61,095.4	26.6
1991	1,129.8	18.3	2041	10,185.2	22.6	2091	63,259.2	26.7
1992	1,182.2	18.1	2042	10,553.8	22.6	2092	65,500.6	26.8
1993	1,210.7	17.7	2043	10,935.6	22.6	2093	67,822.5	26.8
1994	1,258.8	17.3	2044	11,331.1	22.6	2094	70,175.7	26.9
1995	1,283.6	16.8	2045	11,743.4	22.7	2095	72,629.8	26.9
1996	1,319.4	16.3	2046	12,176.0	22.7	2096	75,208.3	27.0
1997	1,357.1	15.8	2047	12,624.3	22.8	2097	77,879.4	27.1
1998	1,411.3	15.6	2048	13,089.0	22.8	2098	80,646.8	27.2
1999	1,472.1	15.3	2049	13,580.1	22.9	2099	83,513.8	27.2
2000	1,566.0	15.3	2050	14,085.3	23.0	2100	86,414.4	27.3

Annex Table 12: Federal Government Net Interest (Central Scenario)								
	$ billions	% GDP		$ billions	% GDP		$ billions	% GDP
1950	4.8	1.6						
1951	4.7	1.3	2001	206.2	1.9	2051	3,598.1	5.7
1952	4.7	1.3	2002	170.9	1.6	2052	3,797.2	5.8
1953	5.2	1.3	2003	153.1	1.3	2053	4,006.8	5.9
1954	4.8	1.2	2004	160.2	1.3	2054	4,227.4	6.0
1955	4.9	1.1	2005	184.0	1.4	2055	4,459.7	6.2
1956	5.1	1.1	2006	226.6	1.6	2056	4,704.3	6.3
1957	5.4	1.1	2007	237.1	1.6	2057	4,962.1	6.4
1958	5.6	1.2	2008	252.8	1.7	2058	5,233.9	6.5
1959	5.8	1.1	2009	186.9	1.3	2059	5,520.6	6.7
1960	6.9	1.3	2010	196.2	1.3	2060	5,823.1	6.8
1961	6.7	1.2	2011	230.0	1.5	2061	6,141.9	6.9
1962	6.9	1.1	2012	220.4	1.4	2062	6,477.6	7.1
1963	7.7	1.2	2013	220.9	1.3	2063	6,830.6	7.2
1964	8.2	1.2	2014	229.0	1.3	2064	7,201.4	7.4
1965	8.6	1.2	2015	223.2	1.2	2065	7,591.0	7.5
1966	9.4	1.2	2016	240.0	1.3	2066	8,000.3	7.6
1967	10.3	1.2	2017	262.6	1.3	2067	8,430.1	7.8
1968	11.1	1.2	2018	325.0	1.6	2068	8,881.6	7.9
1969	12.7	1.2	2019	375.6	1.8	2069	9,355.4	8.1
1970	14.4	1.3	2020	277.3	1.4	2070	9,852.6	8.2
1971	14.8	1.3	2021	216.1	1.0	2071	10,374.5	8.4
1972	15.5	1.2	2022	238.4	1.0	2072	10,922.4	8.6
1973	17.3	1.2	2023	253.7	1.1	2073	11,497.2	8.7
1974	21.4	1.4	2024	266.7	1.1	2074	12,099.7	8.9
1975	23.2	1.4	2025	279.2	1.1	2075	12,731.2	9.0
1976	26.7	1.4	2026	354.3	1.3	2076	13,393.0	9.2
1977	29.9	1.4	2027	437.7	1.6	2077	14,085.8	9.4
1978	35.5	1.5	2028	533.1	1.9	2078	14,810.2	9.5
1979	42.6	1.6	2029	641.4	2.2	2079	15,566.9	9.7
1980	52.5	1.8	2030	762.3	2.5	2080	16,357.2	9.8
1981	68.8	2.1	2031	900.5	2.8	2081	17,182.6	10.0
1982	85.0	2.5	2032	1,056.2	3.2	2082	18,044.5	10.2
1983	89.8	2.5	2033	1,183.2	3.5	2083	18,944.1	10.3
1984	111.1	2.8	2034	1,271.7	3.6	2084	19,882.6	10.5
1985	129.5	3.0	2035	1,365.6	3.7	2085	20,861.4	10.7
1986	136.0	3.0	2036	1,465.1	3.9	2086	21,882.6	10.8
1987	138.6	2.9	2037	1,570.4	4.0	2087	22,948.3	11.0
1988	151.8	2.9	2038	1,684.2	4.1	2088	24,060.4	11.2
1989	169.0	3.0	2039	1,805.3	4.3	2089	25,220.8	11.3
1990	184.3	3.1	2040	1,934.0	4.4	2090	26,431.7	11.5
1991	194.4	3.2	2041	2,061.6	4.6	2091	27,695.4	11.7
1992	199.3	3.1	2042	2,184.5	4.7	2092	29,014.8	11.9
1993	198.7	2.9	2043	2,313.4	4.8	2093	30,392.3	12.0
1994	202.9	2.8	2044	2,448.4	4.9	2094	31,829.5	12.2
1995	232.1	3.0	2045	2,589.9	5.0	2095	33,328.5	12.4
1996	241.1	3.0	2046	2,738.3	5.1	2096	34,892.6	12.5
1997	244.0	2.8	2047	2,894.0	5.2	2097	36,525.0	12.7
1998	241.1	2.7	2048	3,057.4	5.3	2098	38,228.4	12.9
1999	229.8	2.4	2049	3,228.9	5.4	2099	40,005.8	13.0
2000	222.9	2.2	2050	3,408.9	5.6	2100	41,859.6	13.2

	$ billions	% GDP		$ billions	% GDP		$ billions	% GDP
			Annex Table 13: Federal Government Primary Balance (Central Scenario)					
1950	1.7	0.6						
1951	10.8	3.1	2001	334.4	3.2	2051	-3,591.5	-5.7
1952	3.2	0.9	2002	13.2	0.1	2052	-3,785.1	-5.8
1953	-1.3	-0.3	2003	-224.5	-2.0	2053	-3,988.3	-5.9
1954	3.7	0.9	2004	-252.5	-2.1	2054	-4,201.2	-6.0
1955	1.9	0.4	2005	-134.4	-1.0	2055	-4,423.5	-6.1
1956	9.0	2.0	2006	-21.6	-0.2	2056	-4,673.1	-6.2
1957	8.8	1.8	2007	76.4	0.5	2057	-4,935.0	-6.4
1958	2.8	0.6	2008	-205.8	-1.4	2058	-5,223.2	-6.5
1959	-7.1	-1.4	2009	-1,225.8	-8.5	2059	-5,526.3	-6.7
1960	7.2	1.3	2010	-1,098.2	-7.3	2060	-5,848.6	-6.8
1961	3.4	0.6	2011	-1,069.6	-6.9	2061	-6,170.6	-7.0
1962	-0.3	0.0	2012	-856.2	-5.3	2062	-6,492.6	-7.1
1963	3.0	0.5	2013	-458.9	-2.7	2063	-6,813.6	-7.2
1964	2.3	0.3	2014	-255.8	-1.5	2064	-7,149.8	-7.3
1965	7.2	1.0	2015	-218.8	-1.2	2065	-7,501.0	-7.4
1966	5.7	0.7	2016	-344.6	-1.8	2066	-7,868.6	-7.5
1967	1.6	0.2	2017	-402.9	-2.1	2067	-8,253.8	-7.6
1968	-14.1	-1.5	2018	-454.2	-2.2	2068	-8,657.8	-7.7
1969	15.9	1.6	2019	-608.8	-2.8	2069	-9,060.7	-7.8
1970	11.5	1.1	2020	-3,421.2	-16.8	2070	-9,494.5	-7.9
1971	-8.2	-0.7	2021	-2,411.6	-11.1	2071	-9,955.8	-8.1
1972	-7.9	-0.6	2022	-1,287.3	-5.6	2072	-10,440.0	-8.2
1973	2.4	0.2	2023	-817.4	-3.4	2073	-10,923.6	-8.3
1974	15.3	1.0	2024	-684.0	-2.7	2074	-11,404.9	-8.4
1975	-30.0	-1.8	2025	-769.1	-3.0	2075	-11,940.1	-8.5
1976	-47.0	-2.5	2026	-863.5	-3.2	2076	-12,465.8	-8.6
1977	-23.8	-1.1	2027	-971.1	-3.5	2077	-12,987.2	-8.6
1978	-23.7	-1.0	2028	-1,081.7	-3.8	2078	-13,502.1	-8.7
1979	1.9	0.1	2029	-1,181.6	-4.0	2079	-14,008.1	-8.7
1980	-21.3	-0.7	2030	-1,283.7	-4.2	2080	-14,556.6	-8.8
1981	-10.2	-0.3	2031	-1,384.3	-4.3	2081	-15,123.4	-8.8
1982	-42.9	-1.3	2032	-1,481.1	-4.5	2082	-15,696.5	-8.9
1983	-118.0	-3.2	2033	-1,573.7	-4.6	2083	-16,293.0	-8.9
1984	-74.3	-1.8	2034	-1,672.0	-4.7	2084	-16,876.9	-8.9
1985	-82.8	-1.9	2035	-1,778.7	-4.9	2085	-17,500.0	-9.0
1986	-85.2	-1.9	2036	-1,883.1	-5.0	2086	-18,174.3	-9.0
1987	-11.1	-0.2	2037	-1,982.2	-5.0	2087	-18,875.9	-9.1
1988	-3.4	-0.1	2038	-2,071.5	-5.1	2088	-19,605.7	-9.1
1989	16.3	0.3	2039	-2,159.5	-5.1	2089	-20,364.4	-9.2
1990	-36.7	-0.6	2040	-2,242.6	-5.1	2090	-21,154.8	-9.2
1991	-74.8	-1.2	2041	-2,331.2	-5.2	2091	-22,014.8	-9.3
1992	-91.0	-1.4	2042	-2,424.5	-5.2	2092	-22,909.5	-9.4
1993	-56.3	-0.8	2043	-2,522.5	-5.2	2093	-23,840.1	-9.4
1994	-0.3	0.0	2044	-2,625.4	-5.2	2094	-24,756.1	-9.5
1995	68.2	0.9	2045	-2,736.0	-5.3	2095	-25,725.2	-9.5
1996	133.6	1.7	2046	-2,857.0	-5.3	2096	-26,768.5	-9.6
1997	222.1	2.6	2047	-2,984.0	-5.4	2097	-27,853.6	-9.7
1998	310.4	3.4	2048	-3,117.0	-5.4	2098	-28,982.2	-9.8
1999	355.4	3.7	2049	-3,265.5	-5.5	2099	-30,156.0	-9.8
2000	459.2	4.5	2050	-3,416.9	-5.6	2100	-31,306.6	-9.9

Annex Table 14: Federal Government Overall Balance (Central Scenario)								
	$ billions	% GDP		$ billions	% GDP		$ billions	% GDP
1950	-3.1	-1.0						
1951	6.1	1.8	2001	128.2	1.2	2051	-7,189.6	-11.3
1952	-1.5	-0.4	2002	-157.8	-1.4	2052	-7,582.3	-11.6
1953	-6.5	-1.7	2003	-377.6	-3.3	2053	-7,995.0	-11.8
1954	-1.2	-0.3	2004	-412.7	-3.4	2054	-8,428.6	-12.0
1955	-3.0	-0.7	2005	-318.3	-2.4	2055	-8,883.1	-12.3
1956	3.9	0.9	2006	-248.2	-1.8	2056	-9,377.3	-12.5
1957	3.4	0.7	2007	-160.7	-1.1	2057	-9,897.0	-12.8
1958	-2.8	-0.6	2008	-458.6	-3.1	2058	-10,457.1	-13.1
1959	-12.8	-2.5	2009	-1,412.7	-9.8	2059	-11,046.9	-13.3
1960	0.3	0.1	2010	-1,294.4	-8.6	2060	-11,671.7	-13.6
1961	-3.3	-0.6	2011	-1,299.6	-8.4	2061	-12,312.5	-13.9
1962	-7.1	-1.2	2012	-1,076.6	-6.6	2062	-12,970.2	-14.2
1963	-4.8	-0.7	2013	-679.8	-4.0	2063	-13,644.2	-14.4
1964	-5.9	-0.9	2014	-484.8	-2.8	2064	-14,351.2	-14.7
1965	-1.4	-0.2	2015	-442.0	-2.4	2065	-15,092.1	-14.9
1966	-3.7	-0.5	2016	-584.7	-3.1	2066	-15,868.9	-15.2
1967	-8.6	-1.0	2017	-665.4	-3.4	2067	-16,684.0	-15.4
1968	-25.2	-2.7	2018	-779.1	-3.8	2068	-17,539.4	-15.7
1969	3.2	0.3	2019	-984.4	-4.6	2069	-18,416.1	-15.9
1970	-2.8	-0.3	2020	-3,698.5	-18.1	2070	-19,347.1	-16.2
1971	-23.0	-2.0	2021	-2,627.7	-12.1	2071	-20,330.2	-16.5
1972	-23.4	-1.8	2022	-1,525.8	-6.6	2072	-21,362.3	-16.7
1973	-14.9	-1.0	2023	-1,071.2	-4.5	2073	-22,420.8	-17.0
1974	-6.1	-0.4	2024	-950.7	-3.8	2074	-23,504.6	-17.2
1975	-53.2	-3.2	2025	-1,048.4	-4.1	2075	-24,671.3	-17.5
1976	-73.7	-4.6	2026	-1,217.8	-4.6	2076	-25,858.8	-17.7
1977	-53.7	-2.6	2027	-1,408.8	-5.1	2077	-27,073.1	-18.0
1978	-59.2	-2.5	2028	-1,614.8	-5.6	2078	-28,312.4	-18.2
1979	-40.7	-1.6	2029	-1,823.0	-6.1	2079	-29,575.0	-18.4
1980	-73.8	-2.6	2030	-2,046.0	-6.7	2080	-30,913.8	-18.6
1981	-79.0	-2.5	2031	-2,284.8	-7.2	2081	-32,306.0	-18.8
1982	-128.0	-3.8	2032	-2,537.3	-7.7	2082	-33,741.0	-19.0
1983	-207.8	-5.7	2033	-2,756.9	-8.1	2083	-35,237.1	-19.2
1984	-185.4	-4.6	2034	-2,943.7	-8.3	2084	-36,759.5	-19.4
1985	-212.3	-4.9	2035	-3,144.3	-8.6	2085	-38,361.4	-19.6
1986	-221.2	-4.8	2036	-3,348.3	-8.8	2086	-40,056.8	-19.8
1987	-149.7	-3.1	2037	-3,552.5	-9.0	2087	-41,824.1	-20.1
1988	-155.2	-3.0	2038	-3,755.7	-9.2	2088	-43,666.1	-20.3
1989	-152.6	-2.7	2039	-3,964.7	-9.4	2089	-45,585.2	-20.5
1990	-221.0	-3.7	2040	-4,176.6	-9.6	2090	-47,586.5	-20.7
1991	-269.2	-4.4	2041	-4,392.8	-9.7	2091	-49,710.3	-21.0
1992	-290.3	-4.5	2042	-4,609.0	-9.9	2092	-51,924.3	-21.2
1993	-255.1	-3.7	2043	-4,835.9	-10.0	2093	-54,232.3	-21.5
1994	-203.2	-2.8	2044	-5,073.8	-10.1	2094	-56,585.5	-21.7
1995	-164.0	-2.1	2045	-5,325.9	-10.3	2095	-59,053.8	-21.9
1996	-107.4	-1.3	2046	-5,595.4	-10.4	2096	-61,661.1	-22.1
1997	-21.9	-0.3	2047	-5,878.0	-10.6	2097	-64,378.6	-22.4
1998	69.3	0.8	2048	-6,174.4	-10.8	2098	-67,210.6	-22.6
1999	125.6	1.3	2049	-6,494.4	-11.0	2099	-70,161.9	-22.9
2000	236.2	2.3	2050	-6,825.8	-11.1	2100	-73,166.2	-23.1

Annex Table 15: Federal Government Debt held by the Public (Central Scenario)							
	$ billions	% GDP		$ billions	% GDP		$ billions	% GDP
1950	219.0	73.0						
1951	214.3	61.8	2001	3,319.6	31.4	2051	149,060.9	235.1
1952	214.8	58.5	2002	3,540.4	32.4	2052	157,298.8	239.9
1953	218.4	56.1	2003	3,913.4	34.2	2053	165,971.9	244.8
1954	224.5	57.5	2004	4,295.5	35.2	2054	175,101.6	249.8
1955	226.6	53.3	2005	4,592.2	35.2	2055	184,709.7	254.8
1956	222.2	49.4	2006	4,829.0	35.0	2056	194,836.6	259.9
1957	219.3	46.3	2007	5,035.1	34.8	2057	205,508.6	265.2
1958	226.3	47.0	2008	5,803.1	39.4	2058	216,767.0	270.5
1959	234.7	45.0	2009	7,544.7	52.2	2059	228,642.3	276.0
1960	236.8	43.7	2010	9,018.9	60.2	2060	241,170.6	281.6
1961	238.4	42.4	2011	10,128.2	65.2	2061	254,368.6	287.2
1962	248.0	41.1	2012	11,281.1	69.6	2062	268,254.4	293.0
1963	254.0	39.8	2013	11,982.7	71.4	2063	282,845.0	298.8
1964	256.8	37.5	2014	12,779.9	72.9	2064	298,174.8	304.7
1965	260.8	35.1	2015	13,116.7	72.0	2065	314,278.6	310.6
1966	263.7	32.4	2016	14,167.6	75.7	2066	331,193.5	316.6
1967	266.6	31.0	2017	14,665.4	75.1	2067	348,958.9	322.7
1968	289.5	30.8	2018	15,749.6	76.5	2068	367,616.3	328.8
1969	278.1	27.3	2019	16,800.7	78.4	2069	387,188.2	335.0
1970	283.2	26.4	2020	20,736.1	101.7	2070	407,730.0	341.3
1971	303.0	26.0	2021	23,572.9	108.6	2071	429,295.5	347.6
1972	322.4	25.2	2022	25,361.3	110.4	2072	451,934.7	353.9
1973	340.9	23.9	2023	26,743.7	111.8	2073	475,675.4	360.4
1974	343.7	22.2	2024	27,980.6	112.3	2074	500,544.2	366.9
1975	394.7	23.4	2025	29,358.2	113.7	2075	526,625.4	373.5
1976	477.4	25.5	2026	30,914.2	115.7	2076	553,941.5	380.1
1977	549.1	26.4	2027	32,801.5	118.6	2077	582,520.5	386.8
1978	607.1	25.8	2028	34,973.3	122.3	2078	612,389.0	393.5
1979	640.3	24.4	2029	37,319.6	125.9	2079	643,572.0	400.2
1980	711.9	24.9	2030	40,006.9	130.2	2080	676,147.2	407.0
1981	789.4	24.6	2031	42,956.4	135.0	2081	710,169.5	413.8
1982	924.6	27.7	2032	46,182.4	140.1	2082	745,683.6	420.6
1983	1,137.3	31.3	2033	49,652.4	145.4	2083	782,752.2	427.4
1984	1,307.0	32.4	2034	53,333.9	150.8	2084	821,403.6	434.2
1985	1,507.3	34.7	2035	57,241.1	156.2	2085	861,719.1	441.0
1986	1,740.6	38.0	2036	61,377.7	161.8	2086	903,794.1	447.8
1987	1,889.8	38.9	2037	65,858.8	167.7	2087	947,702.4	454.7
1988	2,051.6	39.2	2038	70,632.6	173.6	2088	993,520.8	461.6
1989	2,190.7	38.8	2039	75,711.8	179.8	2089	1,041,328.7	468.5
1990	2,411.6	40.4	2040	80,743.2	185.2	2090	1,091,210.6	475.4
1991	2,689.0	43.7	2041	85,587.4	189.6	2091	1,143,291.3	482.3
1992	2,999.7	46.0	2042	90,663.6	194.1	2092	1,197,663.3	489.3
1993	3,248.4	47.4	2043	95,983.0	198.5	2093	1,254,423.4	496.3
1994	3,433.1	47.1	2044	101,557.1	203.0	2094	1,313,619.2	503.2
1995	3,604.4	47.2	2045	107,400.7	207.5	2095	1,375,368.7	510.2
1996	3,734.1	46.3	2046	113,531.6	212.0	2096	1,439,813.7	517.2
1997	3,772.3	44.0	2047	119,963.7	216.5	2097	1,507,067.3	524.2
1998	3,721.1	41.1	2048	126,711.2	221.1	2098	1,577,247.2	531.2
1999	3,632.4	37.7	2049	133,798.3	225.7	2099	1,650,475.5	538.2
2000	3,409.8	33.3	2050	141,237.3	230.4	2100	1,726,808.9	545.2

Annex Table 16: Federal Government Net Operating Result					
	Revenue		Operating costs		Net operating result
	$ billions	% GDP	$ billions	% GDP	$ billions	% GDP
1994	1,386.1	19.0	1,515.7	20.8	-129.6	-1.8
1995	1,346.0	17.6	1,491.4	19.5	-145.4	-1.9
1996	1,448.6	17.9	1,646.5	20.4	-197.9	-2.5
1997	1,579.0	18.4	1,603.3	18.7	-24.3	-0.3
1998	1,720.2	19.0	1,830.1	20.2	-109.9	-1.2
1999	1,832.9	19.0	1,731.6	18.0	101.3	1.1
2000	2,044.8	19.9	2,005.2	19.6	39.6	0.4
2001	2,013.7	19.0	2,528.5	23.9	-514.8	-4.9
2002	1,877.7	17.2	2,242.6	20.5	-364.9	-3.3
2003	1,796.0	15.7	2,461.0	21.5	-665.0	-5.8
2004	1,912.7	15.7	2,528.3	20.7	-615.6	-5.0
2005	2,185.5	16.8	2,945.7	22.6	-760.2	-5.8
2006	2,440.8	17.7	2,890.3	20.9	-449.5	-3.3
2007	2,627.3	18.2	2,902.8	20.1	-275.5	-1.9
2008	2,661.4	18.1	3,670.5	24.9	-1,009.1	-6.9
2009	2,198.4	15.2	3,452.1	23.9	-1,253.7	-8.7
2010	2,216.5	14.8	4,296.8	28.7	-2,080.3	-13.9
2011	2,363.8	15.2	3,676.4	23.7	-1,312.6	-8.4
2012	2,518.2	15.5	3,834.5	23.7	-1,316.3	-8.1
2013	2,842.5	16.9	3,647.6	21.7	-805.1	-4.8
2014	3,066.1	17.5	3,857.4	22.0	-791.3	-4.5
2015	3,334.0	18.3	3,853.7	21.1	-519.7	-2.9
2016	3,345.3	17.9	4,397.0	23.5	-1,051.7	-5.6
2017	3,374.6	17.3	4,531.3	23.2	-1,156.7	-5.9
2018	3,384.3	16.4	4,543.3	22.1	-1,159.0	-5.6
2019	3,621.0	16.9	5,066.1	23.6	-1,445.1	-6.7

Annex Table 17: Federal Government Balance Sheet						
	Assets		Liabilities		Net Worth	
	$ billions	% GDP	$ billions	% GDP	$ billions	% GDP
1994	1,350.9	18.5	5,357.1	73.5	-4,006.2	-55.0
1995	1,689.4	22.1	5,841.0	76.5	-4,151.6	-54.3
1996	1,723.9	21.4	6,073.4	75.2	-4,349.5	-53.9
1997	1,601.5	18.7	6,604.5	77.0	-5,003.0	-58.3
1998	852.8	9.4	6,987.2	77.1	-6,134.4	-67.7
1999	883.0	9.2	6,909.2	71.7	-6,026.2	-62.6
2000	911.5	8.9	6,856.9	66.9	-5,945.4	-58.0
2001	926.1	8.8	7,384.9	69.8	-6,458.8	-61.0
2002	996.5	9.1	7,816.7	71.5	-6,820.2	-62.4
2003	1,393.9	12.2	8,498.6	74.2	-7,104.7	-62.0
2004	1,397.3	11.4	9,107.1	74.6	-7,709.8	-63.1
2005	1,447.9	11.1	9,914.8	76.1	-8,466.9	-64.9
2006	1,496.5	10.8	10,412.9	75.4	-8,916.4	-64.5
2007	1,581.1	10.9	10,786.9	74.6	-9,205.8	-63.7
2008	1,974.7	13.4	12,178.2	82.8	-10,203.5	-69.4
2009	2,667.9	18.5	14,123.8	97.8	-11,455.9	-79.3
2010	2,883.8	19.2	16,356.6	109.1	-13,472.8	-89.9
2011	2,707.3	17.4	17,492.7	112.5	-14,785.4	-95.1
2012	2,748.3	17.0	18,849.3	116.4	-16,101.0	-99.4
2013	2,968.3	17.7	19,877.6	118.4	-16,909.3	-100.7
2014	3,065.3	17.5	20,766.0	118.5	-17,700.7	-101.0
2015	3,229.8	17.7	21,451.7	117.7	-18,221.9	-100.0
2016	3,480.7	18.6	23,896.9	127.7	-20,416.2	-109.1
2017	3,534.8	18.1	22,831.6	117.0	-19,296.8	-98.9
2018	3,836.7	18.6	25,357.4	123.2	-21,520.7	-104.6
2019	3,992.0	18.6	26,944.8	125.7	-22,952.8	-107.1

Annex Table 18: Federal Government Intertemporal Balance Sheet						
	Net Worth		NPV future Prim Def		Intertemporal Net Wor	
	$ billions	% GDP	$ billions	% GDP	$ billions	% GDP
1994	-4,006.2	-55.0	...	...	...	...
1995	-4,151.6	-54.3	...	...	...	...
1996	-4,349.5	-53.9	...	...	...	...
1997	-5,003.0	-58.3	...	...	...	...
1998	-6,134.4	-67.7	...	...	...	...
1999	-6,026.2	-62.6	...	...	...	...
2000	-5,945.4	-58.0	...	...	...	...
2001	-6,458.8	-61.0	...	...	...	...
2002	-6,820.2	-62.4	...	...	...	...
2003	-7,104.7	-62.0	...	...	...	...
2004	-7,709.8	-63.1	...	...	...	...
2005	-8,466.9	-64.9	...	...	...	...
2006	-8,916.4	-64.5	...	...	...	...
2007	-9,205.8	-63.7	...	...	...	...
2008	-10,203.5	-69.4	...	...	...	...
2009	-11,455.9	-79.3	...	...	...	...
2010	-13,472.8	-89.9	...	...	...	...
2011	-14,785.4	-95.1	-6,400.0	-41.2	-21,185.4	-136.3
2012	-16,101.0	-99.4	-16,500.0	-101.9	-32,601.0	-201.3
2013	-16,909.3	-100.7	-4,000.0	-23.8	-20,909.3	-124.6
2014	-17,700.7	-101.0	-4,700.0	-26.8	-22,400.7	-127.8
2015	-18,221.9	-100.0	-4,100.0	-22.5	-22,321.9	-122.5
2016	-20,416.2	-109.1	-16,200.0	-86.6	-36,616.2	-195.7
2017	-19,296.8	-98.9	-10,600.0	-54.3	-29,896.8	-153.2
2018	-21,520.7	-104.6	-46,200.0	-224.5	-67,720.7	-329.1
2019	-22,952.8	-107.1	-49,000.0	-228.7	-71,952.8	-335.8

Acknowledgments

I have benefited from many critical and constructive comments from friends and colleagues who have been so kind to plow through earlier drafts of this book. I would like to acknowledge in particular the efforts of Leslie Lipschitz, Harold James, and Harald Hirschhofer. I have also benefited from conversations with George Papaconstaninou, Megan Green, and Erin McPike.

A precursor to this book was an unpublished paper, prepared in 2006-2007 (unwittingly at that time, in the runup to the global financial crisis) in which I expressed concern about the sustainability of the Bush Jr. fiscal and economic policies. This paper triggered substantial reactions from my colleagues in the IMF. Invariably, this book incorporates many comments and suggestions that came out of that discussion. Indeed, I owe much gratitude to the staff of the IMF. My former colleagues have shown me how one can analyze a macroeconomy, while being mindful of the uncertainties that always accompany such an exercise.

I stress, though, that this book was written independently and on personal title and does not reflect the views of the Board of Directors of the IMF, its management, or the staff of the IMF. Responsibility for any errors or oversights in this book rest solely with the author.

Finally, I wish to thank my wife for her proofreading of the text, and my children for their support. The next generation of Americans includes my own children and grandchildren. They will need to pay the bills that we leave behind.

About the Author

Mr. Traa is an independent macroeconomic consultant. His research interests center on how to make macroeconomies sustainable and resilient for all citizens in view of demographic slowing, incremental resource depletion and environmental stress, especially in a period where political support for international organizations and policy cooperation is faltering.

In 2019, he was the interim president of the Central Bank of Curacao and St Maarten.

Prior to March 2018, Mr. Traa was a senior staff member of the International Monetary Fund (IMF) where his career spanned 33 years. He has extensive experience in macroeconomic and debt crisis management and financial programming for the IMF in multiple countries, including Brazil, Argentina, Uruguay, Paraguay, Ecuador, Germany, Sweden, The Netherlands, Israel, Switzerland, Spain, and Greece. Mr. Traa also worked on Sri Lanka, Zambia, French Africa (CEMAC and WAEMU), Ethiopia, and Saudi Arabia. Mr. Traa was the senior Resident Representative for the IMF in Athens, Greece, during the euro crisis in the period 2010-2013.

Mr. Traa lives in Washington DC. He is married and has three children.

Mr. Traa has published a book on the Macroeconomy of Greece (available in Greek and English) and one on the Macroeconomy of Ecuador (available in Spanish and English). All books in English are available on Amazon.

Made in the USA
Middletown, DE
20 December 2020